MATLAB for Machine Learning

Functions, algorithms, and use cases

Giuseppe Ciaburro

BIRMINGHAM - MUMBAI

MATLAB for Machine Learning

First published: August 2017

Production reference: 1230817

Published by Packt Publishing Ltd.
Livery Place
35 Livery Street
Birmingham
B3 2PB, UK.
ISBN 978-1-78839-843-5

www.packtpub.com

Credits

Author
Giuseppe Ciaburro

Copy Editors
Safis Editing
Vikrant Phadkay

Reviewers
Ankit Dixit
Ruben Oliva Ramos
Juan Tomás Oliva Ramos
Prashant Verma

Project Coordinator
Nidhi Joshi

Commissioning Editor
Veena Pagare

Proofreader
Safis Editing

Acquisition Editor
Varsha Shetty

Indexer
Tejal Daruwale Soni

Content Development Editor
Cheryl Dsa

Graphics
Tania Dutta

Technical Editor
Suwarna Patil

Production Coordinator
Arvindkumar Gupta

About the Author

Giuseppe Ciaburro holds a master's degree in chemical engineering from Università degli Studi di Napoli Federico II, and a master's degree in acoustic and noise control from Seconda Università degli Studi di Napoli. He works at the Built Environment Control Laboratory - Università degli Studi della Campania "Luigi Vanvitelli".

He has over 15 years of work experience in programming, first in the field of combustion and then in acoustics and noise control. His core programming knowledge is in Python and R, and he has extensive experience of working with MATLAB. An expert in acoustics and noise control, Giuseppe has wide experience in teaching professional computer courses (about 15 years), dealing with e-learning as an author. He has several publications to his credit: monographs, scientific journals, and thematic conferences. He is currently researching machine learning applications in acoustics and noise control.

About the Reviewers

Ankit Dixit is a data scientist and computer vision engineer from Mumbai, India; He has a B.Tech in biomedical engineering and a master's degree in computer vision specialization. He has been working in the field of computer vision and machine learning for more than 6 years.

He has worked with various software and hardware platforms for design and development of machine vision algorithms and has experience of machine learning algorithms such as decision trees, random forest, support vector machines, artificial neural networks, and deep neural networks. Currently, he is working on designing computer vision and machine learning algorithms for medical imaging data for Aditya Imaging and Information Technologies (part of Sun Pharmaceutical Advance Research Center), Mumbai. He does this with the use of advanced technologies such as ensemble methods and deep learning based models.

Ruben Oliva Ramos is a computer systems engineer with a master's degree in computer and electronic systems engineering, teleinformatics and networking, specialization from the University of Salle Bajio in Leon, Guanajuato, Mexico. He has more than 5 years of experience in developing web applications to control and monitor devices connected with Arduino and Raspberry Pi, and using web frameworks and cloud services to build the Internet of Things applications.

He is a mechatronics teacher at the University of Salle Bajio and teaches students of the master's degree in design and engineering of mechatronics systems. Ruben also works at Centro de Bachillerato Tecnologico Industrial 225 in Leon, teaching subjects such as electronics, robotics and control, automation, and microcontrollers.

He is a technician, consultant, and developer of monitoring systems and datalogger data using technologies such as Android, iOS, Windows Phone, HTML5, PHP, CSS, Ajax, JavaScript, Angular, ASP .NET databases (SQlite, MongoDB, and MySQL), web servers, Node.js, IIS, hardware programming (Arduino, Raspberry Pi, Ethernet Shield, GPS, and GSM/GPRS), ESP8266, and control and monitor systems for data acquisition and programming.

He has written a book for *Internet of Things Programming with JavaScript, Packt*.

I would like to thank my savior and lord, Jesus Christ for giving me strength and courage to pursue this project, to my dearest wife, Mayte, our two lovely sons, Ruben and Dario, To my father (Ruben), my dearest mom (Rosalia), my brother (Juan Tomas), and my sister (Rosalia) whom I love, for all their support while reviewing this book, for allowing me to pursue my dream and tolerating not being with them after my busy day job.

Juan Tomás Oliva Ramos is an environmental engineer from the University of Guanajuato, with a master's degree in administrative engineering and quality. He has more than 5 years of experience in the management and development of patents, technological innovation projects, and the development of technological solutions through the statistical control of processes.

He is a teacher of statistics, entrepreneurship, and the technological development of projects since 2011. He has always maintained an interest in the improvement and innovation in processes through technology. He became an entrepreneur mentor and technology management consultant, and started a new department of technology management and entrepreneurship at Instituto Tecnologico Superior de Purisima del Rincon.

He has worked on the book *Wearable designs for Smart watches, Smart TV's and Android mobile devices*. He has developed prototypes through programming and automation technologies for improvement of operations that have been registered for patents.

I want to thank God for giving me the wisdom and humility to review this book.
I thank Rubén for inviting me to collaborate on this adventure.
I also thank my wife, Brenda, our two magic princesses, Regina and Renata, and our next member, Tadeo. All of you are my strength, happiness, and my desire to look for the best for you.

Prashant Verma started his IT career in 2011 as a Java developer at Ericsson, working in the telecoms domain. After a couple of years of Java EE experience, he moved into the big data domain, and has worked on almost all the popular big data technologies such as Hadoop, Spark, Flume, Mongo, Cassandra. He has also played with Scala. Currently, he works with QA Infotech as a lead data engineer, working on solving e-learning problems with analytics and machine learning.

Prashant has worked for many companies with domain knowledge of telecom and e-learning. He has also worked as a freelance consultant in his free time. He has worked as a reviewer on *Spark For Java Developer*.

I want to thank Packt Publishing for giving me the chance to review this book as well as my employer and my family for their patience while I was busy working on this book.

www.PacktPub.com

For support files and downloads related to your book, please visit www.PacktPub.com.

Did you know that Packt offers eBook versions of every book published, with PDF and ePub files available? You can upgrade to the eBook version at www.PacktPub.com and as a print book customer, you are entitled to a discount on the eBook copy. Get in touch with us at service@packtpub.com for more details.

At www.PacktPub.com, you can also read a collection of free technical articles, sign up for a range of free newsletters and receive exclusive discounts and offers on Packt books and eBooks.

https://www.packtpub.com/mapt

Get the most in-demand software skills with Mapt. Mapt gives you full access to all Packt books and video courses, as well as industry-leading tools to help you plan your personal development and advance your career.

Why subscribe?

- Fully searchable across every book published by Packt
- Copy and paste, print, and bookmark content
- On demand and accessible via a web browser

Customer Feedback

Thanks for purchasing this Packt book. At Packt, quality is at the heart of our editorial process. To help us improve, please leave us an honest review on this book's Amazon page at `https://www.amazon.com/dp/1788398432`.

If you'd like to join our team of regular reviewers, you can e-mail us at `customerreviews@packtpub.com`. We award our regular reviewers with free eBooks and videos in exchange for their valuable feedback. Help us be relentless in improving our products!

Table of Contents

Preface

For humans, learning from mistakes is a fundamental rule. Why should it not be the same for machines? Machine learning algorithms will do just that: learn from experience. Machine learning gives computers the ability to learn without being explicitly programmed. It starts with real examples, extracts the models (that is, the rules that govern their operation), and uses them to make predictions about new examples.

MATLAB provides essential tools for understanding the amazing world of machine learning. Solving machine learning problems becomes extremely easy with the use of the tools available in the MATLAB environment. This is because MATLAB is a strong environment for interactive exploration.

For each topic, after a concise theoretical basis, you will be involved in real-life solutions. By the end of the book, you will be able to apply machine learning techniques and leverage the full capabilities of the MATLAB platform through real-world examples.

What this book covers

Chapter 1, *Getting Started with MATLAB Machine Learning*, introduces the basic concepts of machine learning, and then we take a tour of the different types of algorithms. In addition, some introduction, background information, and basic knowledge of the MATLAB environment will be covered. Finally, we explore the essential tools that MATLAB provides for understanding the amazing world of machine learning.

Chapter 2, *Importing and Organizing Data in MATLAB*, teaches us how to import and organize our data in MATLAB. Then we analyze the different formats available for the data collected and see how to move data in and out of MATLAB. Finally, we learn how to organize the data in the correct format for the next phase of data analysis.

Chapter 3, *From Data to Knowledge Discovery*, is where we begin to analyze data to extract useful information. We start from an analysis of the basic types of variable and the degree of cleaning the data. We analyze the techniques available for the preparation of the most suitable data for analysis and modeling. Then we go to data visualization, which plays a key role in understanding the data.

Chapter 4, *Finding Relationships between Variables - Regression Techniques*, shows how to perform accurate regression analysis in the MATLAB environment. We explore the amazing MATLAB interface for regression analysis, including fitting, prediction, and plotting.

Chapter 5, *Pattern Recognition through Classification Algorithms*, covers classification and much more. You'll learn how to classify an object using nearest neighbors. You'll understand how to use the principles of probability for classification. We'll also cover classification techniques using decision trees and rules.

Chapter 6, *Identifying Groups of Data Using Clustering Methods*, shows you how to divide the data into clusters, or groupings of similar items. You'll learn how to find groups of data with k-means and k-medoids. We'll also cover grouping techniques using hierarchical clustering.

Chapter 7, *Simulation of Human Thinking - Artificial Neural Networks*, teaches you how to use a neural network to fit data, classify patterns, and do clustering. You'll learn preprocessing, postprocessing, and network visualization for improving training efficiency and assessing network performance.

Chapter 8, *Improves the Performance of the Machine Learning Model - Dimensionality Reduction*, shows you how to select a feature that best represents the set of data. You will learn feature extraction techniques for dimensionality reduction when the transformation of variables is possible.

Chapter 9, *Machine Learning in Practice*, starts with a real-world fitting problem. Then you'll learn how to use a neural network to classify patterns. Finally, we perform clustering analysis. In this way, we'll analyze supervised and unsupervised learning algorithms.

What you need for this book

In this book, machine learning algorithms are implemented in the MATLAB environment. So, to reproduce the many examples in this book, you need a new version of MATLAB (R2017a recommended) and the following toolboxes: statistics and machine learning toolbox, neural network toolbox, and fuzzy logic toolbox.

Who this book is for

This book is for data analysts, data scientists, students, or anyone who is looking to get started with machine learning and wants to build efficient data-processing and predicting applications. A mathematical and statistical background will really help in following this book well.

Conventions

In this book, you will find a number of text styles that distinguish between different kinds of information. Here are some examples of these styles and an explanation of their meaning.

Code words in text, database table names, folder names, filenames, file extensions, pathnames, dummy URLs, user input, and Twitter handles are shown as follows: "MATLAB performs the math task and assigns the result to the ans variable."

A block of code is set as follows:

```
PC1 = 0.8852* Area + 0.3958   * Perimeter + 0.0043 * Compactness +
   0.1286 * LengthK + 0.1110 * WidthK - 0.1195 * AsymCoef + 0.1290 *
   LengthKG
```

Any command-line input or output is written as follows:

```
>>10+90
ans =
    100
```

New terms and **important words** are shown in bold. Words that you see on the screen, for example, in menus or dialog boxes, appear in the text like this: "A reference page in the **Help** browser."

Warnings or important notes appear in a box like this.

Tips and tricks appear like this.

Reader feedback

Feedback from our readers is always welcome. Let us know what you think about this book-what you liked or disliked. Reader feedback is important for us as it helps us develop titles that you will really get the most out of.

To send us general feedback, simply e-mail feedback@packtpub.com, and mention the book's title in the subject of your message.

If there is a topic that you have expertise in and you are interested in either writing or contributing to a book, see our author guide at `www.packtpub.com/authors`.

Customer support

Now that you are the proud owner of a Packt book, we have a number of things to help you to get the most from your purchase.

Downloading the example code

You can download the example code files for this book from your account at `http://www.packtpub.com`. If you purchased this book elsewhere, you can visit `http://www.packtpub.com/support` and register to have the files emailed directly to you. You can download the code files by following these steps:

1. Log in or register to our website using your email address and password.
2. Hover the mouse pointer on the **SUPPORT** tab at the top.
3. Click on **Code Downloads & Errata**.
4. Enter the name of the book in the **Search** box.
5. Select the book for which you're looking to download the code files.
6. Choose from the drop-down menu where you purchased this book from.
7. Click on **Code Download**.

Once the file is downloaded, please make sure that you unzip or extract the folder using the latest version of:

- WinRAR / 7-Zip for Windows
- Zipeg / iZip / UnRarX for Mac
- 7-Zip / PeaZip for Linux

The code bundle for the book is also hosted on GitHub at `https://github.com/PacktPublishing/MATLAB-for-Machine-Learning`. We also have other code bundles from our rich catalog of books and videos available at `https://github.com/PacktPublishing/`. Check them out!

Errata

Although we have taken every care to ensure the accuracy of our content, mistakes do happen. If you find a mistake in one of our books-maybe a mistake in the text or the code-we would be grateful if you could report this to us. By doing so, you can save other readers from frustration and help us improve subsequent versions of this book. If you find any errata, please report them by visiting http://www.packtpub.com/submit-errata, selecting your book, clicking on the **Errata Submission Form** link, and entering the details of your errata. Once your errata are verified, your submission will be accepted and the errata will be uploaded to our website or added to any list of existing errata under the Errata section of that title. To view the previously submitted errata, go to https://www.packtpub.com/books/content/support and enter the name of the book in the search field. The required information will appear under the **Errata** section.

Piracy

Piracy of copyrighted material on the internet is an ongoing problem across all media. At Packt, we take the protection of our copyright and licenses very seriously. If you come across any illegal copies of our works in any form on the internet, please provide us with the location address or website name immediately so that we can pursue a remedy. Please contact us at copyright@packtpub.com with a link to the suspected pirated material. We appreciate your help in protecting our authors and our ability to bring you valuable content.

Questions

If you have a problem with any aspect of this book, you can contact us at questions@packtpub.com, and we will do our best to address the problem.

1
Getting Started with MATLAB
Machine Learning

Why is it so difficult for you to accept my orders if you're just a machine? Just a machine? That's like saying that you are just an ape. This is a short dialog between the leading actor and a robot, taken from the movie *Automata*. In this movie, the robots have two unalterable protocols; the first obliges them to preserve human life and the second limits them from repairing themselves. Why should humans limit the ability of robots to repair themselves? Because robots have a great capacity for self-learning that could lead them to take control of humans, over time maybe.

At least that is what happens in the movie.

But what do we really mean by self-learning? A machine has the ability to learn if it is able to improve its performance through its activities. Therefore, this ability can be used to help humans solve specific problems such as extracting knowledge from large amounts of data. In this chapter, we will be introduced to the basic concepts of machine learning, and then we will take a tour of the different types of algorithm. In addition, an introduction, some background information, and a basic knowledge of the MATLAB environment will be covered. Finally, we will explore the essential tools that MATLAB provides for understanding the amazing world of machine learning.
In this chapter, we will cover the following topics:

- Discovering the machine learning capabilities in MATLAB for classification, regression, clustering, and deep learning, including apps for automated model training and code generation
- Taking a tour of the most popular machine learning algorithms to choose the right one for our needs
- Understanding the role of statistics and algebra in machine learning

At the end of the chapter, you will be able to recognize the different machine learning algorithms and the tools that MATLAB provides to handle them.

ABC of machine learning

Defining machine learning is not a simple matter; to do that, we can start from the definitions given by leading scientists in the field:

> *"Machine Learning: Field of study that gives computers the ability to learn without being explicitly programmed."*
>
> *– Arthur L. Samuel(1959)*

Otherwise, we can also provide a definition as:

> *"Learning denotes changes in the system that are adaptive in the sense that they enable the system to do the same task or tasks drawn from the same population more efficiently and more effectively the next time."*
>
> *– Herbert Alexander Simon (1984)*

Finally, we can quote the following:

> *"A computer program is said to learn from experience E with respect to some class of tasks T and performance measure P, if its performance at tasks in T, as measured by P, improves with experience E".*
>
> *– Tom M. Mitchell(1998)*

In all cases, they refer to the ability to learn from experience without any outside help. Which is what we do humans in most cases. Why should it not be the same for machines?

Arthur L. Samuel   Herbert Alexander Simon   Tom M. Mitchell

Figure 1.1: The history of machine learning

Machine learning is a multidisciplinary field created by intersection and synergy between computer science, statistics, neurobiology, and control theory. Its emergence has played a key role in several fields and has fundamentally changed the vision of software programming. If the question before was, *How to program a computer?* now the question becomes, *How will computers program themselves?*

Thus, it is clear that machine learning is a basic method that allows a computer to have its own intelligence.

As it might be expected, machine learning interconnects and coexists with the study of, and research on, human learning. Like humans, whose brain and neurons are the foundation of insight, **Artificial Neural Networks (ANNs)** are the basis of any decision-making activity of the computer.

From a set of data, we can find a model that describes it by the use of machine learning. For example, we can identify a correspondence between input variables and output variables for a given system. One way to do this is to postulate the existence of some kind of mechanism for the parametric generation of data, which, however, does not know the exact values of the parameters. This process typically makes reference to statistical techniques such as **Induction**, **Deduction**, and **Abduction**, as shown in the following figure:

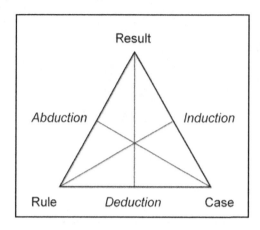

Figure 1.2: Peirce's triangle - scheme of the relationship between reasoning patterns

The extraction of general laws from a set of observed data is called **induction**; it is opposed to **deduction,** in which, starting from general laws, we want to predict the value of a set of variables. Induction is the fundamental mechanism underlying the scientific method, in which we want to derive general laws (typically described in a mathematical language) starting from the observation of phenomena.

This observation includes the measurement of a set of variables and therefore the acquisition of data that describes the observed phenomena. Then, the resulting model can be used to make predictions on additional data. The overall process in which, starting from a set of observations, we want to make predictions for new situations is called **inference**.

Therefore, inductive learning starts from observations arising from the surrounding environment and generalizes obtaining knowledge that will be valid for not-yet-observed cases; at least we hope so.

We can distinguish two types of inductive learning:

- **Learning by example**: Knowledge gained by starting from a set of positive examples that are instances of the concept to be learned and negative examples that are non-instances of the concept.
- **Learning regularity**: This is not a concept to learn. The goal is to find regularity (common characteristics) in the instances provided.

The following figure shows the types of inductive learning:

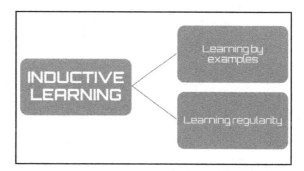

Figure 1.3: Types of inductive learning

A question arises spontaneously: Why do machine learning systems work while traditional algorithms fail? The reasons for the failure of traditional algorithms are numerous and typically due to the following:

- **Difficulty in problem formalization**: For example, each of us can recognize our friends from their voice. But probably none can describe a sequence of computational steps enabling them to recognize the speaker from the recorded sound.
- **High number of variables at play**: When considering the problem of recognizing characters from a document, specifying all parameters that are thought to be involved can be particularly complex. In addition, the same formalization applied in the same context but on a different idiom could prove inadequate.
- **Lack of theory**: Imagine you have to predict exactly the performance of financial markets in the absence of specific mathematical laws.
- **Need for customization**: The distinction between interesting and uninteresting features depends significantly on the perception of the individual user.

Here is a flowchart showing inductive and deductive learning:

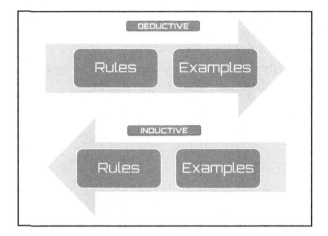

Figure 1.4: Inductive and deductive learning flowchart

Discover the different types of machine learning

The power of the machine learning is due to the quality of its algorithms, which have been improved and updated over the years; these are divided into several main types depending on the nature of the signal used for learning or the type of feedback adopted by the system. They are:

- **Supervised learning**: The algorithm generates a function that links input values to a desired output through the observation of a set of examples in which each data input has its relative output data, and that is used to construct predictive models.
- **Unsupervised learning** : The algorithm tries to derive knowledge from a general input without the help of a set of pre-classified examples that are used to build descriptive models. A typical example of the application of these algorithms are search engines.
- **Reinforcement learning**: The algorithm is able to learn depending on the changes that occur in the environment in which it is performed. In fact, since every action has some effect on the environment concerned, the algorithm is driven by the same feedback environment. Some of these algorithms are used in speech or text recognition.

The following is a figure depicting the different types of machine learning algorithms:

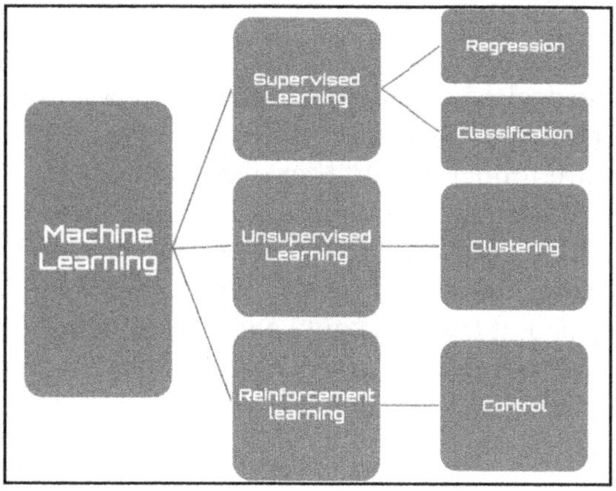

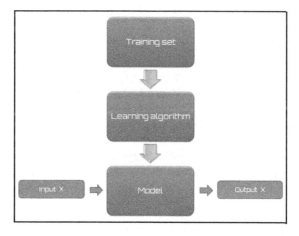

Figure 1.5: Types of machine learning algorithms

Supervised learning

Supervised learning is a machine learning technique that aims to program a computer system so that it can resolve the relevant tasks automatically. To do this, the input data is included in a set *I*, (typically vectors). Then the set of output data is fixed as set *O*, and finally it defines a function f that associates each input with the correct answer. Such information is called a **training set**. This workflow is presented in the following figure:

Figure 1.6: Supervised learning workflow

All supervised learning algorithms are based on the following thesis: if an algorithm provides an adequate number of examples, it will be able to create a derived function B that will approximate the desired function A.

If the approximation of the desired function is adequate, when the input data is offered to the derived function, this function should be able to provide output responses similar to those provided by the desired function and then acceptable.These algorithms are based on the following concept: similar inputs correspond to similar outputs.
Generally, in the real-world, this assumption is not valid; however, some situations exist in which it is acceptable. Clearly, the proper functioning of such algorithms depends significantly on the input data. If there are only a few training inputs, the algorithm might not have enough experience to provide a correct output. Conversely, many inputs may make it excessively slow since the derivative function generated by a large number of inputs could be very complicated.

Moreover, experience shows that this type of algorithm is very sensitive to noise; even a few pieces of incorrect data can make the entire system unreliable and lead to wrong decisions.

In supervised learning, it's possible to split problems based on the nature of the data. If the output value is categorical, such as membership/non-membership to a certain class, it is a classification problem. If the output is a continuous real value in a certain range, then it is a regression problem.

Unsupervised learning

The aim of unsupervised learning is to automatically extract information from databases. This process occurs without prior knowledge of the contents to be analyzed. Unlike supervised learning, there is no information on membership classes of the examples or generally on the output corresponding to a certain input. The goal is to get a model that is able to discover interesting properties: groups with similar characteristics (clustering) for instance. Search engines are an example of an application of these algorithms. Given one or more keywords, they are able to create a list of links related to our search.

The validity of these algorithms depends on the usefulness of the information they can extract from the databases. These algorithms work by comparing data and looking for similarities or differences. Available data concerns only the set of features that describe each example.

The following figure shows supervised learning and unsupervised learning examples:

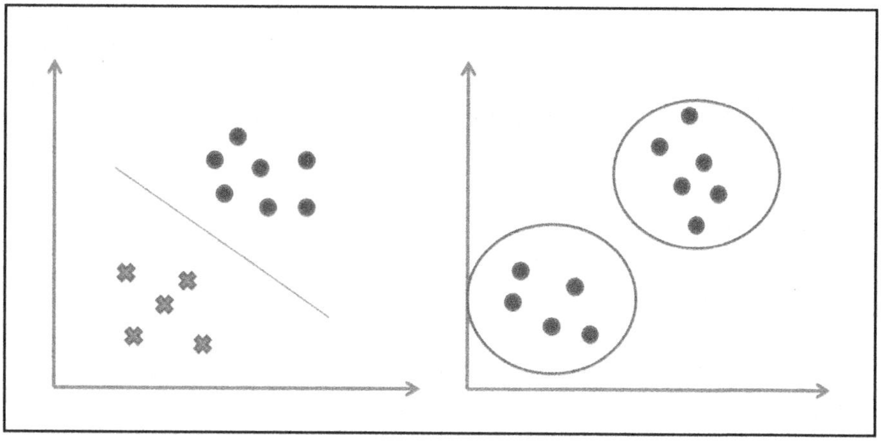

Figure 1.7: Supervised learning versus unsupervised learning

They show great efficiency with elements of numeric type, but are much less accurate with non-numeric data. Generally, they work properly in the presence of data that contains an order or a clear grouping and is clearly identifiable.

Reinforcement learning

Reinforcement learning aims to create algorithms that can learn and adapt to environmental changes. This programming technique is based on the concept of receiving external stimuli depending on the algorithm choices. A correct choice will involve a premium while an incorrect choice will lead to a penalty. The goal of system is to achieve the best possible result, of course.

In supervised learning, there is a teacher that tells the system which is the correct output (learning with a teacher). This is not always possible. Often we have only qualitative information (sometimes binary, right/wrong, or success/failure).

The information available is called reinforcement signals. But the system does not give any information on how to update the agent's behavior (that is, weights). You cannot define a cost function or a gradient. The goal of the system is to create the smart agents that have a machinery able to learn from their experience.

This flowchart shows reinforcement learning:

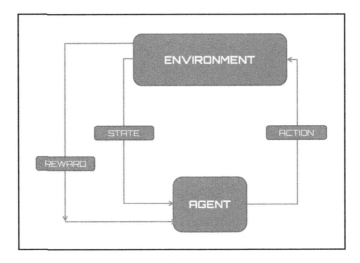

Figure 1.8: How to reinforcement learning interact with the environment

Choosing the right algorithm

In the previous section, we learned the difference between various types of machine learning algorithms. So, we understood the basic principles that underlie the different techniques. Now it's time to ask ourselves the following question: What is the right algorithm for my needs?

Unfortunately there is no common answer for everyone, except the more generic: *It depends*. But what does it depend on? It mainly depends on the data available to us: the size, quality, and nature of the data. It depends on what we want to do with the answer. It depends on how the algorithm has been expressed in instructions for the computer. It depends on how much time we have. There is no best method or one-size-fits-all. The only way to be sure that the algorithm chosen is the right one is to try it.

However, to understand what is most suitable for our needs, we can perform a preliminary analysis. Beginning from what we have (data), what tools we have available (algorithms), and what objectives we set for ourselves (the results), we can obtain useful information on the road ahead.

If we start from what we have (data), it is a classification problem, and two options are available:

- **Classify based on input**: We have a supervised learning problem if we can label the input data. If we cannot label the input data but want to find the structure of the system, then it is unsupervised. Finally, if our goal is to optimize an objective function by interacting with the environment, it is a reinforcement learning problem.
- **Classify based on output**: If our model output is a number, we have to deal with a regression problem. But it is a classification problem if the output of the model is a class. Finally, we have a clustering problem if the output of the model is a set of input groups.

The following is a figure that shows two options available in the classification problem:

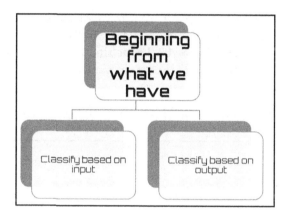

Figure 1.9: Preliminary analysis

After classifying the problem, we can analyze the tools available to solve the specific problem. Thus, we can identify the algorithms that are applicable and focus our study on the methods to be implemented to apply these tools to our problem.

Having identified the tools, we need to evaluate their performance. To do this, we simply apply the selected algorithms on the datasets at our disposal. Subsequently, on the basis of a series of carefully selected evaluation criteria, we carry out a comparison of the performance of each algorithm.

How to build machine learning models step by step

Finally, the algorithm to apply to our data is chosen; it is now time to get down to work without delay. Before you tackle such a job, it is appropriate to devote some time to the workflow setting. When developing an application that uses machine learning, we will follow a procedure characterized by the following steps:

1. **Collect the data**: Everything starts from the data, no doubt about it; but one might wonder where so much data comes from. In practice, it is collected through lengthy procedures that may, for example, derive from measurement campaigns or face-to-face interviews. In all cases, the data is collected in a database so that it can then be analyzed to derive knowledge.

 If we do not have specific requirements, and to save time and effort, we can use publicly available data. In this regard, a large collection of data is available in the **UCI Machine Learning Repository** at the following link: `http://archive.ics.uci.edu/ml`.

The following figure shows how to build machine learning models step by step:

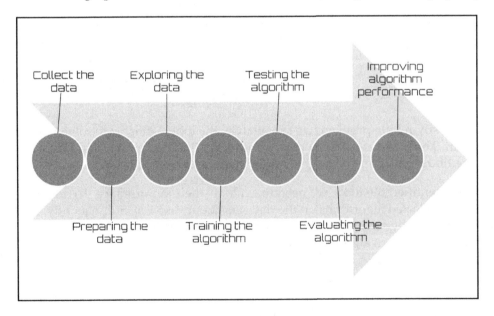

Figure 1.10: Machine learning workflow

2. **Preparing the data**: We have collected the data; now we have to prepare it for the next step. Once we have this data, we must make sure it is in a format usable by the algorithm we want to use. To do this, you may need to do some formatting. Recall that some algorithms need data in an integer format, whereas others require data in the form of strings, and finally others need to be in a special format. We will get to this later, but the specific formatting is usually simple compared to data collection.

3. **Exploring the data**: At this point, we can look at data to verify that it is actually working and we do not have a bunch of empty values. In this step, through the use of plots, we can recognize patterns or whether there are some data points that are vastly different from the rest of the set. Plotting data in one, two, or three dimensions can also help.

4. **Training the algorithm**: Now let's get serious. In this step, the machine learning begins to work with the definition of the model and the next training. The model starts to extract knowledge from large amounts of data that we had available, and that nothing has been explained so far. For unsupervised learning, there's no training step because you don't have a target value.

5. **Testing the algorithm**: In this step, we use the information learned in the previous step to see if the model actually works. The evaluation of an algorithm is for seeing how well the model approximates the real system. In the case of supervised learning, we have some known values that we can use to evaluate the algorithm. In unsupervised learning, we may need to use some other metrics to evaluate success. In both cases, if we are not satisfied, we can return to the previous steps, change some things, and retry the test.

6. **Evaluating the algorithm**: We have reached the point where we can apply what has been done so far. We can assess the approximation ability of the model by applying it to real data. The model, preventively trained and tested, is then valued in this phase.

7. **Improving algorithm performance**: Finally we can focus on the finishing steps. We've verified that the model works, we have evaluated the performance, and now we are ready to analyze the whole process to identify any possible room for improvement.

Introducing machine learning with MATLAB

So far, we have learned what machine learning algorithms do; we have also understood how to recognize the different types, how to locate the right solution for our needs, and finally how to set a proper workflow. It's time to learn how to do all this in the MATLAB environment.

Solving machine learning problems becomes extremely easy with the use of the tools available in the MATLAB environment. This is because MATLAB is a strong environment for interactive exploration. It has numerous algorithms and apps to help you get started using machine learning techniques. Some examples include:

- Clustering, classification, and regression algorithms
- Neural network app, curve fitting app, and Classification Learner app

MATLAB is a software platform optimized for solving scientific problems and design. In MATLAB, calculation, visualization, and programming are integrated in an easy-to-use environment, where problems and solutions are expressed in familiar mathematical notation.

The name MATLAB is an acronym of the term **matrix laboratory**. MATLAB was originally written to provide easy access to software of matrices; then it evolved in the years to come, thanks to numerous user inputs. The MATLAB programming language is based on matrices that represent the most natural way to express computational mathematics. Its desktop environment invites experimentation, exploration, and discovery. The integrated graphics are easy to view and provide an in-depth understanding of the data.

The MATLAB desktop is shown in the following screenshot:

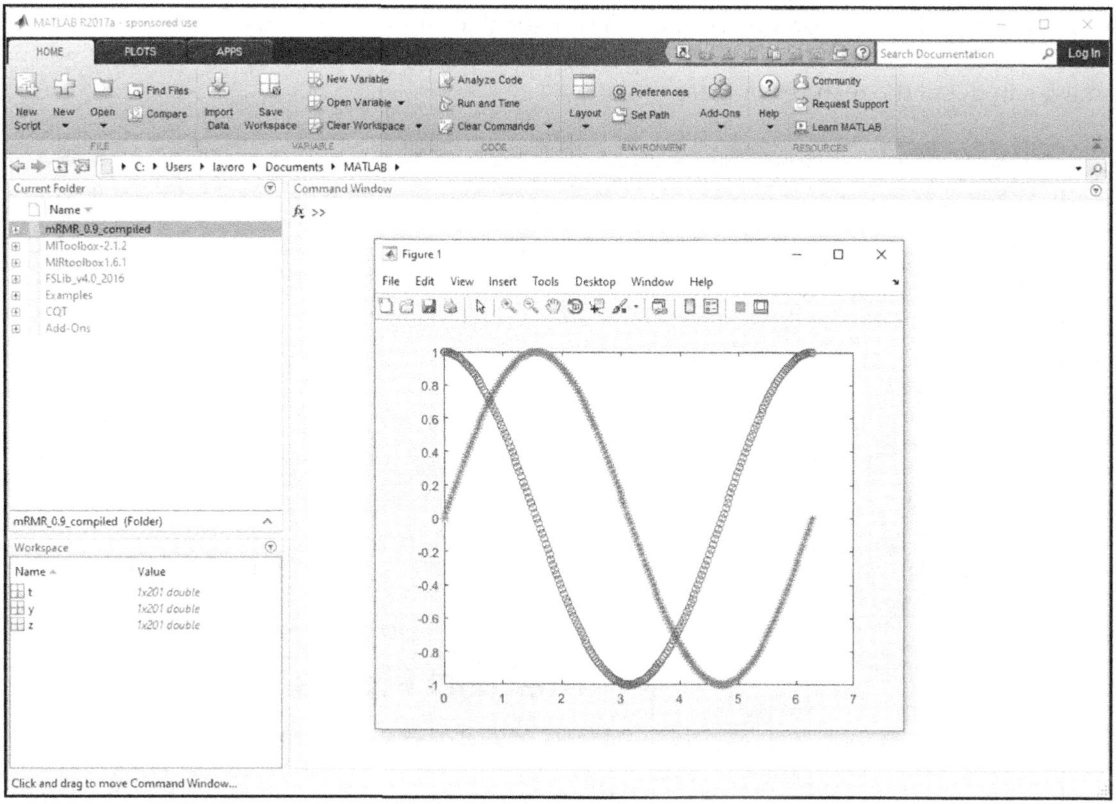

Figure 1.11: MATLAB desktop

MATLAB is also characterized by the presence of specific solutions to application problems called toolboxes. Very useful for most users, MATLAB toolboxes represent solutions for many practical problems and provide the basis for applying these instruments to the specialized technology. These toolboxes are collections of MATLAB functions (referred to as M-files) that extend the MATLAB environment in order to solve particular classes of problems.

MATLAB has two specific toolboxes for processing machine learning problems. They are the Statistics and Machine Learning Toolbox and Neural Network Toolbox. While the first solves machine learning problems through statistical techniques and algorithms most widely used in this field, the second is specific to ANNs. In the following sections, we will analyze in detail the features of these tools.

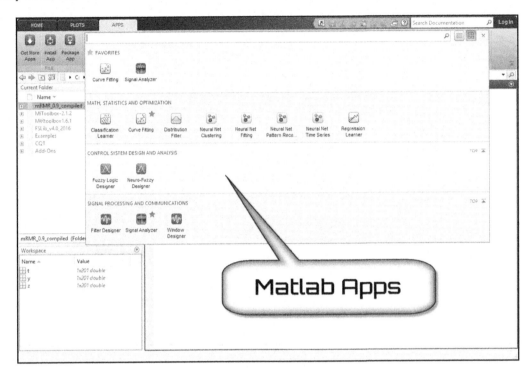

Figure 1.12: Some apps available in MATLAB

System requirements and platform availability

To be used efficiently, all computer software needs certain hardware components or other software resources to be present on a computer. Thus, MATLAB requires specific hardware to be installed and working properly on our computer. Fortunately, we can start from the assumption that MATLAB is available for all popular software platforms in both professional and student editions. In fact, it is available for the Windows, macOS, and Linux platforms. But we can rest assured that what MATLAB requires is widely supported by new computers.

So the hardware requirements for Windows are:

- **Operating systems**: Windows 10, Windows 8.1, Windows 8, Windows 7 Service Pack 1, Windows Server 2016, Windows Server 2012 R2, Windows Server 2012, and Windows Server 2008 R2 Service Pack 1.
- **Processors**: Any Intel or AMD x86-64 processor; AVX2 instruction set support is recommended; with Polyspace, 4-core is recommended.
- **Disk Space**: 2 GB for MATLAB only, 4–6 GB for a typical installation.
- **RAM**: 2 GB; with Simulink, 4 GB is required; with Polyspace, 4 GB per core is recommended.
- **Graphics**: No specific graphics card is required. A hardware-accelerated graphics card supporting OpenGL 3.3 with 1 GB GPU memory is recommended.

 To discover the hardware requirements for other platforms, visit the manufacturer's website at the following link: https://www.mathworks. com/support/sysreq.html.

In the following screenshot, the hardware requirements for Windows are listed:

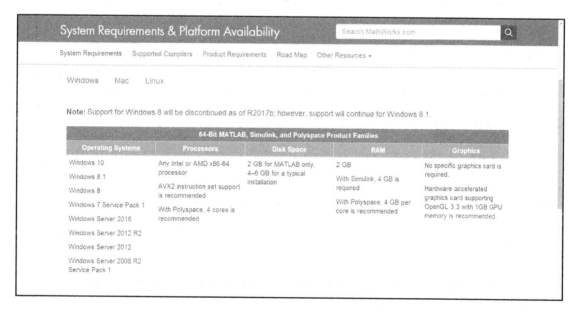

Figure 1.13: Windows hardware requirements for MATLAB.

MATLAB ready for use

Installing **MathWorks** products requires a valid software license, which we can obtain by purchasing products or downloading a product trial. To download products, we must log in to our MathWorks account or create a new one.

Once we have the MathWorks installer, to start the installation, we run this file and select the products we want to use. To run the installer, we need the following:

- Our email address and our MathWorks account password. We need them to log in to our account during installation.
- Correct permissions to install the software. If you have questions about permissions, ask your system administrator.
- Consider disabling anti-virus software and Internet security applications on your system during installation. These applications can slow down the installation process or cause it to appear unresponsive.

Later we should simply follow the usual software installation procedure. In the end, we will get a version of MATLAB ready for use.

 For more information about the installation procedure, visit the manufacturer's website at the following link:

`https://www.mathworks.com/help/install/index.html`

Statistics and Machine Learning Toolbox

The Statistics and Machine Learning Toolbox contains all the tools necessary to extract knowledge from large datasets. It provides functions and apps to analyze, describe, and model data. Starting exploratory data analysis becomes a breeze with the descriptive statistics and graphs contained in the toolbox. Furthermore, fitting probability distributions to data, generating random numbers, and performing hypothesis tests will be extremely easy. Finally through the regression and classification algorithms, we can draw inferences from data and build predictive models.

For data mining, the Statistics and Machine Learning Toolbox offers feature selection, stepwise regression, **Principal Component Analysis (PCA)**, regularization, and other dimensionality reduction methods that allow the identification of variables or functions that impact your model.

In this toolbox are developed supervised and unsupervised machine learning algorithms, including **Support Vector Machines (SVMs)**, decision trees, **k-Nearest Neighbor (KNN)**, k-means, k-medoids, hierarchical clustering, **Gaussian Mixture Models (GMM)**, and **hidden Markov models (HMM)**. Through the use of such algorithms, calculations on datasets that are too large to be stored in memory can be correctly executed. In the following screenshot, product capabilities of the Statistics and Machine Learning Toolbox are shown, extracted from the MathWorks site:

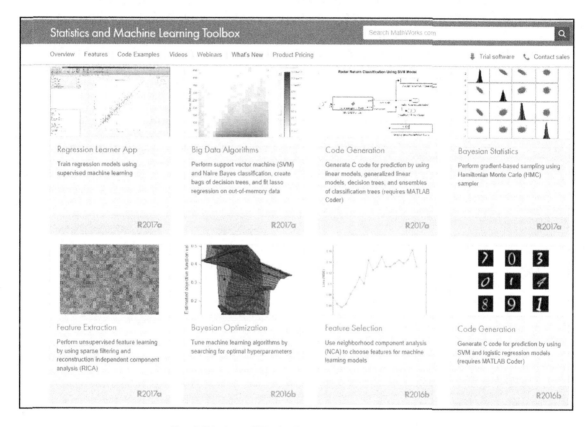

Figure 1.14: Product capabilities of the Statistics and Machine Learning Toolbox

Here is a descriptive list of the key features of this tool; you will find the main topics of the machine learning field:

- Regression techniques, including linear, generalized linear, nonlinear, robust, regularized, ANOVA, repeated measures, and mixed-effects models
- Big data algorithms for dimension reduction, descriptive statistics, k-means clustering, linear regression, logistic regression, and discriminant analysis

- Univariate and multivariate probability distributions, random and quasi-random number generators, and Markov chain samplers
- Hypothesis tests for distributions, dispersion, and location; **Design of Experiments (DOE)** techniques for optimal, factorial, and response surface designs
- Classification Learner app and algorithms for supervised machine learning, including SVMs, boosted and bagged decision trees, KNN, Naive Bayes, discriminant analysis, and Gaussian process regression
- Unsupervised machine learning algorithms, including k-means, k-medoids, hierarchical clustering, Gaussian mixtures, and HMMs
- Bayesian optimization for tuning machine learning algorithms by searching for optimal hyperparameters

The following are the product resources of the **Statistics and Machine Learning Toolbox:**

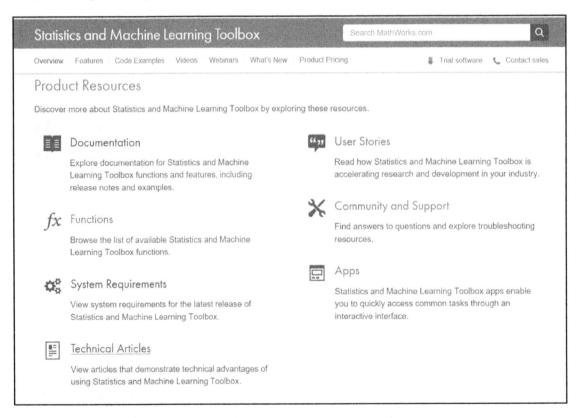

Figure 1.15: Product resources of the Statistics and Machine Learning Toolbox

For a more comprehensive overview of the Statistics and Machine Learning Toolbox's capabilities, you can connect to the manufacturer's website at the following link: `https://www.mathworks.com/products/statistics.html`.

Datatypes

Before we start working with the Statistics and Machine Learning Toolbox, we should learn how to format the data to be processed by MATLAB. The Statistics and Machine Learning Toolbox supports only some specific datatypes for input arguments. MATLAB might return an error or unexpected results if we specify data in an unsupported type.

Supported datatypes

The datatypes supported are as follow:

- Numeric scalars, vectors, matrices, or arrays having single or double precision entries. These data forms have the single or double datatype.
- Cell arrays of character vectors; character, logical, or categorical arrays; or numeric vectors for categorical variables representing grouping data. These data forms have the cellstr, char, logical, categorical, and single or double datatype, respectively.
- Some functions support tabular arrays for heterogeneous. The table datatype contains variables of any of the datatypes previously listed.
- Some functions accept `gpuArray` input arguments so that they execute on the GPU.

Unsupported datatypes

These are as follows:

- Complex numbers.
- Custom numeric datatypes, for example, a variable that is double precision and an object.
- Signed or unsigned numeric integers for non-grouping data, for example, `unint8` and `int16`.
- Sparse matrices, for example, matrix `ONE` such that `issparse(ONE)` returns `1`. To use data that is of datatype sparse, recast the data to a matrix using `full`.

What can you do with the Statistics and Machine Learning Toolbox?

In the previous section, we analyzed the main features of the Statistics and Machine Learning Toolbox and how to format the data for following processes. It is now legitimate to ask: What can we really do with all the functions that MATLAB makes available to us? In this section, we will see a series of real case solutions through the use of such tools. Let us see some applications.

Data mining and data visualization

Data mining is the process of finding correlations among several fields of large relational databases. Through this process, data is analyzed from different perspectives and summarized into useful information. This information will then be used to adopt the necessary strategies to solve a problem.

MATLAB has several tools that allow us to perform a data mining analysis. In particular, the Statistics and Machine Learning Toolbox presents many techniques that give us the opportunity to obtain useful information from data. Good examples of these tools are:

- Statistical plotting with interactive graphics
- Descriptive statistics for large datasets

An example of visualizing multivariate data is shown in the following figure:

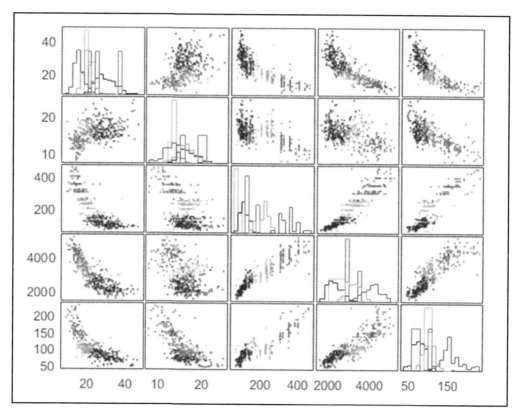

Figure 1.16: Visualizing multivariate data

For example, we can start our analysis from visual exploration of data through a statistical plotting with interactive graphics. In this regard, MATLAB has many graphs and charts ready for use. In addition, the Statistics and Machine Learning Toolbox augments MATLAB plot types with probability plots, box plots, histograms, scatter histograms, 3D histograms, control charts, and quantile-quantile plots. For multivariate analysis, dendrograms, biplots, parallel coordinate charts, and Andrews plots are included in the toolbox.

In some cases, we must visualize multivariate data. Many statistical analyses require only two variables: A **predictor variable** (independent variable) and a **response variable** (dependent variable). The relationships between the two types of variables is easy to visualize using 2D scatter plots, bivariate histograms, boxplots, and so on. Similarly it is possible to extend the analysis to trivariate data and display it with 3D scatter plots, or 2D scatter plots with a third variable encoded. However, many datasets involve a larger number of variables, making direct visualization more difficult. In MATLAB, it's possible to visualize multivariate data using various statistical plots, through the Statistics and Machine Learning Toolbox (*Figure 1.16*).

Finally we can extract useful information using a descriptive statistic. A descriptive statistic identifies a set of techniques and tools aimed at fulfilling one of the top priorities of the statistic: describe, represent, and summarize the observed data to analyze a certain phenomenon. The Statistics and Machine Learning Toolbox includes functions for calculating:

- Measures of central tendency, including average, median, and various means
- Measures of dispersion, including range, variance, standard deviation, and mean or median absolute deviation
- Linear and rank correlation
- Results based on data with missing values
- Percentile and quartile estimates
- Density estimates using a kernel-smoothing function

Regression analysis

Regression analysis is a technique used to analyze a series of data that consists of a dependent variable and one or more independent variables. The purpose is to estimate a possible functional relationship between the dependent variable and the independent variables. Using this technique, we can build a model in which a continuous response variable is a function of one or more predictors.

In the Statistics and Machine Learning Toolbox, there are a variety of regression algorithms, including:

- Linear regression
- Nonlinear regression
- Generalized linear models
- Mixed-effects models

A scatter plot of the linear regression model is shown in the following figure.

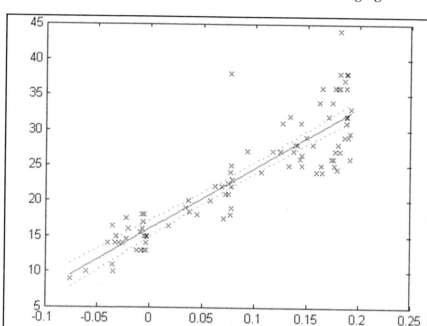

Figure 1.17: Scatter plot of linear regression model

To study the relationship between two variables, a scatter plot is useful, in which we show the values of the independent variable X on the horizontal axis and the values of the dependent variable Y on the vertical axis. Using a regression model, we can express the relationship between two variables with functions that are more or less complex. Simple linear regression is suitable when the values of X and Y are distributed along a straight line in the scatter plot (*Figure 1.17*).

Classification

Classification models are supervised learning methods and are aimed at predicting a categorical target. From a set of observations for which the class is known, a model that allows us to make predictions is generated.

The Statistics and Machine Learning Toolbox offers apps and functions that cover a variety of parametric and non-parametric classification algorithms, such as:

- Logistic regression
- Boosted and bagged decision trees, including AdaBoost, LogitBoost, GentleBoost, and RobustBoost
- Naive Bayes classification
- KNN classification
- Discriminant analysis (linear and quadratic)
- SVM (binary and multiclass classification)

The Classification Learner app is a very useful tool that executes more request activities such as interactively explore data, select features, specify cross-validation schemes, train models, and assess results. We can use it to perform common tasks such as:

- Importing data and specifying cross-validation schemes
- Exploring data and selecting features
- Training models using several classification algorithms
- Comparing and assessing models
- Sharing trained models for use in applications such as computer vision and signal processing

Using the Classification Learner app, we can choose between various algorithms to train and validate classification models. After the training, compare the models' validation errors and choose the best one on the basis of results.

The following figure shows the Classification Learner app:

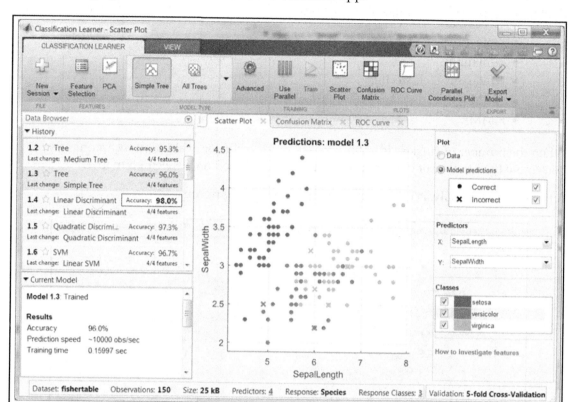

Figure 1.18: The Classification Learner with a history list containing various classifier types

Cluster analysis

Cluster analysis is a multivariate analysis technique through which it is possible to group the statistical units so as to minimize the logic distance of each group and the logic distance between the groups. The logic distance is quantified by means of measures of similarity/dissimilarity between the defined statistical units.

The Statistics and Machine Learning Toolbox provides several algorithms to carry out cluster analysis. Available algorithms include:

- k-means
- k-medoids
- Hierarchical clustering
- GMM
- HMM

When the number of clusters is unknown, we can use cluster evaluation techniques to determine the number of clusters present in the data based on a specified metric.

A typical cluster analysis result is shown in the following figure:

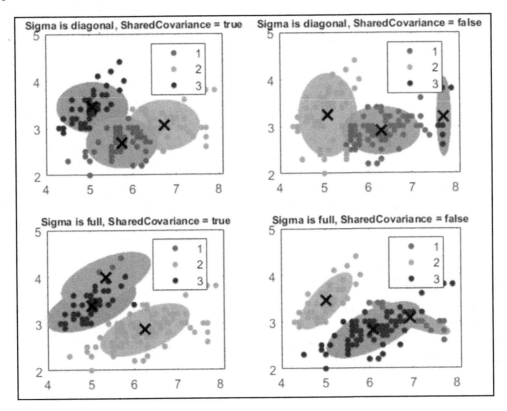

Figure 1.19: A cluster analysis example

In addition, the Statistics and Machine Learning Toolbox allows viewing clusters by creating a dendrogram plot to display a hierarchical binary cluster tree. Then, we optimize the leaf order to maximize the sum of the similarities between adjacent leaves. Finally, for grouped data with multiple measurements for each group, we create a dendrogram plot based on the group means computed using a multivariate analysis of variance.

Dimensionality reduction

Dimensionality reduction is the process of converting a set of data with many variables into data with lesser dimensions but ensuring similar information. It can help improve model accuracy and performance, improve interpretability, and prevent overfitting. The Statistics and Machine Learning Toolbox includes many algorithms and functions for reducing the dimensionality of our datasets. It can be divided into feature selection and feature extraction. Feature selection approaches try to find a subset of the original variables. Feature extraction reduces the dimensionality in the data by transforming data into new features.

As already mentioned, feature selection finds only the subset of measured features (predictor variables) that give the best predictive performance in modeling the data. The Statistics and Machine Learning Toolbox includes many feature selection methods, as follows:

- **Stepwise regression**: Adds or removes features until there is no improvement in prediction accuracy. Especially suited for linear regression or generalized linear regression algorithms.
- **Sequential feature selection**: Equivalent to stepwise regression, this can be applied with any supervised learning algorithm.
- Selecting features for classifying high-dimensional data.
- **Boosted and bagged decision trees**: Calculate the variable's importance from out-of-bag errors.
- **Regularization**: Remove redundant features by reducing their weights to zero.

Otherwise, feature extraction transforms existing features into new features (predictor variables) where less-descriptive features can be ignored.

The Statistics and Machine Learning Toolbox includes many feature extraction methods, as follows:

- **PCA**: This can be applied to summarize data in fewer dimensions by projection onto a unique orthogonal basis
- **Non-negative matrix factorization**: This can be applied when model terms must represent non-negative quantities
- **Factor analysis**: This can be applied to build explanatory models of data correlations

The following are step-wise regression example charts:

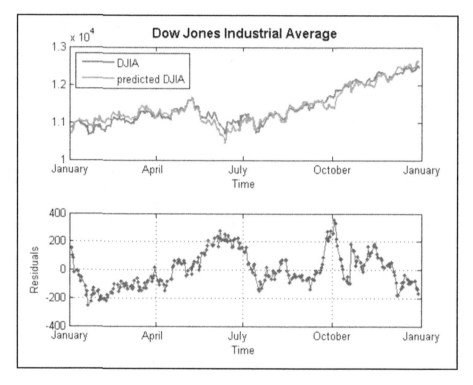

Figure 1.20: Step-wise regression example

Neural Network Toolbox

ANNs are a computational model used in computer science, built on a large series of simple neural units, called **artificial neurons**, which draw inspiration from the behavior observed in the axons of a human brain. Each neural unit is connected with many others, and such link defines the activation status of the adjacent neural units. Every single neural unit performs calculations using the summation function. The models based on ANNs are self-learning and training, rather than explicitly programmed, which his is particularly suitable in cases where the solution function is hard to express in a traditional computer program.

The Neural Network Toolbox provides algorithms, pre-trained models, and apps to create, train, visualize, and simulate neural networks with one hidden layer (called shallow neural network) and neural networks with several hidden layers (called deep neural networks). Through the use of the tools offered, we can perform classification, regression, clustering, dimensionality reduction, time series forecasting, and dynamic system modeling and control.

Deep learning networks include **convolutional neural networks** (**CNNs**) and autoencoders for image classification, regression, and feature learning. For training sets of moderated sized, we can quickly apply deep learning by performing transfer learning with pre-trained deep networks. To make working on large amounts of data faster, we can use the **Parallel Computing Toolbox** (another MATLAB toolbox) to distribute computations and data across multicore processors and GPUs on the desktop, and we can scale up to clusters and clouds with **MATLAB Distributed Computing Server**.

Here is a descriptive list of the key features of this tool; you will find the main topics of the machine learning field here:

- Deep learning with CNNs (for classification and regression) and autoencoders (for feature learning)
- Transfer learning with pre-trained CNNs models and models from the **Caffe model zoo**
- Training and inference with CPUs or multi-GPUs on desktops, clusters, and clouds
- Unsupervised learning algorithms, including self-organizing maps and competitive layers

In the following screenshot, the product capabilities of the **Neural Networks Toolbox** are shown, extracted from the MathWorks site:

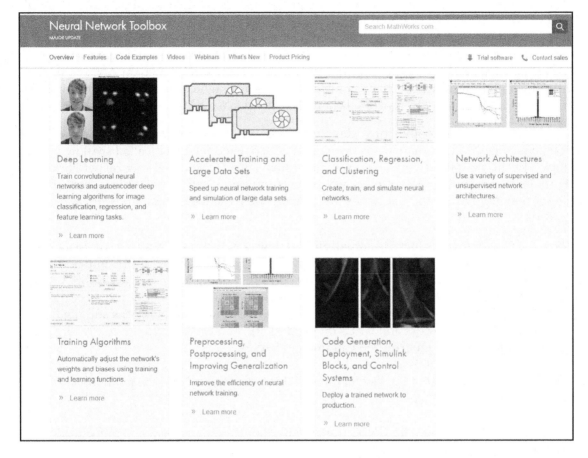

Figure 1.21: Product capabilities of the Neural Networks Toolbox

- Supervised learning algorithms, including multilayer, radial basis, **Learning Vector Quantization** (**LVQ**), time-delay, **nonlinear autoregressive** (**NARX**), and **Recurrent Neural Network** (**RNNs**)
- Apps for data fitting, pattern recognition, and clustering
- Preprocessing, postprocessing, and network visualization for improving training efficiency and assessing network performance

For a more comprehensive overview of the Neural Network Toolbox's capabilities, you can connect to the manufacturer's website at the following link: `https://www.mathworks.com/products/ neural-network.html`.

Statistics and algebra in MATLAB

Machine learning is an interdisciplinary field; it includes statistics, probability theory, algebra, computer science, and much more. These disciplines come together in algorithms capable of learning iteratively from data and finding hidden insights that can be used to create intelligent applications. In spite of the immense possibilities offered by machine learning, a thorough mathematical understanding of many of these disciplines is necessary for a good understanding of the inner workings of the algorithms and getting good results.

There are many reasons why the statistics and algebra is important to build a machine learning system. Some of them are highlighted as follows:

- Select the right algorithm in terms of accuracy, training time, number of parameters, number of features, and complexity of the model
- Correctly set the parameters and choose validation strategies
- Recognize underfitting and overfitting
- Put appropriate confidence interval and uncertainty

MATLAB offers several functions that allow us to perform statistical analyses and algebraic operations on our data. For example, in MATLAB, computing descriptive statistics from sample data really is a breeze. It is possible to measure central tendency, dispersion, shape, correlation, covariance, quantiles, percentiles and much more. In addition, we can tabulate and cross-tabulate data, and compute summary statistics for grouped data. In case of missing (NaN) values, MATLAB arithmetic operation functions return NaN. To solve this problem, available functions in Statistics and Machine Learning Toolbox ignore these missing values and return a numerical value calculated using the remaining values.

Furthermore we can use statistical visualization to understand how data is distributed and how that compares to other datasets and distributions. In MATLAB, we may explore single-variable distributions using univariate plots such as box plots and histograms. As well as we can discover the relationships between variables applying bivariate plots such as grouped scatter plots and bivariate histograms. We visualize the relationship between multiple variables using multivariate plots such as Andrews and glyph plots. Finally we may customize our plot by adding case names, least-squares lines, and reference curves.

As for statistical analysis, and also for linear algebra, MATLAB offers many solutions ready to use. To remind you, linear algebra is the study of linear equations and their properties and is based on numerical matrices. MATLAB offers many tools for manipulating matrices, easily understood by people who are not experts in them. MATLAB makes it easy to perform computations with vectors and matrices.

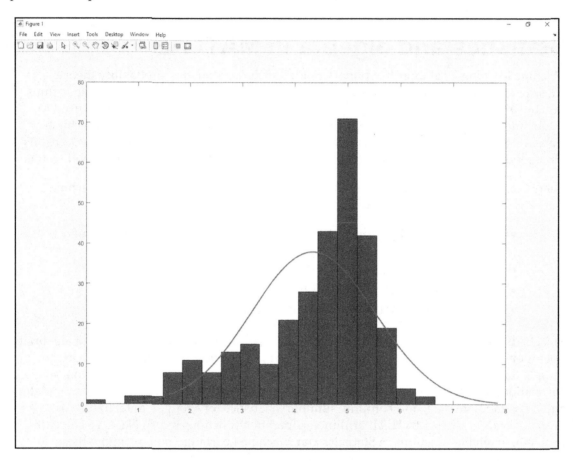

Figure 1.22: Histogram of the sample data with a normal density fit

MATLAB provides several functions for:

- Matrix operations and transformations
- Linear equations
- Matrix factorization and decomposition

- Eigenvalues and eigenvectors
- Matrix analysis and vector calculus
- Normal forms and special matrices
- Matrix functions

With the help of these functions, performing linear algebra tasks in a MATLAB environment is really easy.

Summary

In this chapter, we explored the amazing world of machine learning and took a tour of the most popular machine learning algorithms to choose the right one for our needs. To understand what is most suitable for our needs, we learned to perform a preliminary analysis. Then we analyzed how to build machine learning models step by step.

Afterwards, we discovered the machine learning capabilities in MATLAB for classification, regression, clustering, and deep learning, including apps for automated model training and code generation. We verified the MATLAB system requirements and platform availability for a correct installation.

Finally, we introduced the Statistics and Machine Learning Toolbox and Neural Network Toolbox. We learned what we can do with these tools, and what algorithms we need to use to solve our problems. We understood the role of statistics and algebra in machine learning and how MATLAB can help us.

In the next chapter, we will learn how to easily interact with the MATLAB workspace, import and organize our data in MATLAB, export data from the workspace, and organize the data in the correct format for the next phase of data analysis.

2
Importing and Organizing Data in MATLAB

Today, the amount of data generated is enormous; smartphones, credit cards, televisions, computers, home appliances, sensors, domotic systems, public and private transport, and so on are just a few examples of devices that generate data seamlessly. Such data is stored and then used for various purposes. One of these is data analysis using machine learning algorithms.

In the previous chapter, we analyzed how to build machine learning models step by step. At the start of the workflow, there is organization of data. Indeed, after collecting data, we typically need to import and preprocess. This first step is crucial for the proper functioning of the model that we will build and then for the final result.

In this chapter, we will have a look at how to import and organize our data in MATLAB. To do this, you should familiarize yourself with the MATLAB workspace in order to make the operations as simple as possible. Then we will analyze the different formats available for the data collected and how to move data into and out of MATLAB. We will also explore datatypes for working with grouping variables and categorical data and how to export data from the workspace, including cell array, structure array, and tabular data, and save it in a MATLAB-supported file format. Finally we will understand how to organize the data in the correct format for the next phase of data analysis.

We will cover the following topics:

- How to work with the MATLAB workspace
- How to use the MATLAB import tool to select and import data interactively
- The different datatypes supported by MATLAB
- How to export text, images, audio, video, and scientific data from MATLAB
- Discovering different ways to transform data
- Exploring the wide world of MATLAB data
- How to organize your data

At the end of the chapter, we will be able to import, format and organize our data correctly so that we can go on to next step: the exploratory data analysis.

Familiarizing yourself with the MATLAB desktop

MATLAB is an interactive working environment based on the matrix, the most natural way to express computational mathematics. Moreover, it is a programming language designed for technical computing, mathematical analysis, and system simulation. The integrated graphics make it easy to view and acquire knowledge from the data. Finally, a large library of prebuilt toolboxes allows us to immediately start with programming.

After installing, to start MATLAB, simply double-click on the icon on the desktop; or from the system prompt, type `matlab`. At first startup, MATLAB will show us a desk of contents with all the necessary items for its proper and smooth operation. *Figure 2.1* shows the MATLAB desktop in the R2017a version:

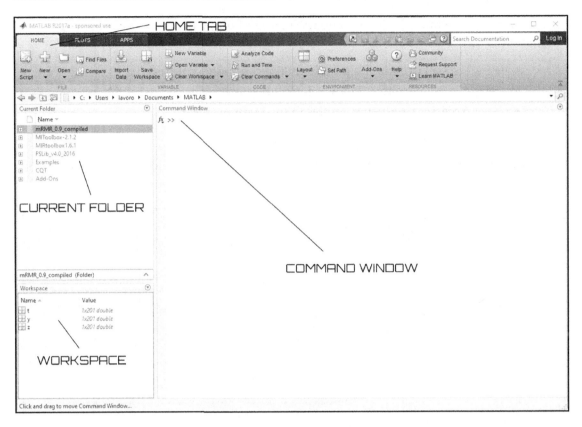

Figure 2.1: MATLAB R2017a desktop for Windows 10

The MATLAB desktop includes the following panels:

- **Current Folder**: Shows the files that are stored in this folder (we can change it)
- **Command Window**: At the prompt (>>), any MATLAB command or expression can be entered, so it can be used interactively
- **Workspace**: Shows variables that have been created or imported from data files or other programs
- **Command History**: Displays commands that have been entered (they can be called up quickly)

For a comprehensive introduction to the MATLAB desktop, we can use the following commands:

- `help`: Lists all primary help topics in the command window
- `lookfor`: Searches for a keyword in all help entries
- `demo`: Accesses product examples in the **Help** browser
- `doc`: A reference page in the **Help** browser

To exit from MATLAB, either type `quit` or `exit` at the prompt or click the **Close** box in the MATLAB desktop. The following figure shows the **MATLAB Toolstrip**:

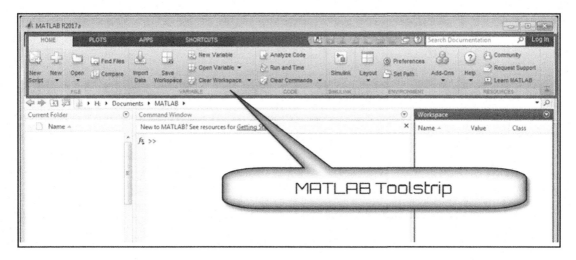

Figure 2.2: MATLAB Toolstrip

MATLAB now uses the typical toolstrip ribbon interface found in the recent Microsoft Windows applications. At the top of desktop window is the MATLAB Toolstrip (*Figure 2.2*). The toolstrip organizes MATLAB functionality in a series of tabs. Tabs are divided into sections that contain a series of related controls. The controls are buttons, drop-down menus, and other user interface elements that we will use to perform operations in MATLAB.

For example, the **HOME** tab includes icons used to perform operations on files, variables, code, and so on. The **PLOTS** tab shows tools for creating graphic presentations of our formulas and the **APPS** tab allows us to get new applications to use with MATLAB.

The first way--and a simple way--to interact with MATLAB is by using it as a calculator. Suppose we want to find the sum of two numbers, 10 and 90. To perform this operation, just position the cursor to the right of the symbol >> (MATLAB prompt), write precisely 10+90, and then press the *Enter* key, thereby obtaining the result:

```
>>10+90
ans =
    100
>>
```

The following screenshot shows a typical math task in the MATLAB desktop:

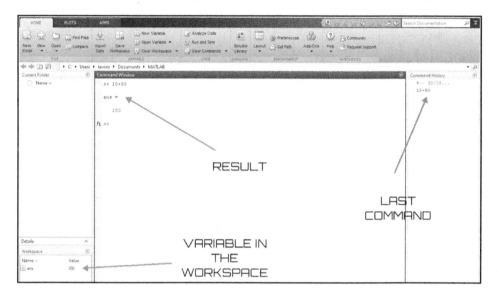

Figure 2.3: Typical math task in the MATLAB desktop

MATLAB performs the math task and assigns the result to the ans variable. Since we did not specify an output variable, MATLAB uses a default variable, precisely ans (short for answer), to store the results of the calculation. This operation is performed by default for every subsequent operation, with the result that the content of this ans variable, which could be defined as a working variable, is overwritten at each occurrence.

In order to avoid losing such information, starting from the next calculation, we will define new variables.

After this simple task, MATLAB starts to fill its windows; in fact, in the **Workspace Window** appears the `ans` variable, while the **Command History** window shows the operation performed so far (*Figure 2.3*).

To define a new variable in order to preserve the contents, we can use an assignment statement. For example, create two variables named FIRST and SECOND by typing the following statement in the command line:

```
>> FIRST = 10
FIRST =
         10
>> SECOND = 90
SECOND =
         90
>>
```

Now we can add these two variables and save the result in a third variable named THIRD:

```
>> THIRD = FIRST + SECOND
THIRD =
       100
>>
```

As we know, the basic elements of MATLAB are arrays, so all of the entered information is stored in the form of arrays. Thus, the variables FIRST, SECOND, and THIRD are arrays with a single value. To create an array with ten elements in a single row (row vector), separate the elements with either a space as shown in the following code or a comma (,):

```
>> vector = [10 20 30 40 50 60 70 80 90 100]
vector =
        10   20   30   40   50   60   70   80   90   100
>>
```

Similarly, to create a matrix that has multiple rows, separate the rows with semicolons, as follows:

```
>> matrix = [10 20 30; 40 50 60 ;70 80 90]
matrix =
        10   20   30
        40   50   60
        70   80   90
>>
```

To access the elements of an array, use indexing; for example, we can specify row and column subscripts so as to select the element in the first row and second column:

```
>> matrix (1,2)
ans =
    20
>>
```

To select multiple elements of an array, use the colon operator, specifying a interval of the form start:end. For example, for selecting the elements in the first three rows and the third column we can use the following code:

```
>> matrix (1:3,3)
ans =
    30
    60
    90
>>
```

Omitting start or end values, we will specify all the elements in that dimension. Thus, the previous result can also be obtained in the following way:

```
>> matrix (:,3)
ans =
    30
    60
    90
>>
```

The colon operator can also be used to create an equally spaced vector of values using the more general form start:step:end. For example, to create an array containing even numbers from 0 to 20, we can do this:

```
>> vector_even = 0:2:20
 vector_even =
             0   2   4   6   8   10   12   14   16   18   20
>>
```

To manipulate the data in the workspace, the following three commands are particularly useful: who, whos, and clear. The first and second list the contents of the workspace with the difference in the report details, while the third one cleans it by deleting all the variables. So far we have used some variables; let's see:

```
>> who
Your variables are:
FIRST          SECOND        THIRD          matrix        vector
vector_even
```

```
>> whos
  Name              Size              Bytes  Class     Attributes
  FIRST             1x1                   8  double
  SECOND            1x1                   8  double
  THIRD             1x1                   8  double
  matrix            3x3                  72  double
  vector            1x10                 80  double
  vector_even       1x11                 88  double
>>
```

So, we have verified that the whos command shows details of the variables contained in the workspace. How is it possible to check? The variables present in the whos report actually represent those contained in the MATLAB workspace, as shown in the *Figure 2.4*:

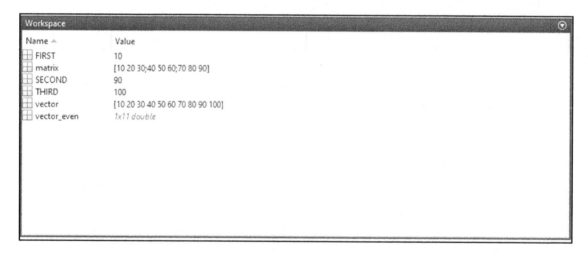

Figure 2.4: Workspace variables list.

It's time to tidy up the workspace, removing all of its contents. To do this, we will use the clear command, as follows:

```
>> clear
>> who
>>
```

Later, we use the `who` command to confirm that the workspace is empty. Use the `clear` command with caution. The variables that you erase may be impossible to recover. It's a good practice to save contents of the workspace before we exit MATLAB because variables do not persist later. Save your data for later use with the `save` command, shown as follows:

```
>> save filename.mat
```

With this command all the contents of the workspace is saved in a compressed file with a `.mat` extension, called a MAT-file, and all the contents of the workspace. To restore data from a MAT-file into the workspace, simply use the `load` command:

```
>> load filename.mat
```

MATLAB provides a large number of functions that perform computational tasks. For example, we calculate the average of the values contained in the array previously used. To call a function such as `mean()`, enclose its input arguments in parentheses, as shown here:

```
>> vector
vector =
    10    20    30    40    50    60    70    80    90   100
>> mean(vector)
ans =
    55
>>
```

Importing data into MATLAB

In data analysis, a fundamental role is assumed by the exchange of such data between the analysis environment and external devices. We start from data collection and importing in MATLAB for whatever analysis we are going to do--always. As well, we will finish our activities by exporting the results. There are several ways to import and export data in the MATLAB environment depending on the different formats in which data is available. In this section, we will cover data import.

The Import Wizard

We can import files into MATLAB both interactively and programmatically. Interactively, we can import data from a disk file or the system clipboard. From a file, do any one of these three actions:

- On the **HOME** tab, in the **Variable** section, select **Import Data**.
- Double-click on a filename in the **Current Folder** browser.
- Call the `uiimport()` function via the command line.

From the clipboard, do any one of the two following actions:

- On the **Workspace** browser title bar, click on the triangle icon and then select **Paste**.
- Call the `uiimport()` function via the command line.

In both cases, it will be invoked by **Import Wizard**. The import wizard is very useful for beginners since we are helped in the data import process, and depending on the nature of the data, various ways of importing are offered. This tool will guide us step by step in the data import process. So we can specify the type of data that we are going to import from many different recognizable file types. Among these, we can also import images, audio, and video data. The wizard allows us to view the contents of a file in order to select the variables to be imported, and possibly discard those deemed unnecessary.

The commands used in the **Import Wizard** can be saved in a script or function so that they can be reused to import other similar files. To understand how the **Import Wizard** works, let's look at a practical example. Suppose we want to import a spreadsheet in the MATLAB workspace (each field contains a variable). To do this, we use the **Import Wizard** in the following way:

1. Let's start **Import Wizard** in one of the ways that we've suggested.
2. For example, by selecting the **Import Data** button, we will open the **Import Data** dialog box.

3. After selecting the file (in our case, `IrisData.csv`), the **IMPORT** tool opens, as shown in *Figure 2.5*:

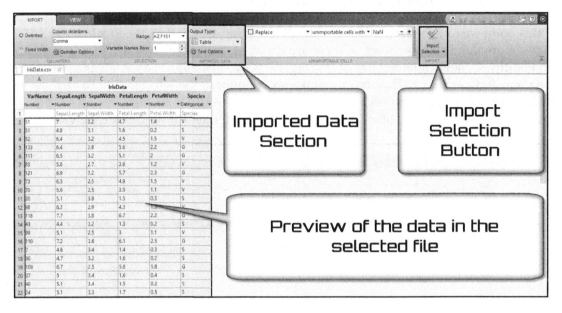

Figure 2.5: The IMPORT tool window

4. The **IMPORT** tool (*Figure 2.5*) shows a preview of the data in the selected file; we only select the ones that interest us, or do nothing to import the entire file content.

5. In the **Imported Data** section (*Figure 2.5*), in the drop-down menu below the **Output Type** label, it's possible to select how we want the data to be imported. The following options are available:

- **Table**: Import selected data as a table
- **Column vectors**: Import each column of the selected data as an individual *m-by-1* vector
- **Numeric Matrix**: Import selected data as an *m-by-n* numeric array
- **String Array**: Import selected data as a string array; each element that can contain a *1-by-N* character vector
- **Cell Array**: Import selected data as a cell array that can contain multiple datatypes, such as numeric data and text

6. Select the **Column vectors** option, for example.
7. Now just click on the **Import Selection** button (*Figure 2.5*); in this way the **IMPORT** tool creates variables in our workspace.

At this point we can check whether it worked; to do this, let's look at the **Workspace** browser, are there new variables? If there are variables, then it has worked. In our case, we can identify six new variables: `PetalLength`, `PetalWidth`, `SepalLength`, `SepalWidth`, `Species`, and `VarName1`. They represent the six columns of the selected file. To analyze the contents of each variable, besides recalling it from the MATLAB prompt, we can simply double-click on it. This will open the variables window, in which we can see the values:

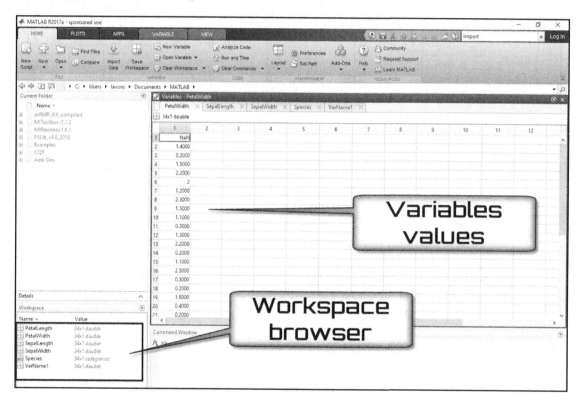

Figure 2.6: Variables inspection

Our variables have been correctly imported into MATLAB; now we will be able to use them to perform all the calculations we need for our purposes.

Importing data programmatically

As anticipated, we can import files into MATLAB programmatically. This way of importing data is very important as it can be inserted into a script and rendered automatically, while the wizard requires the presence of an operator. To import data programmatically, we will use the import functions available in MATLAB. Each import function has features that make it more suitable for a particular type of data, so it is crucial to choose the right one.

Loading variables from file

Previously, we've already seen some of these. In particular, we worked with the load() and save() functions to load and save workspace data using command-line functions. Let's review these functions:

```
>> save filename.mat
>> load filename.mat
```

 Recall that these functions operate on .mat files but can also be used with ASCII text files.

We've just seen how to upload a .mat file, which we remember represents a specific format to save the contents of the workspace. Let's now take a look at how to load ASCII text files. For this purpose, we can use different functions depending on the kind of delimiter (a character used to separate values) in the text files. If the numeric entries are separated by blank space, comma, semicolon, or tab, then the load() function can be used. Let's try it with an example. Suppose we have a text file named matrix.txt in the following form:

```
10 20 30
40 50 60
70 80 90
```

To import such data as a MATLAB matrix, we will write:

```
>> load matrix.txt
>> matrix
matrix =
    10    20    30
    40    50    60
    70    80    90
>>
```

Reading an ASCII-delimited file

In the previous case, we did not have to add anything; MATLAB automatically saved the contents of the file, naming the variable with the filename. In addition, we can use a little more flexible function: dmlread(). It is more flexible because it allows us to specify the delimiter used in the file and what data to import. In order to use this function, all data in the input file must be numeric. Let's start from a text file named matrix.txt in the following form:

```
10;20;30
40;50;60
70;80;90
```

To import such data using the dmlread() function, we can type:

```
>> MatrixTxt=dlmread('matrix.txt',';')
MatrixTxt =
     10    20    30
     40    50    60
     70    80    90
>>
```

To import the first two rows and two columns only:

```
>> MatrixTxt2=dlmread('matrix.txt',',','A1..B2')
MatrixTxt2 =
     10    20
     40    50
>>
```

Remember, the dlmread() function does not operate on files containing nonnumeric data even if the specified rows and columns for the read contain only numeric data.

Comma-separated value files

Now, we have a file named matrix.csv in the following form:

```
10,20,30
40,50,60
70,80,90
```

This is a particular file where the numbers are separated by commas (**Comma-Separated Values (CSV)**). MATLAB provides the `csvread()` function for this common type of file. This function reads a CSV file, which may only contain numeric values. To import such data using the `csvread()` function, we can type:

```
>> MatrixCsv=csvread('matrix.csv')
MatrixCsv =
    10    20    30
    40    50    60
    70    80    90
>>
```

This function also allows us to import only a selection of rows and columns. To import just a range of data contained in the file `matrix.csv`, type:

```
>> MatrixCsv2=csvread('matrix.csv',0,0,[0,0,1,2])
MatrixCsv2 =
    10    20    30
    40    50    60
>>
```

To understand how to identify the range of data, we must analyze the function argument (what is in the brackets):

```
csvread('matrix.csv',0,0,[0,0,1,2])
```

At the beginning is the name of the file, in the second and third place there are the number of rows and columns from which to start reading, and the fourth is a matrix that specifies the range of values to read. Now let's analyze the matrix:

```
[0,0,1,2]
```

The first and second values represent the upper-left corner of the data to be read, and the third and fourth represent the lower-right corner. In this case, `0,0` specifies the first value in the file (identified by the first row and first column); then `1,2` specifies the value identified by the second row and third column.

Importing spreadsheets

Another common file format is the spreadsheet, specially those created with Microsoft Excel. MATLAB provides a specific function called `xlsread()` to import this type of data. Using this function, we can import mixed numeric and text data into separate arrays. Let's start from a spreadsheet file, `capri.xlsx`, that contains temperature values (in Celsius degrees) recorded last August in Capri (a beautiful island in the Gulf of Naples). In a worksheet called `Temp`, there is the following data (only the first five days for space reasons):

Day	T Mean	T max	T min
1	26	24	29
2	26	24	29
3	26	24	30
4	27	24	30
5	26	23	28

At this point, we use the `xlsread()` function by entering only the filename and the name of the worksheet as arguments:

```
>>values = xlsread('capri.xlsx','Temp')
values =
1      26      24      29
2      26      24      29
3      26      24      30
4      27      24      30
5      26      23      28
>>
```

In this way, MATLAB ignores any leading rows or columns of text in the numeric result, making the result unclear by missing the header row. To retrieve this information, import both numeric data and header data by specifying two output arguments in the call to `xlsread()` in the following way:

```
>>[values,headertxt ]= xlsread('capri.xlsx','Temp')
values =
1       26        24        29
2       26        24        29
3       26        24        30
4       27        24        30
5       26        23        28
>> headertxt=
'Day' 'TMean' 'Tmin' 'Tmax'
>>
```

Two items are thus returned: an array (values) containing the numeric data and a cell array (`headertxt`) containing the text data of the header row. We can also import a specific range of data from the Excel file. The example in the following code reads only the first two rows of the spreadsheet:

```
>>row1_2 = xlsread('capri.xlsx','Temp','A2:D3')
row1_2 =
1       26        24        29
2       26        24        29
>>
```

Similarly, we can only read a specific column:

```
>>column_C = xlsread('capri.xlsx','Temp','C2:C6')
column_C =
24
24
24
24
23
>>
```

Reading mixed strings and numbers

There is more to life than numbers, although we cannot do without them. Very often we'll have to deal with files that can have numerical data as well as some text. In MATLAB, only some of the import functions actually work with strings and numbers. This is the case of the function `readtable()`. This function creates a table from a file. To understand how it works, we analyze the file containing the number of visitors to Italian museums in the last two years (*Figure 2.7*):

	A	B	C	D	E	F
1	N	Museum	City	Visitors2016	Visitors2015	
2	1	Colosseo e Foro Romano	ROMA	6408852	6551046	
3	2	Scavi di Pompei	POMPEI	3283740	2934010	
4	3	Galleria degli Uffizi	FIRENZE	2010631	1971758	
5	4	Galleria dell'Accademia di Firenze	FIRENZE	1461185	1415397	
6	5	Castel Sant'Angelo	ROMA	1234443	1047326	
7	6	Venaria Reale	VENARIA R.	1012033	580786	
8	7	Museo Egizio di Torino	TORINO	881463	863535	
9	8	Circuito Museale Boboli …	FIRENZE	852095	772934	
10	9	Reggia di Caserta	CASERTA	683070	497197	
11	10	Galleria Borghese	ROMA	527937	506442	
12						

Figure 2.7: Number of visitors in Italian museums

The `readtable()` function creates a table by reading column-oriented data from a file. The file formats supported are:

- Delimited text files: `.txt`, `.dat`, `.csv`
- Spreadsheet files: `.xls`, `.xlsb`, `.xlsm`, `.xlsx`, `.xltm`, `.xltx`, `.ods`

One variable for each column in the file will be created, and variable names will read from the first row of the file. By default, the variables created are double when the entire column is numeric and are cell arrays of character vectors when any element in a column is not numeric. The number of visitors to Italian museums is contained in a file named `museum.xls`:

```
>> TableMuseum = readtable('museum.xls')
TableMuseum =
  10×5 table
N    Museum                        City        Visitors_2016 Visitors_2015

1    'Colosseo e Foro Romano'      'ROMA'      6.4089e+06    6.551e+06
2    'Scavi di Pompei'             'POMPEI'    3.2837e+06    2.934e+06
3    'Galleria degli Uffizi'       'FIRENZE'   2.0106e+06    1.9718e+06
4    'Galleria dell'Accademia...'  'FIRENZE'   1.4612e+06    1.4154e+06
```

5	'Castel Sant'Angelo'	'ROMA'	1.2344e+06	1.0473e+06
6	'Venaria Reale'	'VENARIA'	1.012e+06	5.8079e+05
7	'Museo Egizio di Torino'	'TORINO'	8.8146e+05	8.6354e+05
8	'Circuito Museale Boboli ...'	'FIRENZE'	8.521e+05	7.7293e+05
9	'Reggia di Caserta'	'CASERTA'	6.8307e+05	4.972e+05
10	'Galleria Borghese'	'ROMA'	5.2794e+05	5.0644e+05

We can create a table that does not contain variable names as column headings:

```
>> TableMuseum = readtable('museum.xls','ReadVariableNames',false)
TableMuseum =
  10x5 table
Var1 Var2                          Var3        Var4         Var5
____ _____   _____   _____   _____

  1  'Colosseo e Foro Romano'      'ROMA'      6.4089e+06   6.551e+06
  2  'Scavi di Pompei'             'POMPEI'    3.2837e+06   2.934e+06
  3  'Galleria degli Uffizi'       'FIRENZE'   2.0106e+06   1.9718e+06
  4  'Galleria dell'Accademia...'  'FIRENZE'   1.4612e+06   1.4154e+06
  5  'Castel Sant'Angelo'          'ROMA'      1.2344e+06   1.0473e+06
  6  'Venaria Reale'               'VENARIA'   1.012e+06    5.8079e+05
  7  'Museo Egizio di Torino'      'TORINO'    8.8146e+05   8.6354e+05
  8  'Circuito Museale Boboli ...' 'FIRENZE'   8.521e+05    7.7293e+05
  9  'Reggia di Caserta'           'CASERTA'   6.8307e+05   4.972e+05
 10  'Galleria Borghese'           'ROMA'      5.2794e+05   5.0644e+05
```

Another function that can read both strings and numbers in the same dataset is `textscan()`. The `textscan()` function reads data from an open text file and saves its content in a cell array. The text file is indicated by the file identifier (for example, `fileID`). You must use the `fopen()` function to open the file and get the value of the file identifier; you can't simply open the file and work with it. Once you have finished reading from a file, you should close the file by calling the `fclose()` function, by specifying the `fileID`.

Let's remember that a cell array is a datatype with indexed data containers called **cells**. Each cell can contain any type of data. Cell arrays commonly contain text strings (a combination of text and numbers), spreadsheets, text files, or numeric arrays of different sizes, for example.

However, we must define a format specification to use this function. Describe each component with conversion specifiers, such as `%s` for character vectors, `%d` for integers, or `%f` for floating-point numbers.

As an example, we use a file named `Ferrari.txt`, which contains some information about the latest five Ferrari models (*Figure 2.8*). To begin, specify the data format:

```
>> formatSpec = '%u%s%d%d';
```

So let's open our file in read-only mode and assign it to the `fileID` variable. Remember, the variable `fileID` contains the identifier used to access the file:

```
>> fileID = fopen('Ferrari.txt');
```

Let's apply the `textscan()` function to it and assign the result to the variable `Ferrari`:

```
>> Ferrari = textscan(fileID, formatSpec);
```

In the following figure is some information about the latest five Ferrari models:

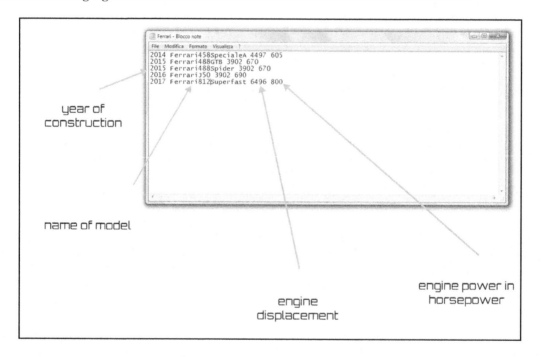

Figure 2.8: Information about the latest five Ferrari models

Now simply close the file:

```
>> fclose(fileID)
```

So we've imported the data contained in the file; let's check whether everything works as designed:

```
>>whos Ferrari
  Name          Size        Bytes  Class   Attributes
  Ferrari       1x4           635  cell
```

To view the datatype of each of the cells in `Ferrari`, simply type:

```
>> Ferrari
Ferrari = 1x4 cell array
    [5x1 uint32]   {5x1 cell}   [5x1 uint32]   [5x1 uint32]
```

Finally, to examine the individual entries:

```
>> celldisp(Ferrari)
Ferrari{1} =
2014
2015
2015
2016
2017
Ferrari{2}{1} =
Ferrari458SpecialeA
Ferrari{2}{2} =
Ferrari488GTB
Ferrari{2}{3} =
Ferrari488Spider
Ferrari{2}{4} =
FerrariJ50
Ferrari{2}{5} =
Ferrari812Superfast
Ferrari{3} =
4497
3902
3902
3902
6496
Ferrari{4} =
605
670
670
690
800
```

Exporting data from MATLAB

Many of the functions we have used to import data into MATLAB have a corresponding function that allows us to export data. At the beginning of the chapter, we learned to save our data for later use with the `save` command:

```
>> save filename.mat
```

Remember, this command saves all contents of the workspace in a compressed file with a `.mat` extension, called a MAT-file.

The `dlmread()` function allows us to handle text files with a specified delimiter. We can use this function to write a matrix to an ASCII-delimited file. To test the function, we start from a matrix of random numbers:

```
>> MyMatrix = rand(5)
MyMatrix =
    0.7577    0.7060    0.8235    0.4387    0.4898
    0.7431    0.0318    0.6948    0.3816    0.4456
    0.3922    0.2769    0.3171    0.7655    0.6463
    0.6555    0.0462    0.9502    0.7952    0.7094
    0.1712    0.0971    0.0344    0.1869    0.7547
```

Now simply write a matrix named `MyMatrix` to a file named `MyMatrix.txt` using the default delimiter (,):

```
>> dlmwrite('MyMatrix.txt', MyMatrix)
```

To view the data in the file, type:

```
>> type('MyMatrix.txt')
0.75774,0.70605,0.82346,0.43874,0.48976
0.74313,0.031833,0.69483,0.38156,0.44559
0.39223,0.27692,0.3171,0.76552,0.64631
0.65548,0.046171,0.95022,0.7952,0.70936
0.17119,0.097132,0.034446,0.18687,0.75469
```

To export data into spreadsheet files, we can use the `xlswrite()` function. This function writes a matrix into a Microsoft Excel spreadsheet. To test the function, we can use the same matrix already used in the previous example, although with different numbers because the `rand()` function creates different numbers for each use:

```
>> MyMatrix = rand(5)
MyMatrix =
    0.2760    0.4984    0.7513    0.9593    0.8407
    0.6797    0.9597    0.2551    0.5472    0.2543
    0.6551    0.3404    0.5060    0.1386    0.8143
    0.1626    0.5853    0.6991    0.1493    0.2435
    0.1190    0.2238    0.8909    0.2575    0.9293
```

To write a matrix named `MyMatrix` to a file named `MyMatrix.xls`, we can use the following command:

```
>> xlswrite('MyMatrix.xls', MyMatrix)
```

Finally, to export data from MATLAB in `.csv` files, use the `csvwrite()` function. Let's start again from a matrix of random numbers:

```
>> MyMatrix = rand(5)
MyMatrix =
    0.3500    0.3517    0.2858    0.0759    0.1299
    0.1966    0.8308    0.7572    0.0540    0.5688
    0.2511    0.5853    0.7537    0.5308    0.4694
    0.6160    0.5497    0.3804    0.7792    0.0119
    0.4733    0.9172    0.5678    0.9340    0.3371
```

To write a matrix named `MyMatrix` into a file named `MyMatrix.csv` as CSV, type:

```
>> csvwrite('MyMatrix.csv', MyMatrix)
```

A quick look at the **Current Folder** to verify the correct creation of the three file types (*Figure 2.9*):

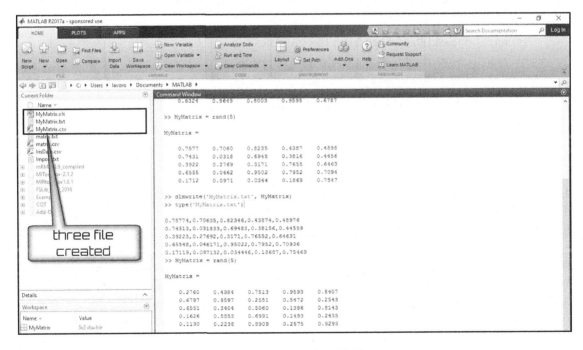

Figure 2.9: Exporting data from MATLAB

Working with media files

Images, videos, and audio files nowadays are an integral part of our lives. We use them widely thanks to the capabilities provided by modern devices that enable us to capture, store, and manipulate them. They often represent the input data we use in our machine learning applications, because through such algorithms, it is possible to extract a lot of information that at first glance is not so obvious. In this section, we will learn to deal with such files in the MATLAB environment.

Handling images

Raster images are made up of a grid of colored pixels. In MATLAB, images can be represented as two-dimensional matrices, where each matrix element corresponds to a single pixel of the displayed image. For example, a *800x600* photo (consisting of *600* lines and *800* columns of pixel of different colors) will be stored as a *600x800* matrix. However, sometimes, a third dimension will be required to store the depth of color. For example, for RGB images, you will need to specify red, green, and blue values to create a color image.

MATLAB provides several functions to operate on and display images. The following list will give a description of the most used functions for image handling:

- `imread`: Read the image from the graphics file
- `imwrite`: Write the image to the graphics file
- `image`: Display the image (create image object)
- `mfinfo`: Get image information from the graphics file
- `imagesc`: Scale data and display as an image
- `ind2rgb`: Convert an indexed image to an RGB image

To import an image in MATLAB, we can use the `imread()` function. This function imports the image from the file specified in brackets, obtaining the format of the file from its contents. Let's see an example:

```
>> Coliseum = imread('coliseum.jpg');
```

This is a beautiful image of the Colosseum, also known as the **Flavian Amphitheatre**, an oval amphitheater in the centre of the city of Rome, Italy. This file has a resolution of *1650x1042* pixels (*Figure 2.10*), so the resulting matrix is actually *1650x1042x3*.

To export an image from MATLAB, we will use the `imwrite()` function. It writes the data contained in a variable into a file specified by the user. The format of the exported file will be derived from the specified extension. The new file will be created in `Current Folder`. The bit depth of the output image will depend on the datatype in the variable and the file format. Then, to export the newly imported image to MATLAB (*Figure 2.10*), we will write:

```
>>imwrite(Coliseum, 'coliseum.jpg');
```

Here is a wonderful image of the Colosseum in Rome, as an example resource to be imported into MATLAB:

Figure 2.10: Importing images into MATLAB

In the following chapters, we will experiment with the use of some of these features through practical examples. In any case, for a detailed description of its operation, please refer to MATLAB's help.

Sound import/export

Sound signals are stored digitally in several file formats. The difference between formats generally depends on the degree of compression that affects sound quality. MATLAB provides several functions to handle audio files that allow us to write data to an audio file, get information about the file, and read data from the audio file. We can also record data from an audio input device and listen to audio files. The following list gives a description of the most used functions for the sound handling:

- `audioread`: Read audio file
- `audioinfo`: Information about the audio file
- `audiowrite`: Write audio file
- `audiodevinfo`: Information about the audio device
- `audioplayer`: Create an object for playing audio
- `audiorecorder`: Create an object for recording audio
- `sound`: Convert a matrix of signal data to sound
- `soundsc`: Scale the data and play as sound
- `beep`: Produce an operating system beep sound

To import audio files use the `audioread()` function. This function can support WAVE, OGG, FLAC, AU, MP3, and MPEG-4 AAC files. As an example, we will import a short audio file that contains the original NASA recording of Apollo 13, in which the famous message is communicated: *Houston, we have a problem.*

```
>>[apollo13,Fs] = audioread('apollo13.wav');
```

In this way, two variables are imported: a matrix of audio data, `apollo13`, and a sample rate, `Fs`. On the other hand, we also can read audio files interactively by selecting **Import Data** from the **HOME** tab or double-clicking on the filename in the **Current Folder** browser. To verify the procedure, we can listen to the audio file using the MATLAB player:

```
>> sound(apollo13,Fs)
```

For greater control during playback, we can use the `audioplayer()` function. It allows us to pause, resume, or define callbacks. To use this feature, create an `audioplayer` object; then call the methods to play the audio:

```
>> Apollo13Obj = audioplayer(apollo13,Fs);
>> play(Apollo13Obj);
```

Now that we have an audio file in MATLAB workspace as a matrix (`apollo13`), we can export it through the use of the `audiowrite()` function:

```
>> audiowrite('apollo13.wav',apollo13,Fs)
```

This command writes the data to a WAVE file named `apollo13.wav` in **Current Folder**. This function can also write to other audio file formats such as OGG, FLAC, and MPEG-4 AAC. Finally we use the `audioinfo()` function to get information about the WAVE file, `apollo13.wav`, that we just created:

```
>> InfoAudio = audioinfo('apollo13.wav')
```

Data organization

So far, for data organization, we have mostly used standard arrays that represent useful data structures for storing a large number of objects, but all of the same type, such as a matrix of numbers or characters. However, such arrays cannot be used if you want to memorize both numbers and strings in the same object. This is a problem that can be solved by so-called cell arrays, structure arrays, and more generally all those structures that the MATLAB programming environment provides us.

Cell array

A cell array is a datatype that has indexed data containers called cells. Each cell can contain any type of data; cell arrays can contain, for example, text strings, combinations of text and numbers, or numeric arrays of different sizes.

To create a cell array, we can simply use the cell array construction operator, that is, the `{ }` operator (braces), we can see as (name and age of my family members):

```
>> MyFamily = {'Luigi', 'Simone', 'Tiziana'; 13, 11, 43}
MyFamily =
  2×3 cell array
    'Luigi'    'Simone'    'Tiziana'
    [   13]    [   11]    [    43]
```

Like all MATLAB arrays, cell arrays are also rectangular, with the same number of cells in each row. For example, the cell array we just created (`MyFamily`) is a 2x3 array.

To perform math operations on this data, we must access the contents. There are two ways to refer to the elements of a cell array:

- Insert the indexes in round parentheses `()`, to provide a reference to cell sets, for example, to define a subset of the array
- Insert the indexes in braces, `{}`, to provide a reference to the text, numbers, or other data within the individual cells

To access the contents of a cell set, we can write, for example:

```
>> MyFamily2= MyFamily(1:2,1:2)
MyFamily2 =
  2×2 cell array
    'Luigi'    'Simone'
    [   13]    [    11]
```

So we've created a new `2x2 cell array` that contains the cells in the first two columns in the starting cell array. Now, we will see how to access the content of the single cell through the use of braces. Let's consider again the cell array that we've created before; we extract the content from the last cell:

```
>> LastCell= MyFamily{2,3}
LastCell =
    43
>> class(LastCell)
ans =
double
```

In this way, we create a numeric variable of the `double` type because the cell contains a double-precision numeric value. We can use the same syntax to modify the contents of the same cell:

```
>> MyFamily2{2,2}=110
MyFamily2 =
  2×2 cell array
    'Luigi'    'Simone'
    [   13]    [   110]
```

When trying to access the content of multiple cells, using the bracket syntax, MATLAB creates a list of contents of these cells, separated by commas:

```
>> MyFamily{1:2,1:3}
ans =
    'Luigi'
ans =
    13
```

```
ans =
    'Simone'
ans =
    11
ans =
    'Tiziana'
ans =
   430
```

To assign any content to a variable, we can type:

```
>> [r1c1, r2c1, r1c2, r2c2, r1c3, r2c3]= MyFamily{1:2,1:3}
r1c1 =
    'Luigi'
r2c1 =
    13
r1c2 =
    'Simone'
r2c2 =
    11
r1c3 =
    'Tiziana'
r2c3 =
   430
```

Then, each variable will be assigned a type depending on the cell content, so the cells in the first line will be of the `char` type and those of the second row will be of the `double` type. Check them:

```
>> class(r1c1)
ans =
    'char'

>> class(r2c1)
ans =
    'double'
```

If each cell contains the same type of data, it will be possible to create a single variable containing the set of such data by applying the array concatenation operator `[]` to the comma-separated list. For example:

```
>> Age = [MyFamily{2,:}]
Age =
    13    11    43
```

To add elements, we can use the concatenation operator, `[]`. In this example, the first cell array (`MyFamily`) is concatenated vertically with a cell array containing the member's gender, separating them with a semicolon:

```
>> MyFamily=[MyFamily;{'M','M','F'}]
MyFamily =
  3×3 cell array

    'Luigi'      'Simone'      'Tiziana'
    [   13]      [   11]       [     43]
    'M'          'M'           'F'
```

Structure array

Structure arrays are similar to cell arrays, as they allow us to group disparate data collections into a single variable. They differ from cell arrays because data is identified by names that are called **fields** instead of being identified by numbers (each field can contain data of any type or size). They also use point notation instead of braces. Let's look at how to define a structure of this type by creating a structure array for a warehouse customer's data, which contains several fields such as name, amount, and data (the data field contains the number of objects purchased by type). This is a structure array with multiple fields. First we define the fields and their values, and then we will create the structure (*Figure 2.10*):

```
>> field1 = 'Name';
>> value1 = {'Luigi','Simone','Tiziana'}
>> field2 = 'Amount';
>> value2 = {150000,250000,50000};
>> field3 = 'Data';
>> value3 = {[25, 65, 43; 150, 168, 127.5; 280, 110, 170],[5, 5, 23; 120,
118, 107.5; 200, 100, 140],[15, 45, 23; 160, 158, 12; 230, 140, 160]};

>> customers = struct(field1,value1,field2,value2,field3,value3)
customers =
  1×3 struct array with fields:
    Name
    Amount
    Data
```

In the following figure, we can see how a structure array is made in the preview provided by MATLAB:

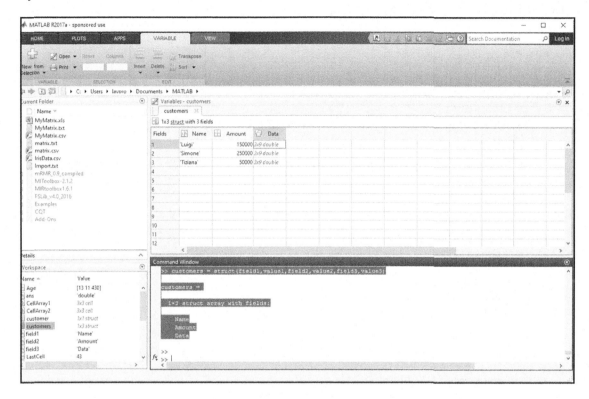

Figure 2.11: Structure array

As we anticipated earlier, it's possible to access data in this type of object using dot notation. Let's see how:

```
>> customers(1).Name
ans =
    'Luigi'

>> customers(1).Amount
ans =
    150000

>> customers(1).Data
ans =
   25.0000    65.0000    43.0000
  150.0000   168.0000   127.5000
  280.0000   110.0000   170.0000
```

The content in brackets is the record number we want to access. Each record of the customers array represents a structure that belongs to the struct class. Like other MATLAB arrays, a structure array can be of any size:

```
>> class(customers)
ans =
    'struct'
```

A structure array has the following properties:

- All records in the array have the same number of fields
- All records have the same field names
- Fields with the same name in different records can contain data of different types or sizes

If a new record is inserted, all unspecified fields will contain empty arrays:

```
>> customers(4).Name='Giuseppe';
>> customers(4)
ans =
  struct with fields:
      Name: 'Giuseppe'
    Amount: []
      Data: []
```

We now analyze how to create a bar graph of the first customer data (*Figure 2.11*):

```
>> bar(customers(1).Data)
>> title(['Data of first customer: ', customers(1).Name])
```

To access a part of a field, you must add the indexes according to the size and type of data in the field. For example, to display only the data field of the first two clients, we write:

```
>> customers(1:2).Data
ans =
    25.0000    65.0000    43.0000
   150.0000   168.0000   127.5000
   280.0000   110.0000   170.0000

ans =
    5.0000     5.0000    23.0000
   120.0000   118.0000   107.5000
   200.0000   100.0000   140.0000
```

Here is the bar plot of the first customer data:

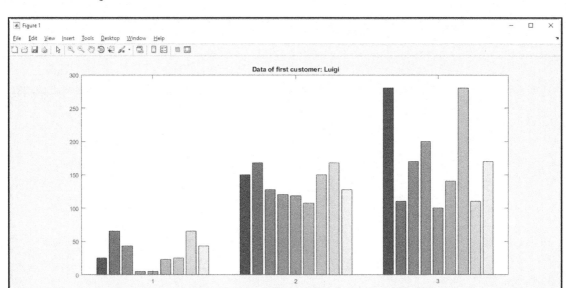

Figure 2.12: Bar plot of the first customer data

While, to access only the first two rows and two columns of values contained in the data field for the first customer, we will write:

```
>> customers(1).Data(1:2,1:2)
ans =
    25    65
   150   168
```

Table

A table in MATLAB represents a datatype for collecting heterogeneous elements with its metadata properties, such as variable names, row and column headers, descriptions, and unit of measurement of the variables, all in one container. Tables are particularly suitable for containing tabular data that is often placed in columns in a text file or spreadsheet. Each variable in the table can host a different type of data, but must have the same number of rows. A typical use of a table is to store experimental data, in which the rows represent the different observations of the phenomenon and the columns represent the different measured variables.

Here is a dataset example:

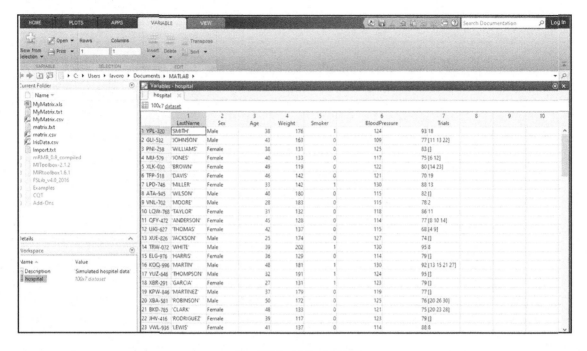

Figure 2.13: Simulated hospital data

Let's consider now how to create a table from variables in the MATLAB workspace and how to proceed with its visualization. Alternatively, we can use the import tool or the `readtable()` function to create a table from an existing spreadsheet or text file. When importing data from an external file with these tools, each column becomes a table variable. To get the data to be included in the table, quickly and easily, we can draw on the many examples in the software distribution. In this case, we load in the MATLAB workspace the MAT-file `hospital.mat` (present in software distribution), which contains simulated hospital data for `100` patients. After doing this we will be able to see all variables contained in the MATLAB workspace (*Figure 2.12*):

```
>> load hospital
>> whos
   Name            Size            Bytes   Class        Attributes
   Description     1x23               46   char
   hospital        100x7           46480   dataset
```

We can access variable data, or select a subset of variables, by using variable (column) names and dot indexing. For our needs we will extract individual fields in separate variables:

```
>> LastName=hospital.LastName;
>> Sex=hospital.Sex;
>> Age=hospital.Age;
>> Weight=hospital.Weight;
```

Now we will create a table and populate it with data contained in the fields (columns) Gender, Smoker, Height, and Weight already present as work variables, so we will only view the top five rows for space reasons:

```
>> TablePatients = table(LastName,Sex,Age,Weight);
>> TablePatients(1:5,:)
ans =
  10x4 table
    LastName        Sex        Age      Weight

    'SMITH'         Male        38       176
    'JOHNSON'       Male        43       163
    'WILLIAMS'      Female      38       131
    'JONES'         Female      40       133
    'BROWN'         Female      49       119
```

We can add new fields using dot notation. First, we extract the blood pressure from the starting dataset, dividing it into two variables:

```
>> BlPrMax=hospital.BloodPressure(:,1);
>> BlPrMin=hospital.BloodPressure(:,2);
```

Now add the two new variables to the table:

```
>> TablePatients.BlPrMax=BlPrMax;
>> TablePatients.BlPrMin=BlPrMin;
```

To confirm the correctness of the operations, we print the first five rows of the table and only three columns:

```
>> TablePatients(1:5,[1 5:6])
ans =
  5x3 table
    LastName        BlPrMax      BlPrMin

    'SMITH'          124          93
    'JOHNSON'        109          77
    'WILLIAMS'       125          83
    'JONES'          117          75
    'BROWN'          122          80
```

We can create a summary table to see the datatype, description, units of measurement, and other descriptive statistics for each variable, using the summary() function:

```
>> summary(TablePatients)
Variables:
    LastName: 100x1 cell array of character vectors
    Sex: 100x1 categorical
        Values:
            Female     53
            Male       47
    Age: 100x1 double
        Values:
            Min        25
            Median     39
            Max        50
    Weight: 100x1 double
        Values:
            Min          111
            Median       142.5
            Max          202
    BlPrMax: 100x1 double
        Values:
            Min          109
            Median       122
            Max          138
    BlPrMin: 100x1 double
        Values:
            Min           68
            Median       81.5
            Max          99
```

Categorical array

Categorical variables are intended to contain data that has values belonging to a finite set of discrete categories. These categories may have a natural order or may be unordered. A variable is **categorical unordered** if the property to be recorded has discrete non-orderable values. To the categories are assigned values that have no meaning other than to identify a category and distinguish it from others (man, woman). Conversely, a variable is said to be **categorical ordered** if the property to be recorded has discrete values that can be ordered. In this case, the categories are assigned a value that reflects the order relationships between them (*1,2,3,4 ..*).

To create a categorical array from a numeric array, a logical array, a cell array, a character array, or an existing categorical array, use the `categorical()` function. As an example, we will use the data already analyzed in the previous paragraph; in particular, we will refer to the `Sex` and `Age` variables, which contain the gender and age of patients in a hospital. Those variables will be converted into categorical arrays by using the commands in the following code:

```
>> SexC=categorical(Sex);
>> categories(SexC)
ans =
  2×1 cell array
    'Female'
    'Male'
>> AgeC=categorical(Age);
>> categories(AgeC)
ans =
  25×1 cell array
    '25''27''28''29''30''31''32''33''34''35''36''37''38''39'
'40''41''42''43''44''45''46''47''48''49'50'
```

We notice that the categories of the `SexC` array are presented in alphabetical order (categorical unordered) while those of `AgeC` are in ascending order (categorical ordered).

In the example that follows, we will discuss the case of creating an ordinal categorical array by binning type numeric data. In this regard, recall that data binning is a preprocessing technique used to reduce the effects of observation errors. The values of the original data that fall within a given range (bin) will be replaced by a representative value of this range, often identified with the central value. To do this, we will use the `Age` variable. We will use the `discretive()` function to create a categorical array by binning `Age` values. We will divide the range of values (25 50) into three bins (25-33, 33-41, 41-50); each bin will include the left extremity but not the right one. We will also provide a name for each of the three bins so identified:

```
>> NameBin = {'FirstBin', 'SecondBin', 'ThirdBin'};
>> AgeBin = discretize(Age,[25 33 41 50],'categorical',NameBin);
```

In this way, we will create a categorical array `100x1` with three categories such that:

```
FirstBin   <   SecondBin   <    ThirdBin
```

Use the `summary()` function to print the number of items in each category:

```
>> summary(AgeBin)
     FirstBin        27
     SecondBin       33
     ThirdBin        40
```

Summary

In this chapter, we started to explore the MATLAB desktop and how to easily interact with it. We took a look at MATLAB Toolstrip and how it is organized into a series of tabs. Then we just used MATLAB as a calculator and learned to manipulate matrices.

Next, we discovered the importing capabilities of MATLAB for reading several input types of data resources. We also learned how to import data into MATLAB interactively and programmatically. Afterwards, we understood how to export data from the workspace and working with media files.

Finally, we introduced data organization. We learned how to work with a cell array, structure array, table, and categorical array.

In the next chapter, we will learn the different datatypes in machine learning and how to clean the data and identify missing data. In addition, we will understand how to work with outliers and derived variables, learn the most used descriptive statistical techniques, and understand some data analysis techniques.

3
From Data to Knowledge Discovery

Modern computer technology, coupled with the availability of more and more powerful sensors, has led to impressive-sized collections of information. Having a lot of data, on one hand, undoubtedly represents an advantage; on the other hand, it is a problem. This is because it imposes obvious management problems, in the sense that more sophisticated tools will be needed to extract knowledge from it.

These pieces of data, taken individually, are in fact pieces of elementary information that describe some particular aspects of a phenomenon, but do not allow us to represent them. To get more knowledge about a phenomenon, a form of analysis is needed that can link the data to some *significant* aspect of the phenomenon itself. It is therefore necessary to follow a path to transform data into an element of knowledge.

The two important steps in this path are the analysis, which extracts information from the raw data, and the model, which allows the information to be included in an interpretative context. This context defines its meaning and establishes correlation with other pieces of information, contributing in this way to the knowledge of the phenomenon.

From this chapter, we begin to analyze data to extract useful information. We start from an analysis of the basic types of variables and the degree of cleaning the data. We will analyze the techniques available for preparation of the most suitable data for analysis and modeling, which includes imputation of missing data, eliminating outliers, and adding derived variables. Through descriptive statistical techniques, it will then be possible to more accurately explain the data. The chapter will focus on some data analysis techniques. Then, we will move on to data visualization, which plays a key role in understanding data.

We will cover the following topics:

- Basic types of variables
- How to treat missing data, outliers, clean the data
- Methods of measuring of central tendency, dispersion, shape, correlation, and covariance
- Discovering techniques to calculate ranges, percentiles, and quartiles
- How to draw box plots, histograms, scatter plots, and a scatter plot matrix

At the end of the chapter, we will be able to distinguish the different datatypes in machine learning, clean the data and identify missing data. Work with outliers and missing entries, use the most common descriptive statistical techniques, understand some data analysis techniques, and display data values on a plot.

Distinguishing the types of variables

Data can be collected in a number of ways; however, the typology of the result can easily be identified by a simple test. If we have to measure a quantity related to a specific event, we collect numbers that identify quantitative variables. If we have to describe the quality of an observed phenomenon, we cannot measure it and we are collecting qualitative variables. Let's understand each one in detail.

Quantitative variables

Quantitative variables (also called **continuous variables**) are an expression of a measure and are presented in the form of numerical data. Some examples of quantitative variables are temperature, pressure, and humidity values of a precise location. Quantitative variables can be further categorized as either interval or ratio variables.

Interval variables are variables that assume numeric values that allow comparisons only by difference. It follows that it is possible to order statistical units based on the answers and also to measure the difference between the values assumed by each of them. Interval scale assumes an arbitrary zero that represents a convention and not the absolute absence of the phenomenon (for example, temperature measured in degrees Celsius). In this case, you can compare the differences between temperatures but not the ratios:

- New York *10 °C*
- Miami *20 °C*
- Mexico City *30 °C*

The difference between the temperature of Mexico City and Miami is the same difference as between Miami and New York (*10* degrees), but the ratio is different.

Ratio variables are variables that assume numeric values that allow comparisons for both the difference and the relationship between the modes that the units assume. It follows that in addition to ordering and comparing the differences, it is possible to relate in proportional terms the values assumed by the different units. The ratio scale assumes an absolute zero that indicates the absolute absence of the phenomenon. The name *ratio* indicates that you can use the ratio of those variables to make a comparison. Thus, for example, a weight of *100* kg is twice the weight of *50* kg, which indicates that weight is a ratio variable.

Qualitative variables

Qualitative variables, also called **categorical variables**, are variables that are not numerical. They do not derive from measurement operations (and do not have units of measurement) but from classification and comparison operations; for instance, they describe data that fits into specific categories. Categorical variables can be further grouped as nominal, dichotomous, or ordinal.

Nominal variables are variables that have two or more categories, but do not have an intrinsic order. For example, the blood group variable, limited to the *ABO* system, can assume values *A, B, AB, O*. If we try to sort the values that this variable can assume (for example, from smallest to largest), we immediately realize that there is no solution. These variables can not be used for mathematical operations, but can be used as a grouping of subjects in a sample. There are no intermediaries and there is no order or hierarchy between them.

The **dichotomous** variables are a special case of nominal variables that have only two categories or levels, for example, gender. This leads us to classify people as *male* or *females*. This is an example of a dichotomous variable as well as a nominal variable.

Ordinal variables are variables that have two or more categories, just like nominal variables, but compared to the former, they can also be ordered or ranked. For example, the presence of blood in urine may take the following values: *absent, traces, +, ++, +++*. In this example, the order in which the values assigned to the variable has been listed to follow a precise logic, proceeding regularly from the absence of blood to the most massive presence. The position occupied in the ordinal scale not only allows us to determine whether there is a difference between two values, but also defines the sign of that difference. In the case of ordinal variables, it is also not possible to define how much a variable value is greater/less than another variable.

Data preparation

Once data collection has been completed and imported into MATLAB, it is finally time to start the analysis process. This is what a novice might think; conversely, we must first proceed to the preparation of data (data wrangling). This is a laborious process that can take a long time, in some cases about *80* percent of the entire data analysis process. However, it is a fundamental prerequisite for the rest of the data analysis workflow, so it is essential to acquire the best practices in such techniques.

Before submitting our data to any machine learning algorithm, we must be able to evaluate the quality and accuracy of our observations. If we cannot access the data stored in MATLAB correctly or if we do not know how to switch from raw data to something that can be analyzed, we cannot go ahead.

A first look at data

Before passing our data to machine learning algorithms, we need to give a first look at what we've imported into MATLAB to see if there are any issues. Often, raw data is messy and poorly formatted. In other cases, it may not have the appropriate details for our study. Correcting the data in progress can be destructive because it can be overwritten without the ability to restore the original data.

 To get started, it's good practice to keep your original data. To do this, every change will be performed on a copy of the dataset.

Putting order in the data is the first step and it will make data cleaning more easily, but let's ask a question. When can we say that our data is tidy? According to Edgar F. Codd, a dataset is tidy if it satisfies the following conditions:

- Observations are in rows
- Variables are in columns
- Data is contained in a single dataset

But what else can we find in raw data? There are various things that can go wrong in collecting data. Here are some of the most commonly found problems:

- A table contains more types of observed phenomena
- A single observed phenomenon is stored in several tables
- Column headers do not contain variable names
- A column contains multiple variables
- Variables are stored in both rows and columns

Let's move on to a practical example, we will use a file designed ad hoc that contains the data for a small sample of observation; it lists the results of a test. We'll grab `CleaningData.xls`, a spreadsheet that contains some of the issues we just listed. To import this file into MATLAB, we navigate to the folder where we saved the file, in my case `MatlabForML`. To do this, we will write (this path is valid in the PC I'm using; in your case, you will need to find the right one):

```
>> cd('C:\Users\lavoro\Documents\MATLAB\MatlabForML')
```

This command fixes the current folder to the folder containing the spreadsheet. Now it's possible to load the data with the help of the following command:

```
>> SampleData = readtable('CleaningData.xlsx');
```

Now that we have the data in a table in the MATLAB workspace, first we print a summary of the main features with this command:

```
>> summary(SampleData)
Variables:
    name: 12x1 cell array of character vectors
    gender: 12x1 cell array of character vectors
    age: 12x1 cell array of character vectors
    right: 12x1 cell array of character vectors
    wrong: 12x1 double
        Values:
            Min        2
            Median     43
            Max        95
```

In the following screenshot, an overview of the MATLAB desktop is shown, with the newly imported spreadsheet in the foreground:

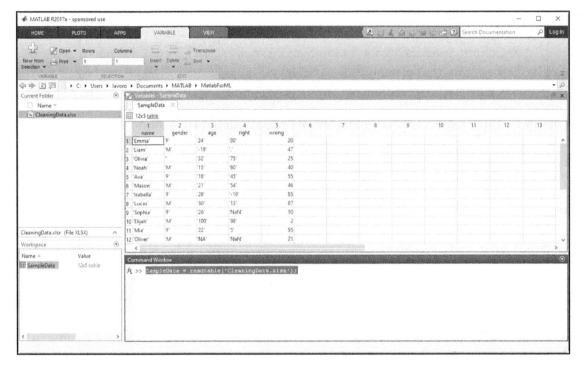

Figure 3.1: Spreadsheet imported into MATLAB

Already we can notice that the `age` variable has one missing value. Missing values of any type of variable are indicated by the NA code, which means not available. The **Not a Number (NaN)** code, on the other hand, indicates invalid numeric values, such as a numeric value divided by zero. If a variable contains missing values, MATLAB can not apply some functions to it. For this reason, it is necessary to process the missing values in advance. Let's look at the table to see what it contains:

```
>> SampleData
SampleData =
  12×5 table
        name       gender     age      right     wrong

       'Emma'       'F'       '24'      '80'       20
       'Liam'       'M'       '-19'     '.'        47
       'Olivia'     ''        '32'      '75'       25
       'Noah'       'M'       '15'      '60'       40
       'Ava'        'F'       '18'      '45'       55
```

'Mason'	'M'	'21'	'54'	46
'Isabella'	'F'	'28'	'-19'	85
'Lucas'	'M'	'30'	'13'	87
'Sophia'	'F'	'26'	'NaN'	30
'Elijah'	'M'	'100'	'98'	2
'Mia'	'F'	'22'	'5'	95
'Oliver'	'M'	'NA'	'NaN'	21

A quick look and we notice that there are some problems:

- Empty cells
- Cell containing a period (.)
- Cell containing the string NA
- Cells containing the string NaN
- Cells containing a negative number (-19)

In this case, we were fast because the file is small--only 12 records--but in the case of large files, we would not have been as quick.

Finding missing values

To find observations with missing values just as fast, we can use the `ismissing()` function. This function displays the subset of observations that have at least one missing value:

```
>> id = {'NA' '' '-19' -19 NaN '.'};
>> WrongPos = ismissing(SampleData,id);
>> SampleData(any(WrongPos,2),:)
ans =
  4×5 table
       name       gender     age      right     wrong
```

name	gender	age	right	wrong
'Liam'	'M'	'-19'	'.'	47
'Olivia'	' '	'32'	'75'	25
'Isabella'	'F'	'28'	'-19'	85
'Oliver'	'M'	'NA'	'NaN'	21

We analyze this code in detail:

- the first line specifies the types of data we want to locate in the table
- the second identifies the location of missing data
- finally, we print only the records with missing data

Remember, the `ismissing()` function recognizes, by default, only the following missing value indicators:

- `NaN` for numeric arrays
- `''` for character arrays
- `<undefined>` for categorical arrays

All the others must be specified in the way we have just seen.

In addition, we can use the `NumericTreatAsMissing` and `StringTreatAsMissing` options to specify other values to treat as missing.

Changing the datatype

Comparing the report provided by the `summary()` function with the content of the `SampleData` table, it is noted that the `age` variable (containing numbers) is stored as a cell array of character vectors. We can correct the problem by converting the char variables that should be numeric using the `str2double()` function:

```
>> SampleData.age = str2double(SampleData.age);
>> summary(SampleData(:,3))
Variables:
 age: 12×1 double
 Values:
 Min -19
 Median 24
 Max 100
 NumMissing 1
```

Now, the `age` variable is a numeric array. During the conversion, the `str2double()` function replaces the nonnumeric elements of the age variable with the value `NaN`. However, there are no changes to the numeric missing value indicator, `-19`. We do the same for the right variable:

```
>> SampleData.right = str2double(SampleData.right);
>> summary(SampleData(:,4))
Variables:
    right: 12×1 double
        Values:
            Min         -19
            Median      54
            Max         98
            NumMissing  3
```

In both cases, a conversion from cell arrays of character vectors to numeric arrays is performed; in fact, the `summary` function also shows simple statistical data (`Min`, `Median`, and `Max`) and the number of missing values.

Replacing the missing value

The next step will allow us to replace the missing value indicators. Then, we will clean the data so that the missing values indicated by the −19 code have the missing numeric value matrix provided by MATLAB, which (as mentioned) is `NaN`. To do this, we can use the `standardizeMissing()` function, which replaces the values specified in parentheses with standard missing values in an array or table:

```
>> SampleData = standardizeMissing(SampleData,-19);
>> summary(SampleData(:,3))
Variables:
    age: 12×1 double
        Values:
            Min            15
            Median         25
            Max            100
            NumMissing     2
```

We may notice that −19 is no longer present, while the missing values are now 2 instead of 1. At this point, we can create a new table, `SampleDataNew`, and replace the missing values with the correct values with the help of the `fillmissing()` function. This function fills missing entries of an array or table with a value indicated, and provides a number of ways to fill in missing values. In this case, we fill missing values with values from previous rows of the table:

```
>> SampleDataNew = fillmissing(SampleData, 'previous')
SampleDataNew =
  12×5 table
```

name	gender	age	right	wrong
'Emma'	'F'	24	80	20
'Liam'	'M'	24	80	47
'Olivia'	'M'	32	75	25
'Noah'	'M'	15	60	40
'Ava'	'F'	18	45	55
'Mason'	'M'	21	54	46
'Isabella'	'F'	28	54	85
'Lucas'	'M'	30	13	87
'Sophia'	'F'	26	13	30
'Elijah'	'M'	100	98	2

```
'Mia'            'F'          22      5        95
'Oliver'         'M'          22      5        21
```

As we can see, there are no missing values; in fact the missing data has been replaced with that of the previous cell (this was performed column by column).

Removing missing entries

In the order to prepare data for subsequent exploration, we may consider it necessary to remove the lines with missing values. Let's create a new table, SampleDataMinor, which contains only the rows without missing values, starting from the table containing the raw data. To this end, we will use the rmmissing() function; it removes missing entries from an array or table:

```
>> SampleDataMinor = rmmissing(SampleData)
SampleDataMinor =
  7x5 table
      name         gender      age     right     wrong

    _____      _____     ___     _____     _____

    'Emma'         'F'          24      80        20
    'Noah'         'M'          15      60        40
    'Ava'          'F'          18      45        55
    'Mason'        'M'          21      54        46
    'Lucas'        'M'          30      13        87
    'Elijah'       'M'         100      98         2
    'Mia'          'F'          22       5        95
```

Thus, the 12-row table has only seven rows, which are the only rows that have all the correct data.

Ordering the table

We're done with the cleaning; now is the time to rearrange the table through the organization of our data. In particular, we will order the rows of the newly created table, SampleDataMinor, in descending order with the age variable. In this case, we will use the sortrows() function, which sorts the rows of a matrix in the order specified in parentheses based on the elements in the column, also specified in parentheses:

```
>> SampleDataOrdered = sortrows(SampleDataMinor,{'age'},{'descend'})
SampleDataOrdered =
  7x5 table
      name         gender      age     right     wrong

    _____      _____     ___     _____     _____
```

'Elijah'	'M'	100	98	2
'Lucas'	'M'	30	13	87
'Emma'	'F'	24	80	20
'Mia'	'F'	22	5	95
'Mason'	'M'	21	54	46
'Ava'	'F'	18	45	55
'Noah'	'M'	15	60	40

The small table now shows the records in decreasing order of age, so the elderly must be first.

Finding outliers in data

Outliers are the values that, compared to others, are particularly extreme. Outliers are a problem because they tend to distort data analysis results, in particular in descriptive statistics and correlations. These should be identified in the data cleaning phase, but can also be dealt in the next step of data analysis. Outliers can be univariate when they have an extreme value for a single variable or multivariate when they have an unusual combination of values on a number of variables.

In MATLAB, an outlier can be identified easily and effectively. Just use the `isoutlier()` function, which actually finds outliers in data. Apply it to the previous example, in particular to the table `SampleDataNew`, which contains the clean data:

```
>> SampleDataOutlier = isoutlier(SampleDataNew(2:end,3:5))
SampleDataOutlier =
  11×3 logical array
   0   0   0
   0   0   0
   0   0   0
   0   0   0
   0   0   0
   0   0   0
   0   0   0
   0   0   0
   1   0   0
   0   0   0
   0   0   0
```

This function returns a logical array whose elements are true when an outlier is detected in the corresponding item in the table. By default, MATLAB identifies an outlier if it is more than three average escalating MADs far from the median. In our case, we applied the function only to the three columns that contained numeric data, and we omitted the first line containing the variable names. The following figure shows the result of the application of the `isoutlier()` function being compared to the original data to locate the outliers:

```
SampleDataNew =

   12×5 table                                   SampleDataOutlier =

      name       gender   age   right   wrong      11×3 logical array

                                                    0   0   0
     'Emma'      'F'      24     80      20         0   0   0
     'Liam'      'M'      24     80      47         0   0   0
     'Olivia'    'M'      32     75      25         0   0   0
     'Noah'      'M'      15     60      40         0   0   0
     'Ava'       'F'      18     45      55         0   0   0
     'Mason'     'M'      21     54      46         0   0   0
     'Isabella'  'F'      28     54      85         0   0   0
     'Lucas'     'M'      30     13      87         0   0   0
     'Sophia'    'F'      26     13      30
     'Elijah'    'M'     100     98       2         1   0   0
     'Mia'       'F'      22      5      95         0   0   0
     'Oliver'    'M'      22      5      21         0   0   0
```

Figure 3.2: Finding outliers in MATLAB

The function works on each column separately. By comparing the table `SampleDataOutlier` with `SampleDataNew`, it can be seen that we have identified an outlier only in the value of **100** (*Figure 3.2*) for the age variable.

Organizing multiple sources of data into one

Suppose we have some data from a survey deriving from two representative samples of the population. These pieces of data are subsequently imported into MATLAB in two separate tables: `SampleData1` and `SampleData2`. Let's see what they contain:

```
>> SampleData1 = SampleDataNew(1:6,:)
SampleData1 =
  6×5 table
```

```
name gender age right wrong
```

_____ _____ ___ _____ _____

```
'Emma'  'F'  24 80 20
'Liam'  'M'  24 80 47
'Olivia' 'M'  32 75 25
'Noah'  'M'  15 60 40
'Ava'   'F'  18 45 55
'Mason' 'M'  21 54 46

>> SampleData2 = SampleDataNew(7:end, :)
SampleData2 =
  6×5 table
  name gender age right wrong
```

_____ _____ ___ _____ _____

```
'Isabella' 'F'  28 54 85
'Lucas'   'M'  30 13 87
'Sophia'  'F'  26 13 30
'Elijah'  'M'  100 98 2
'Mia'    'F'  22 5 95
'Oliver'  'M'  22 5 21
```

Our aim is to submit such data for an exploratory analysis, but as similar data, we first want to merge them into one table. This is a simple concatenation of two matrices. Concatenation is the conjunction process of small matrices to create larger matrices. Concatenating matrices in MATLAB is really a joke. When you create an array, you merely concatenate its individual elements. In MATLAB, the square bracket [] is the concatenation operator. In this case, just type the following command:

```
>> SampleDataComplete = [SampleData1;SampleData2]
SampleDataComplete =
  12×5 table
```

name	gender	age	right	wrong
'Emma'	'F'	24	80	20
'Liam'	'M'	24	80	47
'Olivia'	'M'	32	75	25
'Noah'	'M'	15	60	40
'Ava'	'F'	18	45	55
'Mason'	'M'	21	54	46
'Isabella'	'F'	28	54	85
'Lucas'	'M'	30	13	87
'Sophia'	'F'	26	13	30
'Elijah'	'M'	100	98	2
'Mia'	'F'	22	5	95
'Oliver'	'M'	22	5	21

In addition, we have some data that allows us to add useful information about gender features. In particular, we have data on life expectancy in `Hong Kong` (the country with a higher life expectancy) in a file named `LifeExpectancy.xlsx`. We start importing it into MATLAB:

```
>> LifeExpectancy = readtable('LifeExpectancy.xlsx')
LifeExpectancy =
  2×3 table
        state        Le       gender

    'Hong Kong'     80.91      'M'
    'Hong Kong'     86.58      'F'
```

At this point, we just want to add this data. To do this, we will use the `join()` function; it merge two tables by rows using key variables:

```
>> SampleDataLE = join(SampleDataComplete,LifeExpectancy, 'Keys', 'gender')
SampleDataLE =
  12×7 table
  name        gender    age    right    wrong      state        Le

  'Emma'       'F'        24     80       20      'Hong Kong'    86.58
  'Liam'       'M'        24     80       47      'Hong Kong'    80.91
  'Olivia'     'F'        32     75       25      'Hong Kong'    86.58
  'Noah'       'M'        15     60       40      'Hong Kong'    80.91
  'Ava'        'F'        18     45       55      'Hong Kong'    86.58
  'Mason'      'M'        21     54       46      'Hong Kong'    80.91
  'Isabella'   'F'        28     54       85      'Hong Kong'    86.58
  'Lucas'      'M'        30     13       87      'Hong Kong'    80.91
  'Sophia'     'F'        26     13       30      'Hong Kong'    86.58
  'Elijah'     'M'       100     98        2      'Hong Kong'    80.91
  'Mia'        'F'        22      5       95      'Hong Kong'    86.58
  'Oliver'     'M'        22      5       21      'Hong Kong'    80.91
```

Now, the table can be considered complete; we have cleaned and reorganized it by adding more information, so we can go to the exploratory analysis.

Exploratory statistics - numerical measures

In the exploratory phase of a study, we try to gather a first set of information needed to derive features that can guide us in choosing the right tools to extract knowledge from the data. Those analyses provide a variety of tools for quickly summarizing and gaining insight about a set of data. The purpose of exploratory analysis is to use statistical indicator and visualizations to better understand the data, find clues about data trends and its quality, and formulate hypotheses from our analysis. We do not want to make imaginative or aesthetically pleasing views to surprise the interlocutor; our goal is to try to answer specific questions through data analysis.

Measures of location

The first step in our analysis is to estimate a localization parameter for distribution; that is, to find a typical or central value that best describes the data. MATLAB provides several methods and techniques to execute an effective measure of central tendency through the mathematical formulas derived from the descriptive statistic. To understand such techniques, we will analyze a practical example of a dataset that contains different types of glass defined in terms of its relative oxide content. We start importing the file named `GlassIdentificationDataSet.xlsx` in MATLAB:

```
>> GlassIdentificationDataSet =
readtable('GlassIdentificationDataSet.xlsx');
```

This is a dataset with 214 records and 11 variables (`id`, `refractive index`, `Na`, `Mg`, `Al`, `Si`, `K`, `Ca`, `Ba`, `Fe`, and `type of glass`). The unit of measure of oxide content is the weight percentage in corresponding oxide.

Mean, median, and mode

We begin our explorative analysis by calculating the maximum, mean, and minimum of the newly imported table. MATLAB calculates these statistics independently for each column in the table. For this purpose, we use three useful functions: `max()`, `mean()`, and `min()`.

To find the maximum value of oxide content (from the third column to the eighth, representing oxide content of `Na`, `Mg`, `Al`, `Si`, `K`, and `Ca`), using curly braces, `{}`, simply type the following command:

```
>> Max = max(GlassIdentificationDataSet{:,3:8})
Max =
17.3800    4.4900    3.5000    75.4100    6.2100    16.1900
```

This way, we get the maximum values in each of the specified columns. To calculate the mean of the same columns, we will write the command shown here:

```
>> Mean = mean(GlassIdentificationDataSet{:,3:8})
Mean =
13.4079    2.6845    1.4449    72.6509    0.4971    8.9570
```

To find the minimum value in each column, we use the following command:

```
>> Min = min(GlassIdentificationDataSet{:,3:8})
Min =
10.7300         0    0.2900    69.8100         0    5.4300
```

It may be useful to identify the records in which minimum and maximum are found; to get this information, just specify a second output parameter to return the row index. For example:

```
>> [Max,IndRowMax] = max(GlassIdentificationDataSet{:,3:8})
Max =
17.3800    4.4900    3.5000    75.4100    6.2100    16.1900
IndRowMax =
185      1    164    185    172    108

>> [Min,IndRowMin] = min(GlassIdentificationDataSet{:,3:8})
Min =
10.7300         0    0.2900    69.8100         0    5.4300
IndRowMin =
107    106     22    107     64    186
```

Additionally, using MATLAB's built-in functions, we can calculate median and mode. Recall that the median represents the intermediate value between the extremes of a set of data. MATLAB calculates the median for each column with the `median()` function:

```
>> Median = median(GlassIdentificationDataSet{:,3:8})
Median =
13.3000    3.4800    1.3600    72.7900    0.5550    8.6000
```

The mode is the value that appears most often in a set of data. MATLAB calculates the mode for each column with the `mode()` function:

```
>> Mode = mode(GlassIdentificationDataSet{:,3:8})
Mode =
13.0000         0    1.5400    72.8600         0    8.0300
```

When there are multiple values occurring equally frequently, `mode` returns the smallest of those values.

Quantiles and percentiles

Quantile is one of the classes of values that divide the total frequency of a sample or population into a given number of equal proportions. A special case of quantiles is quartiles, the three points that divide a dataset into four equal groups, each group comprising a quarter of the data. With the data arranged in ascending order, one quarter of the values fall below first quartile. The second quarter (second quartile) is in the center of the distribution and is the same as the median (half of the data is above and the other half below). The top quarter lies between the third quartile and fourth quartile.

In fact, the concept of percentiles is much more widespread. A percentile is the percent of cases occurring at or below a value. The relationship between quartiles and percentiles is:

- first quartile = 25th percentile
- second quartile = 50th percentile = median
- third quartile = 75th percentile
- fourth quartile = 100th percentile

In the Statistics and Machine Learning Toolbox, there are two functions called `quantile()` and `prctile()` that compute quantiles and percentiles. The `prctile()` function calculates the percentiles while the `quantile()` function calculates quantiles. However, the procedure for quantile calculation is entirely identical to that of percentile calculation. Indeed, the quantile at the value A is the same as the percentile at the value $B = 100*A$.

Let's calculate the first three quartiles of our sample distribution. For space reasons, we will limit the calculation to some columns. We will use the function `quantile()` in the following way:

```
>> Quantile = quantile(GlassIdentificationDataSet{:,3:8}, [0.25 0.50 0.75])
Quantile =
    12.9000     2.0900     1.1900    72.2800     0.1200     8.2400
    13.3000     3.4800     1.3600    72.7900     0.5550     8.6000
    13.8300     3.6000     1.6300    73.0900     0.6100     9.1800
```

We can now confirm what was said before about the equivalence between quartiles and percentiles. Then calculate percentiles:

```
>> Percentiles = prctile(GlassIdentificationDataSet{:,3:8}, [25 50 75])
Percentiles =
    12.9000     2.0900     1.1900    72.2800     0.1200     8.2400
    13.3000     3.4800     1.3600    72.7900     0.5550     8.6000
    13.8300     3.6000     1.6300    73.0900     0.6100     9.1800
```

The two results coincide with the confirmation of what has been said--the first three quartiles coincide with the 25th, 50th, and 75th percentiles.

Measures of dispersion

The information provided by the central tendency measures is not sufficient to characterize distribution. We need to integrate this information with other things that take into account the degree of dispersion of the data or variability of them. So, for example, if there are students with different heights in a class, it is said that there is variability in that class. If the heights of the students were all the same, one would say that there is no variability.

Variability can be measured with different types of indicators; MATLAB has special functions to calculate each of these. A first way to express the variability of a distribution is to refer to the range of a distribution (the minimum value and the maximum value). The range depends solely on the extreme values, so if the data sample is small, it can give an erroneous estimate of the population range because the extreme values are rare and may not be represented in a small sample.

The range() function returns the difference between the maximum and the minimum of a sample:

```
>> Range = range(GlassIdentificationDataSet{:,3:8})
Range =
    6.6500    4.4900    3.2100    5.6000    6.2100    10.7600
```

Using this function is extremely easy when calculating the estimate of spread of a sample. But remember, outliers have an undue influence on this statistic, which makes it an unreliable estimator. Let us now calculate the interquartile range with the iqr() function:

```
>> Iqr = iqr(GlassIdentificationDataSet{:,3:8})
Iqr =
    0.9300    1.5100    0.4400    0.8100    0.4900    0.9400
```

Interquartile range represents the difference between the third and the first quartile, that is, the amplitude of the range of values that contains the central half of the observed values. This is a dispersion index, a measure of how much values deviate from a central value. Previously, we calculated both the first and the third quartile; thus we can verify that definition:

```
>> CheckIqr = Quantile(3,:) - Quantile(1,:)
CheckIqr =
    0.9300    1.5100    0.4400    0.8100    0.4900    0.9400
```

The two vectors coincide to confirm that. This index tells us how the 50 percentage of the central distribution behaves and is certainly more robust than the previous one. As it is not affected by abnormal values, in fact, we delete the distribution queues.

The most known variability index is variance; it measures how far a set of numbers are spread out from their mean. It represents the mean of the squares of deviations of individual values from their arithmetic mean. MATLAB calculates the variance for each column with the `var()` function:

```
>> Variance = var(GlassIdentificationDataSet{:,3:8})
Variance =
    0.6668    2.0805    0.2493    0.5999    0.4254    2.0254
```

This function returns a row vector containing the variances corresponding to each column.

Remember that the variance is the expectation of the squared deviation of a random variable from its mean. It represents a measure of the spread of data as a whole and is smaller when values are near the mean. In contrast, variance is higher when values are distant from the mean.

The standard deviation is the square root of the variance and has the desirable property of being in the same units as the data. That is, if the data is in decibels, the standard deviation is in decibels as well. To calculate the standard deviation of each column, type the following command:

```
>> StDev = std(GlassIdentificationDataSet{:,3:8})
StDev =
    0.8166    1.4424    0.4993    0.7745    0.6522    1.4232
```

None of the statistical indices we have just analyzed (variance and standard deviation) prove to be effective against outliers. A single data value far from the others can increase the value of the statistics by an arbitrarily large amount. Even the **Mean Absolute Deviation (MAD)** proves to be sensitive to outliers, but not as much as the standard deviation or variance, in response to defective data. In MATLAB, the mean or median absolute deviation is calculated with the `mad()` function:

```
>> Mad = mad(GlassIdentificationDataSet{:,3:8})
Mad =
    0.5989    1.2094    0.3591    0.5557    0.2944    0.9181
```

There are several statistical measures that can be used to quantify the tendency of two sets of data to move together over time. The two most commonly used measures are correlation and covariance. Covariance provides an unnormalized measure of their tendency to move together, and is estimated by summing the product deviations from the mean for each variable in each period. In MATLAB, covariance is calculated by the cov() function. Let's see an example; we create a *4 x 4* data matrix, as follows:

```
>> a = [1 2 3 4]
a =
     1     2     3     4
>> b = 10*a
b =
    10    20    30    40
>> c = fliplr(a)
c =
     4     3     2     1
>> d = randperm(4,4)
d =
     3     1     4     2
```

In this way, we created 4 row vectors: the first contains the numbers from 1 to 4, the second is obtained from the first by multiplying it by 10, the third is equal to the first but with the inverted values and finally the fourth contains random numbers from 1 to 4. It is clear that between the first and second vector there is a positive linear relationship, as well as between the first and third vector, and this time negative, in the contrary there is no relation between the first and fourth vector, because the fourth vector has been obtained randomly. Now, we build a matrix with the same columns as the newly created vectors.

```
>> MatA = [a' b' c' d']
MatA =
     1    10     4     3
     2    20     3     1
     3    30     2     4
     4    40     1     2
```

At this point we can calculate the covariance matrix.

```
>> CovMatA = cov(MatA)
CovMatA =
     1.6667    16.6667    -1.6667         0
    16.6667   166.6667   -16.6667         0
    -1.6667   -16.6667     1.6667         0
         0          0          0     1.6667
```

Suppose `MatA` columns are each a random variable made up of observations; the covariance matrix `CovMatA` is the pairwise covariance calculation between each column combination. The covariance sign indicates the type of relationship between the two variables. A positive sign indicates that they move in the same direction while a negative indicates that they move in opposite directions. Also, the tighter the relationship between the variables, the greater the covariance. Let's explain what we got in our case: first, this matrix is symmetric ($CovMatA_{ij}$ = $CovMatA_{ji}$), the main diagonal contains the variances of the columns, and finally each term $CovMatA_{ij}$ represents the covariance of the column i with respect to column j.

Based on the previous example, we analyze the first column of the `CovMatA` matrix. The second term (`16.6667`) confirms that there is a sensible positive relationship between the first and the second column. The third term (`-1.6667`) tells us that between the first and the third column there is a relationship, but lower to the previous and negative. Finally, the fourth term (`0`) tells us that between the first and the fourth column there is no relation.

But it is difficult to understand the intensity of the relationship based exclusively on covariance, as it is not a standardized measure. A standardized measurement of the relationship between two variables is instead represented by correlation, which can be calculated starting from covariance. In MATLAB, correlation coefficients are calculated by the `corrcoef()` function; it produces a matrix of sample correlation coefficients for a data matrix (where each column represents a separate quantity).

Remember, the correlation coefficient of two random variables is a measure of their linear dependence.

In the following example, we calculate the correlation coefficients for a *3x3* random data matrix:

```
>> MatB = rand(3)
MatB =
     0.6132    0.0263    0.8312
     0.8202    0.8375    0.4022
     0.5485    0.9608    0.5032

>> Cor = corrcoef(MatB)
Cor =
     1.0000    0.1710   -0.4973
     0.1710    1.0000   -0.9398
    -0.4973   -0.9398    1.0000
```

The correlation coefficients range from −1 to 1, where:

- Values close to 1 indicate that there is a positive linear relationship between the data columns
- Values close to −1 indicate that one column of data has a negative linear relationship to another column of data (anti-correlation)
- Values close to or equal to 0 suggest that there is no linear relationship between the data columns

Previously, we said that the correlation coefficient of two random variables is a measure of their linear dependence. To demonstrate this statement, we will use the same *4x4* matrix used earlier:

```
>> MatA
MatA =
         1      10      4      3
         2      20      3      1
         3      30      2      4
         4      40      1      2
>> CorrMatA = corrcoef(MatA)
  CorrMatA =
         1      1     -1      0
         1      1     -1      0
        -1     -1      1      0
         0      0      0      1
```

Since the second column of MatA is a multiple of the first, these two columns are directly correlated; thus, the correlation coefficient in the (1,2) and (2,1) entries of CorrMatA is 1. The same happens between the first and the third, but this time with a negative sign (−1). Finally, as already provided, no correlation exists between the first column and the fourth (0).

Measures of shape

The location and variability of a frequency distribution are not the only bits of information contained in the data. Two statistical variables may have the same position and the same dispersion but may differ by the weight of the values that are on the queues, that is, those that take measures far away from the average. Descriptive statistics defines some measures concerning the form of a distribution; we will soon see some of them.

Many data distributions are in a normal form. A distribution that has a bell shape and is symmetrical with respect to the central position is said to be normal. Moreover, in normal form, location indicators assume the same value *(mean = median = mode)*. A form is said to be symmetric if, with respect to the central position, it assumes the same structure of frequencies in both the right and the left parts. A normal form is a symmetric distribution, while a symmetric distribution may not always be normal.

In MATLAB, to compute and plot for a normal distribution is very easy. For example, we can compute a standard normal distribution with parameters `mu= 0` and `sigma=1`, named **probability density function (pdf)**:

```
>> a = [-5:.1:5];
>> Norm = normpdf(a,0,1);
```

Now we can plot a bell curve:

```
>> figure;
>> plot(a,Norm)
```

A normal distribution of data is shown here, with the typical bell shape:

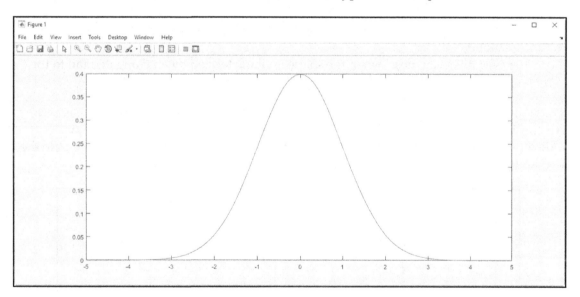

Figure 3.3: Normal distribution of data

Normal distribution is the most used continuous distribution in statistics. Normal distribution is important for three fundamental reasons:

- Several continuous phenomena seem to follow, at least roughly, a normal distribution
- It can be used to approximate numerous discrete probability distributions
- Normal distribution is the basis of classical statistical problems

As can be seen in *Figure 3.3*, the normal distribution is characterized by a perfect symmetry with respect to the central value. This form can be considered as an example to characterize other distributions, as we will see in the next section.

Skewness

Skewness is an asymmetric distribution whose form does not mirror the central position; it measures asymmetry about the mean of the probability distribution of a random variable. The more skewed a distribution is, the greater is the need for using robust estimators such as median and interquartile range. There are two types of skewness:

- Positive skewness, when the shape is characterized by an elongated tail to the right
- Negative skewness, when the shape is characterized by an elongated tail to the left

The skewness of the normal distribution, or any perfectly symmetric distribution, is zero. An empirical method to detect the presence of skewness is to compare the location indicators of the distribution considered. In the following image, negative skewness (to the left) and positive skewness (to the right) are shown:

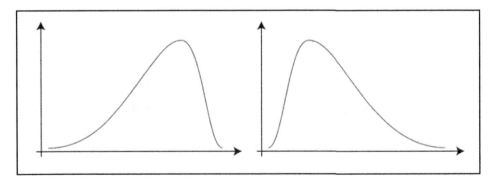

Figure 3.4: Negative skewness to the left and positive skewness to the right

In MATLAB, skewness is computed by the `skewness()` function; as an example, we will refer to the same dataset used earlier:

```
>> GlassIdentificationDataSet =
readtable('GlassIdentificationDataSet.xlsx');
>> SkN = skewness(GlassIdentificationDataSet{:,3:8})
SkN =
    0.4510   -1.1445    0.9009   -0.7253    6.5056    2.0327
```

The columns of data present alternately the left tails (negative skewness) and the right tails (positive skewness).

Kurtosis

Derived from the Greek word **kurtos** (hump), kurtosis refers to the greater or lesser hump of a curve near its maximum, and hence to the greater or lesser length of the tails. Kurtosis is of particular interest in a unimodal frequency distribution, whose curve is bell-shaped. To evaluate this aspect of the shape of a curve, it is compared to a normal curve (also called **mesokurtic distribution**, which would be the extreme case) having the same overall frequency. It can tell us whether the data is heavy-tailed or light-tailed, relative to a normal distribution. Data with high kurtosis tends to have heavy tails, or outliers; data with low kurtosis tends to have light tails, or lack of outliers. The curve is named:

- **leptokurtic** if, with respect to the normal curve, there is an excess frequency in the central classes, a lower frequency in intermediate classes, and a higher frequency in the extreme classes. It is therefore a higher distribution at the center and lower at the sides.
- **platykurtic** if, compared with the normal curve, it has a lower frequency in the central and extreme classes, with a frequency greater than the intermediate ones; it is therefore a lower distribution at the center and higher at the sides.

In the following figure, types of kurtosis in comparison with normal distribution are shown, to highlight the differences:

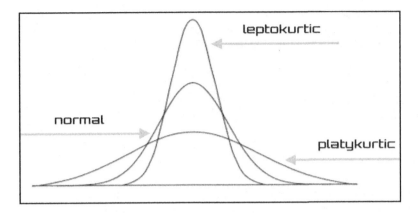

Figure 3.5: Types of kurtosis in comparison with normal distribution

To measure the kurtosis of a bell-shaped unimodal curve, Pearson's kurtosis index is particularly useful; it shows us how outlier-prone a distribution is. This index is equal to three for normal distribution. Distributions that are more outlier-prone than normal distribution have kurtosis greater than three (leptokurtic distribution); distributions that are less outlier-prone have kurtosis less than three (platykurtic distribution).

In MATLAB, to calculate kurtosis, we can use the `kurtosis()` function. As an example, we will refer to the same dataset used earlier:

```
>> Kurt = kurtosis(GlassIdentificationDataSet{:,3:8})
Kurt =
    5.9535    2.5713    4.9848    5.8711    56.3923    9.4990
```

To assign *kurtosis = 0* at the normal distribution, some definitions of kurtosis subtract 3 from the computed value. MATLAB's `kurtosis()` function does not use this convention.

Exploratory visualization

In the previous section, we explored the data using numerical indicators; as a result, we learned several methods of finding important information in the distributions under analysis. Now, we will explore another way to extract knowledge from data through a visual approach. By tracing appropriate charts, from our data, we can identify specific trends even before applying machine learning algorithms. What we will be able to draw from this analysis can serve to focus our study on specific areas rather than performing generic simulations.

Through MATLAB tools, we can explore single-variable distributions using univariate plots such as box plots and histograms, for instance. As well, we can show the relationships between variables using bivariate plots such as grouped scatter plots and bivariate histograms. After plotting, we can customize our plot by adding case names, least squares lines, and reference curves.

The Data Statistics dialog box

We will begin our visual analysis with an example in which we will draw a simple diagram to extract statistical indicators. This will be possible thanks to the **Data Statistics** dialog box; it helps us to calculate and plot descriptive statistics with the data. In the following example, we will first create a plot and then calculate the descriptive statistics. Initially we import the data into the MATLAB workspace (these values represent emergency calls made in 24 hours by users residing on different streets):

```
>> EmergencyCalls = xlsread('EmergencyCalls.xlsx');
```

Now, we save in the appropriate variables the dimensions of the matrix just created, as they will serve to get the chart:

```
>> [rows,cols] = size(EmergencyCalls);
```

Then we define the values on the x axis:

```
>> x = 1:rows;
```

In the following figure, emergency calls' distribution is shown. We can notice that there are two peaks of calls at two specific time bands, and this feature occurs for each street.

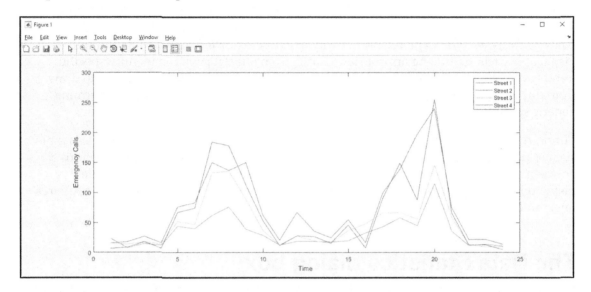

Figure 3.6: Plot of emergency calls

Then, simply plot the data and customize the graph with some annotations:

```
>> plot(x,EmergencyCalls)
>> legend('Street 1','Street 2','Street 3','Street 4')
>> xlabel('Time')
>> ylabel('Emergency Calls')
```

In the code just typed, we set the legend; it contains the name of each dataset as specified by the legend function: Street 1, Street 2, Street 3, and Street 4. A dataset refers to each column of data in the array we plotted. If you do not name the datasets, default names are assigned: data1, data2, and so on.

In the following figure, the **Data Statistics** dialog box is shown:

Data Statistics - 1		
Statistics for Street 1		
Check to plot statistics on figure:		
	X	Y
min	1 ☐	14 ☐
max	24 ☐	240 ☐
mean	12.5 ☐	73.5 ☐
median	12.5 ☐	58.5 ☐
mode	1 ☐	16 ☐
std	7.071 ☐	64.16 ☐
range	23	226

Save to workspace...   Help   Close

Figure 3.7: The Data Statistics dialog box

These commands open a new figure window; by selecting **Tools | Data Statistics**, the **Data Statistics** dialog box will open. In it, we will visualize descriptive statistics for the **X** and **Y** data of our dataset.

As can be seen in *Figure 3.7*, this dialog shows the following statistical indicators: minimum, maximum, mean, median, mode, standard deviation, and range. To display on the plot a specific statistic, select the checkbox next to it and then click on `Save to workspace`. For example, to plot the median, select the median checkbox in the **Y** column. The new feature is now in the chart and its reference is also updated in the legend, as can be seen in the following figure:

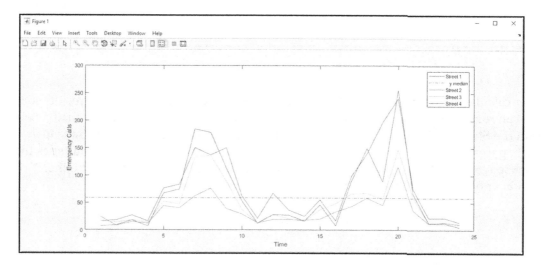

Figure 3.8: Add statistical calculations to the chart

The new feature is now in the chart and its reference is also updated in the legend. To distinguish statistics from the data on the plot, several colors and line styles are used by the **Data Statistics** dialog box. MATLAB allows customizing of the display of descriptive statistics on a plot, such as the color, line width, line style, or marker.

To do this, in the MATLAB Figure window, click on the arrow button in the toolbar. Double-click on the statistic on the plot for which you want to edit display properties. This action shows the **Property Editor** section at the bottom of the Figure window, which enables plot editing, as can be seen in the following figure:

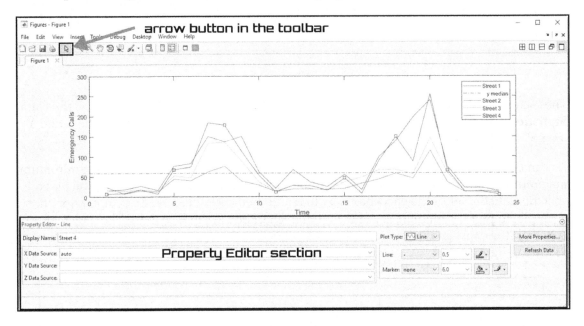

Figure 3.9: Customize the display of descriptive statistics on a plot

After calculating the statistic descriptors from the chart, you should save the results so that you can reuse them later. It's possible to save statistics for each dataset individually. Select it from the **Statistics for** list in the **Data Statistics** dialog box; then click on the **Save to workspace** button shown in that window. It will open in this way the **Save Statistics to Workspace** dialog box (*Figure 3.10*); select the options to save the statistics for either **X** data, **Y** data, or both. Then, enter the corresponding variable names.

In the following figure, the **Save Statistics to Workspace** dialog box is shown:

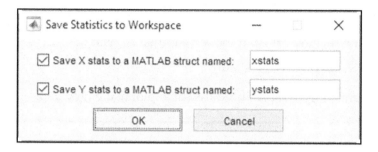

Figure 3.10: Save Statistics to Workspace dialog box

After doing this, simply click on **OK**. In this way, we save the descriptive statistics to a structure. The new variable is added to the MATLAB workspace. To view the new structure variable, type the variable name at the MATLAB prompt:

```
>> ystats
ystats =
  struct with fields:
        min: 14
        max: 240
       mean: 73.5000
     median: 58.5000
       mode: 16
        std: 64.1581
      range: 226
```

Remember, the **Data Statistics** dialog box allows us to select the variable on which to make the calculations; to do so, just click on the drop-down menu at the top of the window to the right of the **Statistics for** label (*Figure 3.7*).

The work done so far has been particularly simple, but it has taken time and needs interactivity with the user. To make the procedure reproducible, we can generate some MATLAB code that will allow us to repeat the entire procedure as many times as we will need.

To do this, simply select **File | Generate Code** in the figure window. In this manner, we will create a function code file and display it in the MATLAB editor. To associate the file we are creating with the code contained therein, it will be appropriate to change the name of the function on the first line of the file, from **create figure** to something more specific. Then, save the file to your current folder with the filename PlotStat.m.

To verify that the procedure works, load new data in the MATLAB workspace:

```
>> EmergencyCallsNew = xlsread('EmergencyCallsNew.xlsx');
```

Reproduce the plot with new data and the recomputed statistics:

```
>> PlotStat (x,EmergencyCallsNew)
```

In the following figure, I have reproduced the same plot using new data:

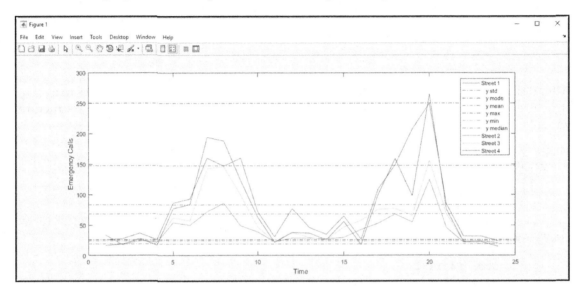

Figure 3.11: Plot reproduction with new data

Analyzing *Figure 3.11*, it can be seen that in addition to displaying the new data, now there are also the statistical descriptors selected in the **Data Statistics** dialog box.

Histogram

A histogram is a graphical representation of a numerical distribution, showing the shape of a distribution. It consists of adjacent rectangles (bins), whose bases are aligned on an axis oriented and equipped with a unit of measure (the axis assumes the unit of measure of the character and can be safely understood as the X axis). The adjacency of the rectangles reflects the continuity of the character. Each rectangle has a base length equal to the width of the corresponding class; the height is calculated as a frequency density, so it is equal to the ratio between the frequencies (absolute) associated with the class and the amplitude of the class.

In the MATLAB environment, it is possible to create histograms with the `histogram()` function, which in the simplest form is written as:

```
>> histogram(x)
```

The x parameter represents a vector of numeric values. The x elements are ordered in 10 bins, equidistant along the x axis, between the maximum and minimum values of x. The `histogram()` function displays each bin as a rectangle, such that the height of each rectangle indicates the number of elements in the respective bin.

If the input is a matrix, the `histogram()` function creates a histogram for each column with different colors. If the input vector is data of the categorical type, each bin represents a category of x.

Let's now look at an example; we will graph a set of values derived from a survey run on a number of users representative of the population. This test provides the results, which we will include as elements of a vector that will represent the argument of the `histogram()` function:

```
>> Vect1=[10,25,12,13,33,25,44,50,43,26,38,32,31,28,30];
>> histogram(Vect1)
```

By not providing any optional arguments, MATLAB has automatically established the number of frequency classes to divide the range of values. In this case, the interval between 10 and 50 (extreme values) was divided into ten classes, as can be seen in the following figure:

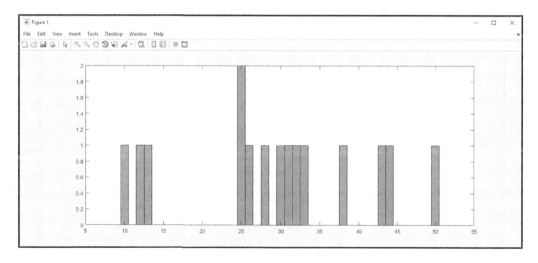

Figure 3.12: Histogram of a continuous distribution

Moreover, nothing has been set relative to the title of the chart on the axis labels. In this case, MATLAB has entered the numbers that refer to the central value of each bin for the horizontal axis and the equivalent values for the vertical axis. Let's see, however, what happens when we set the number of bins (rectangles), a title and label for the axes, and finally the color that the rectangles will have to assume:

```
>> Vect2=[10,25,12,13,33,25,44,50,43,26,38,32,31,28,30,15,16,22,
        35,18];
h = histogram(Vect2,12)
h =
Histogram with properties:
Data: [10 25 12 13 33 25 44 50 43 26 38 32 31 28 30]
Values: [1 0 1 1 0 0 0 0 0 0 0 0 0 0 2 1 0 1 0 1 1 1 1 0 0 0 0 1 0 0 0 0
1 1 0 0 0 0 0 1]
         NumBins: 41
         BinEdges: [1×42 double]
         BinWidth: 1
         BinLimits: [9.5000 50.5000]
    Normalization: 'count'
         FaceColor: 'auto'
         EdgeColor: [0 0 0]
>> xlabel('Results')
>> ylabel('Frequency')
>> title('Customer Satisfaction Survey')
>> h.FaceColor = [0 0.5 0.5];
```

In the following figure, a histogram with number of bins set by the user is shown:

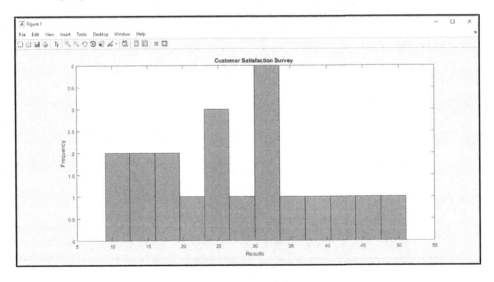

Figure 3.13: Histogram with number of bins set by the user

Let's look at the commands just introduced:

```
>> h = histogram(Vect2,12)
```

We set the bin number, in our case, 12; the following code lines set the labels for the X and Y axes and the title of the chart:

```
>> xlabel('Results')
>> ylabel('Frequency')
>> title('Customer Satisfaction Survey')
```

Finally, to set the color of the rectangles, we attribute to the graphic object identifier the FaceColor property with an RGB value of [0 0.5 0.5], corresponding to green:

```
>> h.FaceColor = [0 0.5 0.5];
```

The result is shown in *Figure 3.13*. Actually, the number of bins in the graph corresponds exactly to the number we specified in the command; this is because the histogram() function accepts several options. In our case, we added the vector containing the data and the bin number. If more control over the exact bin number is required, we can point to breakpoints between them by using an option, giving it a vector that contains a range of values in which we want to divide the data. Let's look at an example: the same vector we used in the previous examples will be represented by dividing the interval into four bins. To do this, we will define a new vector that will contain the entire range from the minimum value to the maximum value with step ten:

```
>> Vect3=[10,25,12,13,33,25,44,50,43,26,38,32,31,28,30,15,16,
            22,35,18];
>> nbin=10:10:50;
>> h = histogram(Vect3,nbin)
h =
Histogram with properties:
Data: [10 25 12 13 33 25 44 50 43 26 38 32 31 28 30 15 16 22 35 18]
            Values: [6 5 6 3]
            NumBins: 4
           BinEdges: [10 20 30 40 50]
           BinWidth: 10
          BinLimits: [10 50]
      Normalization: 'count'
          FaceColor: 'auto'
          EdgeColor: [0 0 0]
>> xlabel('Results')
>> ylabel('Frequency')
>> title('Customer Satisfaction Survey')
>> h.FaceColor = [0 0.5 0.5];
```

Thus, a different breakdown of classes is obtained, as shown in the following figure:

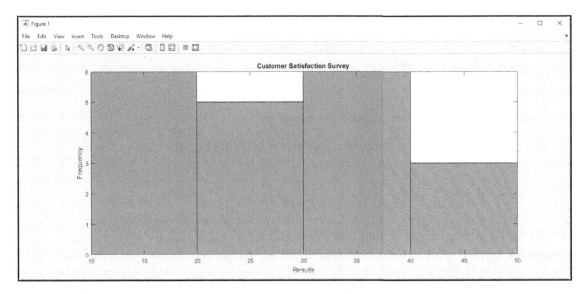

Figure 3.14: Histogram with user-set bin spacing

In data analysis, we are often more interested in the frequency density than frequency. This is because the frequency is related to the size of the sample. So, instead of counting the number of class occurrences of the sample, MATLAB provides probability densities using the Normalization, pdf option. Let us see how to proceed with a simple example; we define a new vector that contains 1000 values automatically and randomly generated by MATLAB, and we plot the relative histogram (*Figure 3.15*):

```
>> Vect4 = randn(1000,1);
>> h = histogram(Vect4,'Normalization','pdf')
h =
Histogram with properties:

              Data: [1000×1 double]
            Values: [1×24 double]
           NumBins: 24
          BinEdges: [1×25 double]
          BinWidth: 0.3000
         BinLimits: [-3.3000 3.9000]
     Normalization: 'pdf'
         FaceColor: 'auto'
         EdgeColor: [0 0 0]
```

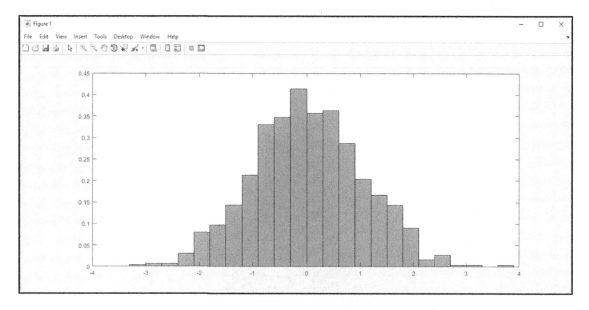

Figure 3.15: Probability density of a normalized distribution

From the *Figure 5.12*, we can note that the *Y* axis now gives us a probability density measurement that a sample falls into that class. If the breakpoints are equidistant, then the height of each rectangle is proportional to the number of points that fall into the class, and hence the sum of all probability densities is equal to one.

To get more detailed information about the results obtained by applying the `histogram()` function, we can save this data to a variable as well as use it to plot the chart. We can do this by saving the output of the function in a variable, thus obtaining not only the output of the histogram but also the graph.

A particular type of histogram is what is plotted with the function `histfit()`; this function plots a histogram using the number of bins equal to the square root of the number of elements in data and fits a normal density function. In the following example, we generate a sample of size `1000` from a normal distribution with mean `50` and variance `3`:

```
>> Vect5 = normrnd(50,3,1000,1);
>> Hist = histfit(Vect5)
```

In the following figure, a distribution fit curve has been added to a histogram with normal distribution:

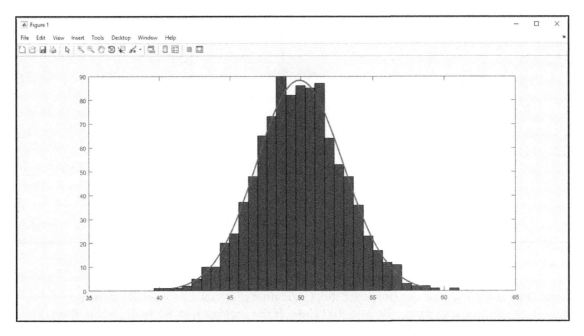

Figure 3.16: Histogram with a distribution fit

Box plots

A box plot, also referred to as a whiskers chart, is a graphical representation used to describe the distribution of a sample by simple dispersion and position indexes. A box plot can be represented either horizontally or vertically by means of a rectangular partition divided by two segments. The rectangle (box) is delimited by the first quartile (25th percentile) and the third quartile (75th percentile), and divided by the median (50th percentile), as shown in the following figure:

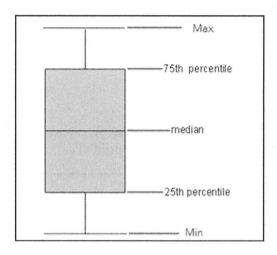

Figure 3.17: Statistical descriptors of a box plot

Segments outside the box (whiskers) represent the minimum and maximum of the sample. In this way, the four equally populated ranges delineated by quartiles are graphically represented. To understand the plot creation process, we will show an example with dummy dataset created by the `normrnd()` function, which generates random sequences of normally distributed data. This function accepts the mean and the standard deviation of the distribution as input parameters. The syntax of this function is as follows:

```
>> normrnd(mu,sigma)
```

In this command, `mu` represents the mean and `sigma` is the standard deviation of the distribution. For example, the following code:

```
>> r=normrnd(3,1,100,1);
```

Generates 100 floats, with a mean of 3 and standard deviation of 1. To generate a dataset for the example, we will use the following instructions:

```
>> data1=normrnd(3,2,100,1);
>> data2=normrnd(2,1,100,1);
>> data3=normrnd(6,2,100,1);
>> data4=normrnd(8,0.5,100,1);
>> data5=normrnd(4,4,100,1);
>> data6=normrnd(5,1,100,1);
>> data=[data1 data2 data3 data4 data5 data6];
```

Finally, we will have a matrix with 100 rows and 6 columns, each column representing the standardized distribution with the mean and standard deviation specified. For box plot creation, we can use the `boxplot()` function in its simplest form by adding the name of the dataset as the only argument:

```
>> boxplot(data)
```

This creates the chart shown in the following figure. As you can see, this is already a good chart, but it is obvious that some adjustments are needed:

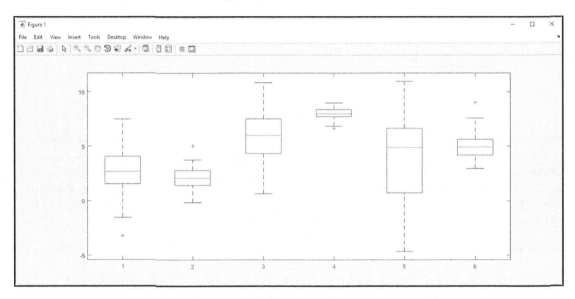

Figure 3.18: Box plot of several standardized distributions

In the chart shown in *Figure 3.18*, the box plot is evenly distributed even though it refers to several observation groups and there are no axis labels; so, it is not tailored to our needs. We need to improve its appearance by setting specific parameters. To label the data we will use the `Labels` option; this option accepts array of characters, cell arrays, or a numeric vector that contains the label names. Thus, we can specify a label for the single value or label for each group. To specify multiple label variables, you will need to use a numeric array or cell array that contains any of the accepted datatypes:

```
>> boxplot(data,'Labels',{'mu = 3','mu = 2','mu = 6','mu = 8','mu = 4','mu = 5'})
```

To shows datum names vertically instead of horizontally, we will use the `LabelOrientation` option. It accepts the following values: inline and horizontal. After adding labels with vertical orientation, calls to the `boxplot()` function become:

```
>> boxplot(dati,'Labels',{'mu = 3','mu = 2','mu = 6','mu = 8','mu = 4','mu = 5'}, 'LabelOrientation', 'inline')
```

The shape of the box can be varied by inserting a recess at the median value. To do this, let's look at another example; we generate two sets of sample data using the `normrnd()` function, again. The first sample, `vect1`, contains random numbers generated by a normal distribution with `mu = 4` and `sigma = 2`. The second sample, `vect2`, contains random numbers generated by a normal distribution with `mu = 7` and `sigma = 0.5`.

```
>> vect1=normrnd(4,2,100,1);
>> vect2=normrnd(7,0.5,100,1);
```

Now, let's create a box plot of a different shape for the two distributions contained in the two newly created vectors:

```
>>figure
>>boxplot([vect1,vect2],'Notch','on','Labels',{'mu = 4','mu = 7'})
>>title('Comparison between two distributions')
```

To make the chart more intuitive, we will label each box with the corresponding value of mu (mean), as shown in the following figure (*Figure 3.19*):

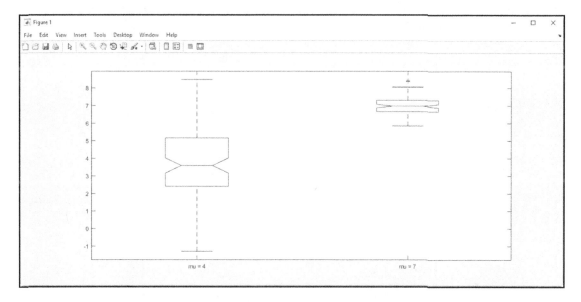

Figure 3.19: Box plot with the Notch option

Scatter plots

Relationships between quantitative variables can be highlighted through a suitable graphical representation, named a scatter plot. A scatter plot helps us to study the relationship between two quantitative variables (correlation), detected on the same units. Let us consider a Cartesian reference where the values of a variable appear on the horizontal axis and those of the other variable on the vertical axis. Each point in the plot is specified by a pair of numerical coordinates that represent values of the two variables detected at a specific observation.

A large number of points can be observed in a single dispersion diagram. More such points are placed around a straight line, the greater the correlation between the two variables. If this straight line goes from the origin out to high x-y values, then it is said that the variables have a positive correlation. If the line moves from a high value on the Y axis to a high value on the X axis, the variables have a negative correlation (*Figure 3.20*).

Through the scatter plots, we can have an idea of the shape and strength of the relationship between the variables. Deviations due to abnormal data, which is specific values that deviate from the general scheme or presence of different clusters, can also be highlighted. In MATLAB, to create a scatter plot, we can use `scatter()` function, which in the simplest form is written:

```
>> scatter(a,b)
```

This command creates a scatter plot with circles at the locations specified by the vectors a and b, as shown in the following figure.

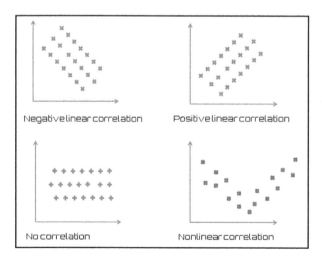

Figure 3.20: Type of correlation between data

To understand the utility of this function, let's look at an example: the height and weight of a group of 26 boys are contained in two vectors. Each boy corresponds to a point $P(x, y)$ in the Cartesian diagram which has, in abscissa, x the height in cm and, in ordinate, the weight in kg of the individual taken into consideration.

```
>> Height = [168   168      168   173   163   174   174   174   175   175
176   165   180   180   182   182   183   186   191   191   192   165   167
174   176   167];
>> Weight = [65      65   65      78   70   68   68   80   70   75
77   69   80   65   79   79   79   80   81   81   82   69   69
77   68   70];
>> scatter(Weight,Height)
>> IdealWeight=Height-100-[(Height-150)/4];
>> hold on
>> plot(IdealWeight,Height)
```

Next we show in the same plot, the straight line showing the ideal weighting according to the Lorenz formula, as shown in the following figure.

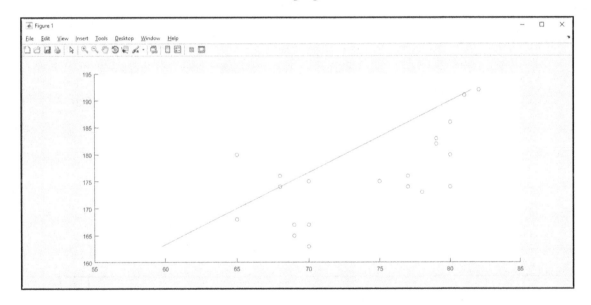

Figure 3.20: Scatter plot of height-weight variables

By analyzing the plot, one can take into account the relationship between the weight and the height in the group under consideration. As the straight line identifies the ideal weight of a normal individual, you can immediately see which individuals are overweight or underweight. In addition, as the data goes around this line, the correlation between the two variables is confirmed.

We have seen that, through scatter plot we can obtain useful information about the possible relationships between two variables. But what happens when the pairs of variables to compare are numerous? In this case we can use the `plotmatrix()` function that gives a scatter plot matrix. But what is the scatter plot matrix? For a set of variables $A_1, A_2, .. , A_k$, the scatter plot matrix shows all the scatter plots of the variables in a matrix format. So, if there are n variables, the scatter plot matrix will have n rows and n columns and the ith row and j^{th} column of this matrix is a plot of A_i versus A_j.

```
>> RandomMatrix = randn(100,4);
>> plotmatrix(RandomMatrix)
```

In the code just seen, for example, we create a scatter plot matrix of random data. The subplot in the ith row, j^{th} column of the matrix is a scatter plot of the ith column of the matrix against the jth column of the matrix. Along the diagonal are histogram plots of each column of the matrix, as shown in the following figure.

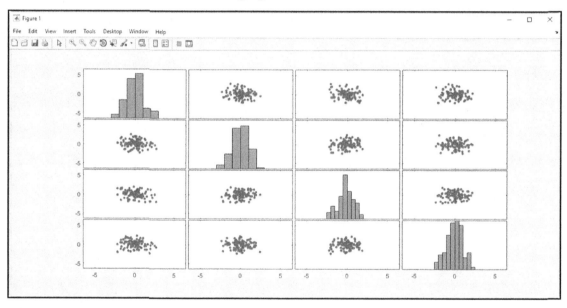

Figure 3.21: Scatter plot matrix of random distribution

Summary

In this chapter, we began exploring the different types of variables: quantitative (interval and ratio) and qualitative variables (nominal, dichotomous, and ordinal). Then, we started the hard work of data preparation; we saw how to find missing values, change the datatype, replace missing values, remove missing entries, order the table, find outliers, and finally, organize multiple sources of data into one.

Next, we discovered the exploratory statistics techniques used to derive features that can guide us in choosing the right tools to extract knowledge from data. We took a look at measures of location such as mean, median, mode, quantiles, and percentiles; measures of dispersion such as range, interquartile range, variance, standard deviation, correlation, and covariance; and measures of shape such as skewness and kurtosis.

Finally, we discussed exploratory visualization to identify specific trends through a visual inspection of data. We learned how to draw histograms, box plots, and scatter plots.

In the next chapter, we will learn the different types of regression techniques, how to apply regression methods to your own data, how the regression algorithm works, and the basic concepts that regression methods use to fit equations to data using MATLAB functions. We will prepare data for regression analysis. We'll also cover topics such as simple linear regression, **Ordinary Least Squares** (**OLS**) estimation, correlation, and multiple linear regression.

4
Finding Relationships between Variables - Regression Techniques

Regression analysis is a statistical process of studying the relationship between a set of independent variables (**explanatory variables**) and the dependent variable (**response variable**). Through this technique, it is possible to understand how the value of the response variable changes when the explanatory variable is varied.

Consider a group of bikers about which some information has been collected: number of years of use, number of kilometers traveled in one year, and number of falls. Through these techniques, we can find that on an average, when the number of kilometers traveled increases, the number of falls also increases. By increasing the number of years of motorcycle usage and so increasing the experience, the number of falls tends to decrease.

A regression analysis can be conducted for a dual purpose:

- Explanatory, to understand and weigh the effects of the independent variable on the dependent variable according to a particular theoretical model
- Predictive, to locate a linear combination of the independent variable to predict the value assumed by the dependent variable-optimally

This chapter shows how to perform an accurate regression analysis in a MATLAB environment. In the Statistics and Machine Learning Toolbox, there are a variety of regression algorithms, including linear regression, nonlinear regression, generalized linear models, and mixed-effects models. We will explore the amazing MATLAB interface for regression analysis including fitting, prediction, and plotting. This interface also provides native support for dataset arrays and categorical data. These new capabilities speed up data analysis, produce more compact and readable MATLAB code, and eliminate the requirement to manually manipulate matrices. We will cover the following topics:

- Simple linear regression
- How to get a **ordinary least squares (OLS)** estimation
- Methods for measuring the intercept and slope of a straight line
- Discovering techniques to perform multiple linear regression and polynomial regression
- How to perform a regression analysis with a Regression Learner App

At the end of the chapter, we will be able to perform different types of regression techniques. We will see how to apply regression methods to our own data and how a regression algorithm works. We will understand the basic concepts that regression methods use to fit equations to data using MATLAB functions, and learn to prepare data for regression analysis. We'll also cover topics such as simple linear regression, ordinary least square estimation, correlations, and multiple linear regressions.

Searching linear relationships

In the previous chapter, we learned that the coefficient of correlation between two quantitative variables, X and Y, provides information on the existence of a linear relation between the two variables. This index, however, does not allow determining whether it is X that affects Y, or it is Y that affects X, or whether both X and Y are consequences of a phenomenon that affects both of them. Only more knowledge of the problem under study can allow some hypothesis of the dependence of a variable on another.

 If a correlation between two variables is not found, it does not necessarily imply that they are independent, because they might have a nonlinear relationship.

Calculating correlation and covariance is a useful way to investigate whether a linear relationship exists between variables, without having to assume or fit a specific model to our data. It can happen that two variables have a small or no linear correlation, meaning a strong nonlinear relationship. As it may happen that the two variables have a strong correlation, it will be necessary to find a model that approximates this trend. This indicates that calculating linear correlation before fitting a model is a great way to identify variables that have a simple relationship.

We have shown that a great way to examine the existence of correlations between pairs of variables is to visualize the observations in a Cartesian plane by a scatter plot. We also said that the stronger the link between the two variables, the greater the tendency of the points to fall in a certain direction.

Remember, covariance quantifies the strength of a linear relationship between two variables and correlation provides a measure of the degree of a linear relationship through a dimensionless quantity.

To describe the form of the link between the variables, we can choose to describe the observation behavior by means of a mathematical function that, upon interpolating the data, can represent its tendency and keep its main information. The linear regression method consists of precisely identifying a line that is capable of representing point distribution in a two-dimensional plane. As it is easy to imagine, if the points corresponding to the observations are near the line, then the chosen model will be able to effectively describe the link between the variables.

In theory, there are an infinite number of lines that may interpolate the observations. In practice, there is only one mathematical model that optimizes the representation of the data. In the case of a linear mathematical relationship, the observations of the variable Y can be obtained by a linear function of observations of the variable X. For each observation, we will have:

$$y = \alpha * x + \beta$$

In this formula, x is the explanatory variable and y is the response variable. Parameters α and β, which represent respectively the intercept with the Y axis and the slope of the line, must be estimated based on the observations collected for the two variables included in the model.

Of particular interest is the slope β, that is, the variation of the mean response for every single increment of the explanatory variable. What about a change in this coefficient? If the slope is positive, the regression line increases from left to right; if the slope is negative, the line decreases from left to right. When the slope is zero, the explanatory variable has no effect on the value of the response. But it is not just the sign of β that establishes the weight of the relationship between the variables; more generally, its value is also important. In the case of a positive slope, the mean response is higher when the explanatory variable is higher; in the case of a negative slope, the mean response is lower when the explanatory variable is higher.

Before looking for the type of relationship between pairs of quantities, it is recommended to conduct a correlation analysis to determine whether there is a linear relationship between the quantities.

MATLAB has several tools for performing simple linear regression. Among these, the MATLAB Basic Fitting interface helps us adapt our data to calculate the coefficients and trace the model. We can also use the `polyfit()` and `polyval()` functions to match data to a pattern that is linear in the coefficients. We will use some of them with specific examples.

Least square regression

To introduce the key concepts, we will get started with a simple linear regression example; we just use a spreadsheet that contains the number of vehicles registered in Italy and the population of the different regions. We will try to find the line that best approximates a relationship that certainly exists between the number of registered vehicles and the population. To do this, we can follow different ways; we will start with the simplest. Previously, we said that a linear relationship is represented by the following formula:

$$y = \alpha * x + \beta$$

If we have a set of observations in the form $(x_1, y_1), (x_2, y_2), \dots (x_n, y_n)$, for each of these pairs, we can write an equation of the type just seen. In this way, we get a system of linear equations. Represent this equation in matrix form as:

$$\begin{bmatrix} y_1 \\ y_2 \\ \dots \\ y_n \end{bmatrix} = \begin{bmatrix} x_1 & 1 \\ x_2 & 1 \\ \dots & \dots \\ x_n & 1 \end{bmatrix} \times \begin{bmatrix} \alpha \\ \beta \end{bmatrix}$$

Assuming:

$$Y = \begin{bmatrix} y_1 \\ y_2 \\ \ldots \\ y_n \end{bmatrix} ; X = \begin{bmatrix} x_1 & 1 \\ x_2 & 1 \\ \ldots & \ldots \\ x_n & 1 \end{bmatrix} ; A = \begin{bmatrix} \alpha \\ \beta \end{bmatrix}$$

This can be re-expressed using a condensed formulation:

$$Y = X \times A$$

This represents a system of linear equations and MATLAB provides a specific function to locate the solution. It is the `mldivide()` function, and it is also performed by the \ operator. To determine the intercept and the slope, just do the following:

$$A = X \backslash Y$$

Let's do it; from the file `VehiclesItaly.xlsx`, import data in table format. Find the linear regression relation between the vehicle registrations in a state and the population of a state using the \ operator. This operator performs a least square regression:

```
>> VehicleData = readtable('VehiclesItaly.xlsx');
>> summary(VehicleData)
Variables:
    Region: 20x1 cell array of character vectors
    Registrations: 20x1 double
        Values:
                Min          1.4526e+05
                Median       1.1171e+06
                Max          5.9235e+06
    Population: 20x1 double
        Values:
                Min          1.2733e+05
                Median       1.8143e+06
                Max          1.0008e+07
```

Now, assuming vehicle registration as the response variable (y) and the population of a state as the explanatory variable (x), we can calculate the slope of the regression line simply by typing:

```
>> y=VehicleData.Registrations;
>> x=VehicleData.Population;
>> alpha=x\y
alpha =
    0.6061
```

The linear relationship between the variables is expressed by the following equation:

$$y = 0.6061 \times x$$

In this case, the intercept is equal to zero.

We will now calculate the number of vehicles checked for each state from the state's population using the newly found relation. After that, we will see the regression by plotting the actual values of y and the calculated values (*Figure 4.1*):

```
>> VehicleRegFit=alpha*x;
>> scatter(x,y)
>> hold on
>> plot(x,VehicleRegFit)
```

Remember, `hold on` command retains plots in the current axes, so that new plots added do not delete existing plots.

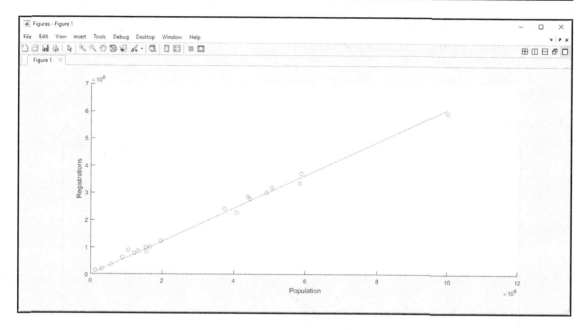

Figure 4.1: Scatter plot of the distribution, with the regression line

As you might expect, there's a positive association between a state population and the vehicle registrations *(Figure 4.1)*.

As just mentioned before, the \ operator performs a least square regression. But how does least square regression work? In the least square method, the coefficients are estimated by finding numerical values that minimize the sum of the squared deviations between the observed responses and the fitted responses.

Given *n* points (x_1, y_1), (x_2, y_2), ... (x_n, y_n), in the observed population, a least square regression line is defined as the equation line:

$$y = \alpha * x + \beta$$

For which the following quantity is minimal:

$$E = \sum_{i=1}^{n} (\alpha x_i + \beta - y_i)^2$$

This quantity represents the sum of squares of distances of each experimental datum (x_i, y_i) from the corresponding point on the straight line:

$$(x_i, \alpha x_i + \beta)$$

This is shown in the following figure (*Figure 4.2*):

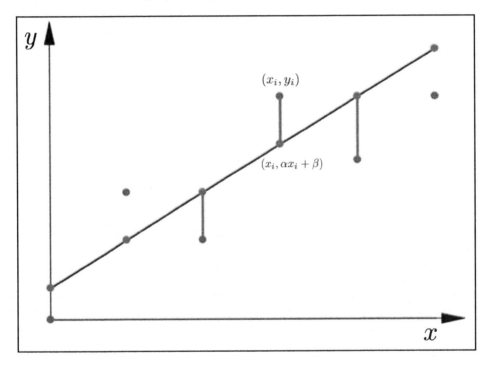

Figure 4.2: Least square regression

To understand this concept, it is easier to draw the distances between these points, formally called **residuals**, for a couple of data. Once the coefficients are obtained, calculating the residuals is really simple. To do this, just calculate the difference between the observed values and the fitted values, that is:

$$r_i = y_i - (\alpha x_i + \beta)$$

In MATLAB, this becomes:

```
>> Residual=y-VehicleRegFit;
>> stem(Residual)
```

The last command shows those values in a chart; for this purpose, we use a `stem` plot. It plots the data sequence as stems that extend from a baseline along the X axis, as shown in the following figure:

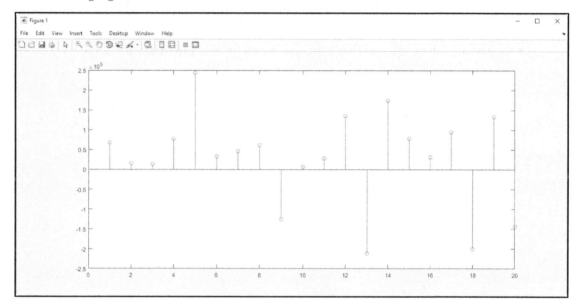

Figure 4.3 : A plot of residuals

A residual is a measure of how well a regression line fits an individual data point. Therefore, if the residuals appear to behave randomly, it suggests that the model fits the data well. However, if the residuals display a systematic pattern, it is a clear sign that the model fits the data poorly.

The analysis of *Figure 4.3* shows that residuals appear randomly scattered around zero, with a good approximation. In *Figure 4.1*, we have seen that the model fits the data very well. But how can we measure this feature? One method to find the better fit is to calculate the coefficient of determination (R-squared). R-squared is a measure of how well a model can predict the data, and it lies between 0 and 1. The higher the value of the coefficient of determination, the better the model at predicting the data.

R-squared (also denoted as R^2) is defined as the proportion of variance in the dependent variable that is predictable from the independent variable. To calculate this coefficient, it is necessary to evaluate two quantities:

- The sum of squares of residuals, also called the **residual sum of squares (RSS)**:

$$SS_{res} = \sum_{i=1}^{n}(y_i - \alpha x_i + \beta)^2$$

- The total sum of squares that is proportional to the variance of the data:

$$SS_{tot} = \sum_{i=1}^{n}(y_i - y_{mean})^2$$

The most general definition of the coefficient of determination is:

$$R^2 = 1 - \frac{SS_{res}}{SS_{tot}} = 1 - \frac{\sum_{i=1}^{n}(y_i - \alpha x_i + \beta)^2}{\sum_{i=1}^{n}(y_i - y_{mean})^2}$$

The better the linear regression fits the data in comparison to the simple average, the closer the value of R^2 is to *1*. Let's see how to calculate it in MATLAB:

```
>> Rsq1 = 1 - sum((y - VehicleRegFit).^2)/sum((y - mean(y)).^2)
Rsq1 =
    0.9935
```

Let's improve the fit by including a y-intercept in our model. To do this, insert a column of one into x and use the \ operator, another time:

```
>> X = [ones(length(x),1) x];
>> alpha_beta = X\y
alpha_beta =
    1.0e+04 *
    7.0549
    0.0001
>> VehicleRegFit2 = X* alpha_beta;
>> scatter(x,y)
>> hold on
```

```
>> plot(x,VehicleRegFit)
>> plot(x,VehicleRegFit2,'--b')
```

Calculate the determination coefficient again to compare the performance of the two models:

```
>> Rsq2 = 1 - sum((y - VehicleRegFit2).^2)/sum((y - mean(y)).^2)
Rsq2 =
    0.9944
```

From the comparison of the two values (Rsq1 and Rsq2), it is evident that the second fit with a y-intercept is better. The following figure shows two linear regression models, with and without intercept, to compare the performance:

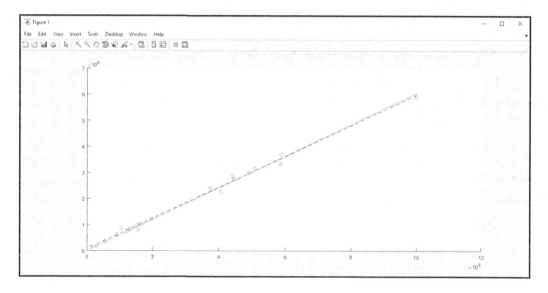

Figure 4.4: Comparison of the two models

The coefficient of determination (R-squared) indicates the proportionate amount of variation in the response variable y explained by the independent variable x in the linear regression model. The larger the R-squared, the more the variability is explained by the linear regression model.

The Basic Fitting interface

What we have done so far has allowed us to perform a linear regression through a *manual* procedure, in the sense that we made calculations step by step without the help of the graphical interface. This approach to the problem was needed to understand the mechanisms underlying the regression techniques. Now that we uderstand the problem perfectly, we can relax and discover the tools that MATLAB provides to perform a regression analysis using the Basic Fitting interface. To present this additional resource, let's look at the example that we analyzed in the previous paragraph from the beginning.

We start by importing data:

```
>> VehicleData = readtable('VehiclesItaly.xlsx');
```

Then, draw a scatter plot of population versus registrations:

```
>> scatter(VehicleData.Population,VehicleData.Registrations)
```

This will be open a figure window. At this point, we only have to use the graphical interface offered by the **Basic Fitting** tool. To open this tool, go to **Tools** | **Basic Fitting** from the menu at the top of the figure window.

In the window that will open, we can select the source data, but above all we choose the type of regression we want to run. We expand the window by clicking on the arrow button in the lower-right corner of the interface to show three panels. Now, we can use these panels to:

- Select a model and plotting options
- Examine and export model coefficients and norms of residuals
- Examine and export interpolated and extrapolated values

In our case, we will perform a linear regression again. In the following figure are shown the **Basic Fitting** window with three panels, the choices made, and the numerical results obtained:

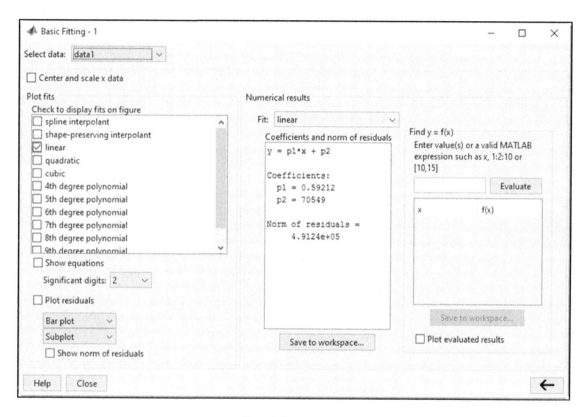

Figure 4.5: The Basic Fitting tool

When we check the plot fit, the line is shown on the plot immediately. In addition, in the **Basic Fitting** window is the equation of the model with the numerical results of coefficient and norm of the residuals. In the last panel to the right of the **Basic Fitting** window, evaluation of the model in the new points is possible (*Figure 4.5*). In the following figure is shown the scatter plot of the distribution with the straight line result of the regression analysis:

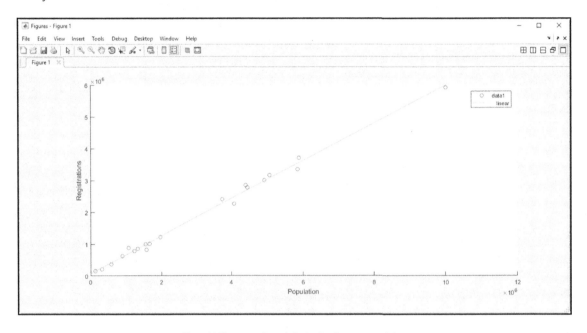

Figure 4.6: Linear regression analysis of registrations versus population

How to create a linear regression model

More generally, to create a linear regression model, use the `fitlm()` function. This function creates a `LinearModel` object. The object in the workspace has a series of properties that can be immediately viewed by simply clicking on it. Methods such as `plot`, `plotResiduals`, and `plotDiagnostics` are available if you want to create plots and perform a diagnostic analysis.

LinearModel is an object comprising training data, model description, diagnostic information, and fitted coefficients for a linear regression.

By default, `fitlm()` takes the last variable in the table or dataset array as the response. Otherwise, we have to specify predictors and response variables, for example, as a formula. In addition, we can set a specific column as the response variable by using the `ResponseVar` name-value pair argument. To use a set of the columns as predictors, use the `PredictorVars` name-value pair argument. Predictor variables can be numeric or of any grouping variable type, such as logical or categorical. The response must be numeric or logical.

A formula string always has the response variable name, followed by ~, followed by one or more terms joined by + or -. Formulas include an intercept term by default. To exclude a constant term from the model, include -1 in the formula. For example:

```
'Y ~ A + B + C'
```

This means a three-variable linear model with intercept.

To understand how `fitlm()` works, we start from the same dataset used before; it contains the number of vehicles registered in Italy and the population of different regions. This dataset contains the following fields:

- Names of Italian regions (named `Region`)
- Vehicle registrations for each region (named `Registrations`)
- Resident population in each region (named `Population`)

Let's start by importing the data into a table:

```
>> VehicleData = readtable('VehiclesItaly.xlsx');
```

Display the first 10 rows of the table.

```
>> VehicleData(1:10,:)
ans =
  10×3 table
          Region             Registrations      Population

    'Valle d'Aosta'            1.4526e+05        1.2733e+05
    'Molise'                   2.0448e+05        3.1203e+05
    'Basilicata'               3.6103e+05        5.7369e+05
    'Umbria'                   6.1672e+05        8.9118e+05
    'Trentino Alto Adige'      8.8567e+05        1.0591e+06
    'Friuli Venezia Giulia'     7.736e+05        1.2212e+06
    'Abruzzo'                  8.5051e+05        1.3265e+06
    'Marche'                   9.9673e+05        1.5438e+06
    'Liguria'                  8.2797e+05        1.5711e+06
    'Sardegna'                 1.0114e+06        1.6581e+06
```

Fit a linear regression model for `Registrations` (vehicle registrations for each region), using `Population` (resident population in each region) as explanatory variables (predictor):

```
>> lrm = fitlm(VehicleData, 'Registrations~Population')
lrm =
Linear regression model:
    Registrations ~ 1 + Population
Estimated Coefficients:
                   Estimate         SE        tStat        pValue

    (Intercept)      70549         41016       1.72         0.10258
    Population      0.59212      0.010488     56.458      1.0323e-21
Number of observations: 20, Error degrees of freedom: 18
Root Mean Squared Error: 1.16e+05
R-squared: 0.994,   Adjusted R-Squared 0.994
F-statistic vs. constant model: 3.19e+03, p-value = 1.03e-21
```

The results show the linear regression model as a formula, estimated coefficients with one row for each term included in the model, and the following columns:

- `Estimate`: The estimated coefficient value for each corresponding term in the model.
- `SE`: The standard error of the estimate.
- `tStat`: The t-statistic for each coefficient for testing the null hypothesis that the corresponding coefficient is zero, against the alternative that it is different from zero, given the other predictors in the model.
- `pValue`: The p-value for the F-statistic of the hypotheses test that the corresponding coefficient is equal to zero or not. In our example, the p-value of the F-statistic for Population is lower than *0.05*, so this term is significant at the 5 percent significance level, given the other terms in the model.

T-test is a parametric test with the purpose of checking whether the average value of a distribution differs significantly from a certain reference value.

In addition, we see the following information about the model created:

- `Number of observations`: The number of records in the data without any `NaN` values. In our example, the number of observations is *20* because we have not identified a `NaN` value for some observations.
- `Error degrees of freedom`: This is equal to the number of observations minus the number of estimated coefficients and is stored as a positive integer value. In our example, the model has two predictors, so the error degrees of freedom are *20 − 2 = 18*.
- `Root Mean Squared Error`: The **Root Mean Squared Error (RMSE)** (residuals); it is stored as a numeric value. The RMSE is the square root of the mean squared error.
- `R-squared`: The proportion of total sum of squares explained by the model. It represents the coefficient of determination. In our example, the R-squared value suggests that the model explains approximately 99 percent of the variability in the registrations response variable.
- `Adjusted R-Squared`: This is a modified version of R-squared that has been adjusted for the number of predictors in the model.
- `F-statistic vs. constant model`: The test statistic for the F-test on the regression model. It tests for a significant linear regression relationship between the response variable and the predictor variables.
- `p-value`: The p-value for the F-test on the model. In our example, the model is significant with a p-value of `1.03e-21`.

Let's look at the result of the last MATLAB command typed. Two values are highlighted on the others: R-squared and p-value. For the first, a very high value was calculated, equal to `0.994`; it means that there is a strong variation in the response variable, explained by the predictor. On the contrary, the p-value is very small, but to understand what this value means, we need to go deep into the subject.

When performing a statistical significance test, the so-called null hypothesis is initially assumed. According to it, there is no difference between the groups regarding the parameter being considered. The groups are equal and the observed difference is attributed to the case.

Obviously, the null hypothesis can be true or false. Now, we have to decide: do we accept or reject the null hypothesis? To decide, we need to analyze our data with a significance test. If the test recommends rejecting the null hypothesis, then the observed difference is declared statistically significant. If, instead, the test advises us to accept the null hypothesis, then the difference is statistically not significant.

As always, the results of a statistical test do not have absolute value and mathematical certainty, but only a probability. Therefore, a decision to reject the null hypothesis is probably right, but it may be wrong. Measuring this risk of falling in error is called the significance level of the test.

> This level (called p-value) represents a quantitative estimate of the probability that the observed differences are due to the case.

P is a probability, and therefore it can only assume values between *0* and *1*. A p-value approaching *0* signifies a low probability that the observed difference can be attributed to the case. The significance level of a test can be chosen by the researcher as desired. However, we usually choose a significance level of *0.05* (5 percent) or *0.01* (1 percent). In our case, we calculated a p-value equal to `1.03e-21`, far below the significance level, indicating that the observed difference is statistically significant.

We previously said that the `fitlm()` function creates a `LinearModel` object, comprising training data, model description, diagnostic information, and fitted coefficients for a linear regression. Now, we will use some of these properties to extract further knowledge from the model.

The least squares method is particularly useful when we have sufficient information about the shape of the model and are interested in finding its parameters. This method is also useful when you want to explore some models. But the method requires manually checking the data to discard the outlier. Now, we will see if there are any outliers in the data that should be excluded from the fit. To do this, there are several residual plots to help us. The most used are the default histogram plot, which shows the range of the residuals and their frequencies, and the probability plot, which shows how the distribution of the residuals compares to a normal distribution with matched variance.

We'll start plotting the residuals through a specific property of the `LinearModel` object:

```
>> plotResiduals(lrm)
```

By analyzing the histogram obtained, we can notice that it has a particular asymmetry at the negative values, as shown in the following figure (*Figure 4.7*):

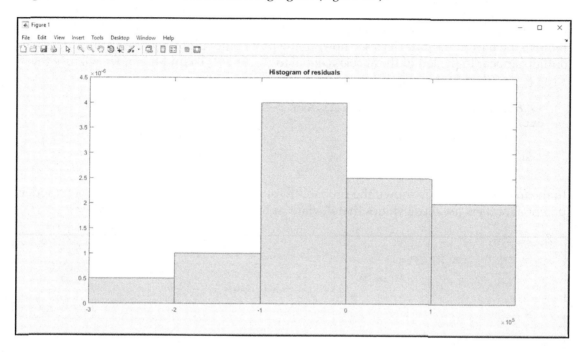

Figure 4.7: Histogram of a residual for a linear regression model

In particular, the observations under -2 $*10^5$ seem to be potential outliers. Looking for better fitting, we will draw the probability plot which, as mentioned before, shows how the distribution of the residuals compares to a normal distribution with matched variance (*Figure 4.8*):

```
>> plotResiduals(lrm, 'probability')
```

Potential outliers appear on this plot as well, notably in the bottom left of the plot shown in *Figure 4.8*, we can notice three values that deviate significantly from the dotted line. Otherwise, for other residual values, the probability plot seems reasonably straight, meaning a reasonable fit for normally distributed residuals. We can identify the outliers and remove them from the data; let's see how. In the probability plot (*Figure 4.8*), three possible outliers appear to the left of the abscissa equal to $-1.5*10^5$. To find them, we will use the `find()` function:

```
>> outliers = find(lrm.Residuals.Raw < -1.5*10^5)
outliers =
      9
     13
     18
```

In the following figure is shown the probability plot of residual for linear regression model: potential outliers are those values that deviate significantly from the dotted line.

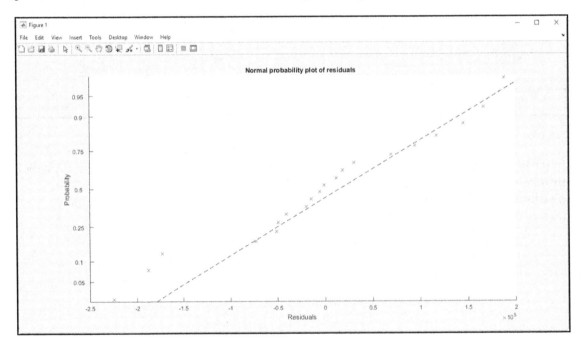

Figure 4.8: Probability plot of residual for a linear regression model

At this point, we can create the model, once again excluding those values:

```
>> lrm2 = fitlm(VehicleData,'Registrations~Population','Exclude',outliers)
lrm2 =
Linear regression model:
    Registrations ~ 1 + Population
Estimated Coefficients:
                    Estimate          SE          tStat        pValue

    (Intercept)       89426          30264        2.9548       0.0098367
    Population       0.59751       0.0078516      76.099       7.9193e-21
Number of observations: 17, Error degrees of freedom: 15
Root Mean Squared Error: 8.25e+04
R-squared: 0.997,   Adjusted R-Squared 0.997
F-statistic vs. constant model: 5.79e+03, p-value = 7.92e-21
```

At first glance, we immediately notice that `R-squared` is clearly improved by recording a value of 0.997, compared to the 0.994 value of the previous model. Let us now examine the probability plot of residual for the new model:

```
>> plotResiduals(lrm2,'probability')
```

In the following figure is shown the probability plot of residual for linear regression model obtained from removing the outliners.

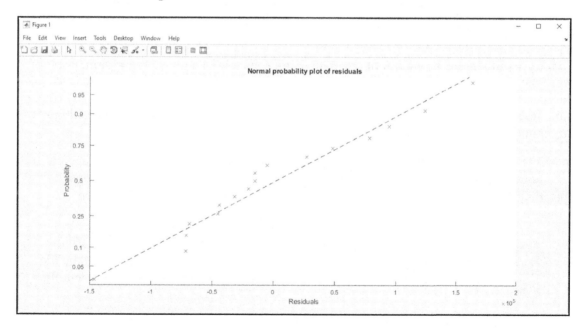

Figure 4.9: Probability plot of residual for linear regression model with outliers removed

The comparison between *Figure 4.8* and *Figure 4.9* (probability plot of two models) highlights the improvement achieved by eliminating outliers. Particularly the probability plot of the second model (*Figure 4.9*) seems reasonably straight, meaning a reasonable fit to normally distributed residuals.

Reducing outlier effects with robust regression

When we use the `fitlm()` function to create a linear model, we can specify the model type. The model specification you give is the model that is fit. If we do not give a model specification, through the parameters of the function, the linear specification will be adopted by default. A linear model contains an intercept and linear terms for each predictor.

The model created is normally affected by the response errors. It is commonly assumed that the response errors follow a normal distribution and that extreme values are rare. However, extreme values called outliers do occur and the linear models are very sensitive to these values. Outliers have a large influence on the fit, because squaring the residuals magnifies the effects of these extreme data points.

Outliers tend to change the direction of the regression line by getting much more weight than they are worth. Thus, the estimate of the regression coefficients is clearly distorted. These effects are difficult to identify since their residuals are much smaller than they would be if the distortion wasn't present.

To reduce outlier effects, we can fit our data using robust least squares regression. Robust regression methods provide an alternative to least squares regression; they attempts to dampen the influence of outlying cases in order to provide a better fit to the majority of the data. Robust regression downweighs the influence of outliers, and makes their residuals larger and easier to identify.

In MATLAB, robust regression can be executed by using the `fitlm()` function. Just add the `RobustOpts` argument to the syntax used so far. Generally, additional options must be specified by one or more `Name,Value` pair arguments. In the case, this pair will be `'RobustOpts','on'`:

Remember: when you use the `fitlm()` function, if you do not specify the predictor and response variables, the last variable in the dataset will be the response variable and the others will be the predictor variables by default.

Let's start from the same dataset used before, containing the number of vehicles registered in Italy and the population of the different regions. In this way, we will be able to compare the results in order to verify any improvements made by the algorithm:

```
>> VehicleData = readtable('VehiclesItaly.xlsx');
```

Now, we create a linear regression model for `Registrations` (vehicle registrations for each region), using `Population` (the resident population in each region) as the explanatory variable (predictor). First, we will do this using the classic least squares method, and then we will add the robust option:

```
>> lrm1 = fitlm(VehicleData, 'Registrations~Population')
lrm1 =
Linear regression model:
    Registrations ~ 1 + Population
Estimated Coefficients:
                   Estimate        SE         tStat       pValue

    (Intercept)      70549        41016        1.72        0.10258
    Population       0.59212      0.010488     56.458      1.0323e-21
Number of observations: 20, Error degrees of freedom: 18
Root Mean Squared Error: 1.16e+05
R-squared: 0.994,  Adjusted R-Squared 0.994
F-statistic vs. constant model: 3.19e+03, p-value = 1.03e-21

>> lrm2 = fitlm(VehicleData, 'Registrations~Population','RobustOpts','on')
lrm2 =
Linear regression model (robust fit):
    Registrations ~ 1 + Population
Estimated Coefficients:
                   Estimate        SE         tStat       pValue

    (Intercept)      25059        27076        0.92549     0.36695
    Population       0.62169      0.0069234    89.796      2.505e-25
Number of observations: 20, Error degrees of freedom: 18
Root Mean Squared Error: 7.64e+04
R-squared: 0.998,  Adjusted R-Squared 0.998
F-statistic vs. constant model: 8.07e+03, p-value = 2.49e-25
```

From the first analysis of the statistical data provided by the command, a performance improvement is already evident. In fact, we can notice that both `R-squared` and `p-value` have better values for the second model (`0.994` versus `0.998` for `R-squared` and `1.03e-21` versus `2.49e-25` for `p-value`).

Note that the R-squared of the Robust model has a value of 0.998. This value is greater than the value obtained in the previous example, after removing the outliers (in that case, we had `R-squared = 0.997`).

To make this improvement more noticeable, plot the residuals of the two models:

```
>> subplot(1,2,1)
>> plotResiduals(lrm1,'probability')
>> subplot(1,2,2)
>> plotResiduals(lrm2,'probability')
```

By comparing the two plots, it is obvious that the Robust model (right half of *Figure 4.10*) is closer to the straight line. Also in this plot, the outliers appear more distant from the straight line and therefore are more highlighted, which helps us in the detection of them. All this is clear in the following figure:

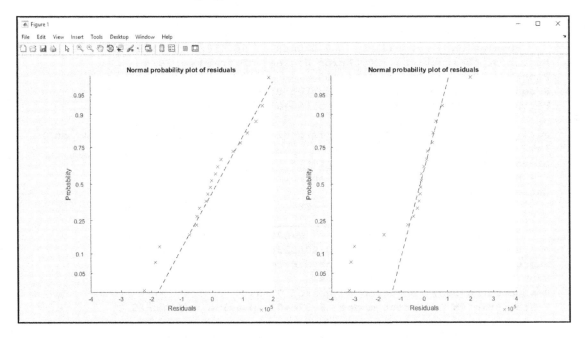

Figure 4.10: Normal probability plot of residuals (standard least squares fit to the left, robust fit to the right)

Analyzing the normal probability plot of residuals for the Robust model (the right half of *Figure 4.10*), we can notice five outliers. Four of these appear to the left of the plot (with residual values lower than $-1.5*10^5$), while the fifth value appears to the right of the plot (with residual value greater than $1.5*10^5$). Now, the elimination of these outliers becomes a child's play:

```
>> outliers = find((lrm2.Residuals.Raw < -1.5*10^5) | (lrm2.Residuals.Raw >
1.5*10^5))
outliers =
      5
      9
     13
     18
     20
```

In the last command, we used the `find()` function with multiple condition. Indeed, we can filter the residuals by applying one or more conditions to these elements. To do this, we have connected them with the logical operator | (or). At this point, we can once again create the model, excluding those values:

```
>> lrm3 =
fitlm(VehicleData, 'Registrations~Population', 'RobustOpts', 'on', 'Exclude', ou
tliers)
lrm3 =
Linear regression model (robust fit):
    Registrations ~ 1 + Population
Estimated Coefficients:
                    Estimate         SE        tStat        pValue

    (Intercept)       25244         19164      1.3172        0.2105
    Population       0.62184     0.0060344     103.05      2.5374e-20
Number of observations: 15, Error degrees of freedom: 13
Root Mean Squared Error: 4.46e+04
R-squared: 0.999,   Adjusted R-Squared 0.999
F-statistic vs. constant model: 1.06e+04, p-value = 2.54e-20
```

Looking at the statistical data provided by the command, we notice a further improvement in performance. In fact, `R-squared` is now equal to 0.999. To show the improvement obtained, plot the residuals of the two models (a robust model versus a robust model without outliers):

```
>> subplot(1,2,1)
>> plotResiduals(lrm2,'probability')
>> subplot(1,2,2)
>> plotResiduals(lrm3,'probability')
```

In the model obtained by eliminating the outlier, the residues fit perfectly on the regression line (right half of *Figure 4.11*). Moreover, there are no residuals that deviate from it, which instead appear in the previous model (left half of *Figure 4.11*). To better understand what has been said so far, let us consider the following figure, in which we report normal probability plot of residuals (a robust fit to the left, a robust fit without outliers to the right):

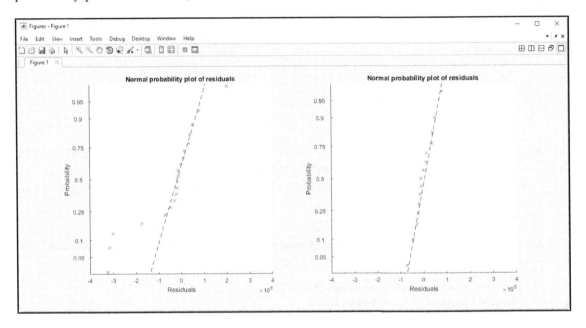

Figure 4.11: Normal probability plot of residuals (robust fit to the left, robust fit without outliers to the right)

The robust regression technique starts by assigning a weight to each data point. Then, a weighting procedure is performed, automatic, and iterative, using a method named **iteratively reweighted least squares**. First, the weights are initialized, placing them all equally. So, model coefficients are estimated using the OLS algorithm. Iteration is then performed; weights are recalculated so that the points farthest from model predictions in the previous iteration are reduced. The model coefficients are then recalculated using weighing least squares. We will continue until the values of the coefficient estimates converge within a specified tolerance.

Multiple linear regression

So far, we have solved simple linear regression problems, which study the relation between the dependent variable y and the independent variable x based on the regression equation:

$$y = \alpha * x + \beta$$

In this equation, x is the explanatory variable and y is the response variable. To solve this problem, we used the least squares method. In this method, the best fitting line can be found by minimizing the sum of the squares of the vertical distance from each data point on the line. In everyday life, it rarely happens that a variable depends solely on another. More often, the response variable depends on at least two predictors. In practice, we will have to create models with response variables that depend on more than one predictor. These models are named multiple linear regressions, a straightforward generalization of the single predictor models. According to multiple linear regression models, the dependent variable is related to two or more independent variables. The general model for n variables is of the form:

$$y = \beta_0 + \beta_1 \times x_1 + \beta_2 \times x_2 + ... + \beta_n x_n$$

Here, $x_1, x_2,.. x_n$ are the n predictors and y is the only response variable. The coefficients β measure the change in the y value associated with a change in x_i, keeping all the other variables constant. The simple linear regression model is used to find the straight line that best fits the data. On the other hand, multiple linear regression models, for example with two independent variables, are used to find the plane that best fits the data, more generally a multidimensional plane. The goal is to find the surface that best fits our predictors in terms of minimizing the overall squared distance between itself and the response. In order to estimate β, similarly to what we did in the simple linear regression case, we want to minimize the following term:

$$\sum_i \left[y_i - (\beta_0 + \beta_1 \times x_{1,i} + \beta_2 \times x_{2,i} + ... + \beta_n x_{n,i}) \right]^2$$

Over all possible values of the intercept and slopes. Just as we did in the case of simple linear regression, we can represent the previous equation in matrix form as:

$$\begin{bmatrix} y_1 \\ y_2 \\ \dots \\ y_n \end{bmatrix} = \begin{bmatrix} 1 & x_{1,1} & x_{1,2} & \dots & x_{1,n} \\ 1 & x_{2,1} & x_{2,2} & \dots & x_{2,n} \\ \dots & & & & \\ 1 & x_{n,1} & x_{n,2} & \dots & x_{n,n} \end{bmatrix} \times \begin{bmatrix} \beta_0 \\ \beta_1 \\ \beta_2 \\ \dots \\ \beta_n \end{bmatrix}$$

Assuming:

$$Y = \begin{bmatrix} y_1 \\ y_2 \\ \dots \\ y_n \end{bmatrix} ; X = \begin{bmatrix} 1 & x_{1,1} & x_{1,2} & \dots & x_{1,n} \\ 1 & x_{2,1} & x_{2,2} & \dots & x_{2,n} \\ \dots & & & & \\ 1 & x_{n,1} & x_{n,2} & \dots & x_{n,n} \end{bmatrix} ; A = \begin{bmatrix} \beta_0 \\ \beta_1 \\ \beta_2 \\ \dots \\ \beta_n \end{bmatrix}$$

This can be re-expressed using a condensed formulation:

$$Y = X \times A$$

This represents a system of linear equations--at least, suppose they are--and just as we did before, in MATLAB we can use the `mldivide()` function to resolve it.

Remember: to solve a system of linear equations in MATLAB, just use the \ operator.

To determine the intercept and the slope, just do the following:

$$A = X \backslash Y$$

To practice these methods, we can draw on the many examples in the software distribution. In this case, we will load in the MATLAB workspace the MAT-file called `hald.mat`; it contains observations of the heat of reaction of various cement mixtures, as shown here:

```
>> load hald
>> whos
  Name              Size            Bytes  Class       Attributes
  Description      22x58             2552  char
  hald             13x5              520  double
  heat             13x1              104  double
  ingredients      13x4              416  double
```

The four columns of the ingredients variable contain the percentage of the following mixture elements:

- **column1**: 3CaO.Al2O3 (tricalcium aluminate)
- **column2**: 3CaO.SiO2 (tricalcium silicate)
- **column3**: 4CaO.Al2O3.Fe2O3 (tetracalcium aluminoferrite)
- **column4**: 2CaO.SiO2 (beta-dicalcium silicate)

The heat variable contains the heat of the reaction of the cement mixtures. From such data, to get the regression coefficients, we have several solutions that can be adopted. We will see some of these, so we can explore many solutions, available in MATLAB, to solve the same problem.

We will start finding the linear regression relation between the ingredients of cement mixtures and the heat of reaction using the \ operator.

Remember that this operator performs a least squares regression.

To determine the intercept and the coefficients, we will add a column of one at the ingredients matrix:

```
>> X = [ones(13,1), ingredients];
>> Y=(heat);
>> A=X\Y
A =
   62.4054
    1.5511
    0.5102
    0.1019
   -0.1441
```

Previously we learned to use the `fitlm()` function to create a `LinearModel` object. We also use it to solve this kind of problem:

```
>> lm=fitlm(ingredients,Y)
lm =
Linear regression model:
    y ~ 1 + x1 + x2 + x3 + x4
Estimated Coefficients:
                  Estimate        SE        tStat       pValue

    (Intercept)     62.405      70.071      0.8906      0.39913
```

x1	1.5511	0.74477	2.0827	0.070822
x2	0.51017	0.72379	0.70486	0.5009
x3	0.10191	0.75471	0.13503	0.89592
x4	−0.14406	0.70905	−0.20317	0.84407

```
Number of observations: 13, Error degrees of freedom: 8
Root Mean Squared Error: 2.45
R-squared: 0.982,  Adjusted R-Squared 0.974
F-statistic vs. constant model: 111, p-value = 4.76e-07
```

By reading the previous table, we can see exact concordance between the results of this function and those obtained with the use of the \ operator. On the other hand, they use the same method: least squares regression.

Finally, we introduce a new function that allows us to solve a regression problem. I mean the regress() function that returns a vector of coefficient estimates for a multiple linear regression of the responses on the predictors:

```
>> b=regress(Y,X)
b =
    62.4054
     1.5511
     0.5102
     0.1019
    -0.1441
```

By comparing the results of the three functions used, it is possible to notice the absolute concordance.

Multiple linear regression with categorical predictor

After dealing with several examples of linear regression, we can certainly claim to have understood the mechanisms underlying this statistical technique. So far, we have used only continuous variables such as predictors. But what happens when the predictors are categorical variables? Don't worry, because the underlying principles of regression techniques remain the same.

Remember: categorical variables are not numerical. They do not derive from measurement operations but from classification and comparison operations. Categorical variables can be further grouped as nominal, dichotomous, or ordinal.

Let's now look at a practical case: in a company, we have been collecting the details of employee wages based on years of experience. We now want to create a model that allows us to get an employee's salary progression over time. Three types of employees were considered: `Management`, `TechnicalStaff`, and `GeneralStaff`. Let's start by importing data into MATLAB; we have a worksheet named `employees.xlsx`:

```
>> EmployeesSalary = readtable('employees.xlsx');
```

Now, we have a table with three variables: `YearsExperience`, `Salary`, and `LevelOfEmployee`. Their content is easily deducible. Now let's see what kinds of variables these are:

```
>> summary(EmployeesSalary)
Variables:
    YearsExperience: 120x1 double
        Values:
            Min             1
            Median         20.5
            Max            40
Salary: 120x1 double
        Values:
            Min            20
            Median         41
            Max            82
LevelOfEmployee: 120x1 cell array of character vectors
```

While the first two are double, the third contains character vectors. In fact, it is easy to understand that this is a categorical variable as it contains the three types of employees already listed before. But MATLAB does not know this, and we have to tell it. In practice, we will have to transform that variable, making it categorical:

```
>>
EmployeesSalary.LevelOfEmployee=categorical(EmployeesSalary.LevelOfEmployee
);
>> class(EmployeesSalary.LevelOfEmployee)
ans =
    'categorical'
```

The time has come to look at the data. In this regard, we draw a simple scatter plot of the salary of the employee versus years of experience, by distinguishing according to the type of employee:

```
>> figure()
>> gscatter(EmployeesSalary.YearsExperience, EmployeesSalary. Salary,
EmployeesSalary.LevelOfEmployee,'bgr','x.o')
>> title('Salary of  Employees versus Years of the Experience, Grouped by
Level of Employee')
```

The results clearly show the wage differences that the three categories have recorded. But in all three cases, the linear trend is equally evident, as is shown in the following figure:

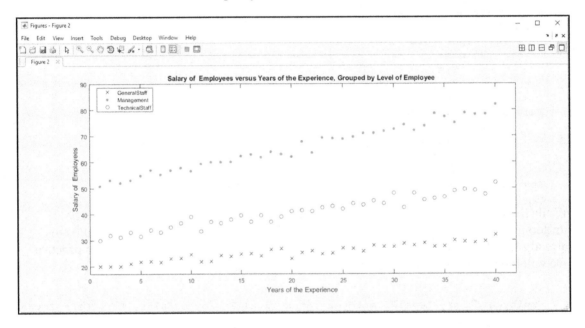

Figure 4.12: Salary of Employees (Salary) versus Years of Experience (YearsExperience), Grouped by Level of Employee (LevelOfEmployee)

Based on the deductions derived from the plot analysis, we can create a model using the `fitlm()` function. The plot suggested a linear trend but highlighted the clear separation between the three types of categorical data. So, we can fit a regression model with `Salary` as the dependent variable and `YearsExperience` and `LevelOfEmployee` as the independent variables. Considering that `LevelOfEmployee` is a categorical variable with three levels (`Management`, `TechnicalStaff`, and `GeneralStaff`), it appears in the model as two indicator variables.

Remember: MATLAB includes categorical predictors as dummy indicator variables. An indicator variable has values *0* and *1*. A categorical variable with *n* categories can be represented by *n – 1* indicator variables.

To take into account the differences between the types of employees, we can include `YearsExperience*LevelOfEmployee` interaction terms:

```
>> LMcat = fitlm(EmployeesSalary,'Salary~YearsExperience*LevelOfEmployee')

LMcat =


Linear regression model:
    Salary ~ 1 + YearsExperience*LevelOfEmployee

Estimated Coefficients:
                                                      Estimate     SE        tStat      pValue
                                                      _____   _____   _____   _____

    (Intercept)                                        20.199     0.40884    49.404     8.0624e-79
    YearsExperience                                    0.25061    0.017378   14.421     1.8358e-27
    LevelOfEmployee_Management                         30.247     0.57819    52.314     1.5568e-81
    LevelOfEmployee_TechnicalStaff                     10.369     0.57819    17.933       5.66e-35
    YearsExperience:LevelOfEmployee_Management         0.48756    0.024576   19.839     9.0452e-39
    YearsExperience:LevelOfEmployee_TechnicalStaff     0.23745    0.024576    9.662     1.7076e-16


Number of observations: 120, Error degrees of freedom: 114
Root Mean Squared Error: 1.27
R-squared: 0.995,  Adjusted R-Squared 0.995
F-statistic vs. constant model: 4.66e+03, p-value = 4.84e-130
```

Figure 4.12a: Differences between types of employees based interaction terms using fitlm()

Based on the results, the model equation is as follows:

```
Salary =
   20.2
 + 0.25 * YearsExperience
 + 30.2 * LevelOfEmployee(Management)
 + 10.4 * LevelOfEmployee(TechnicalStaff)
 + 0.49 * YearsExperience * LevelOfEmployee(Management)
 + 0.24 * YearsExperience * LevelOfEmployee(TechnicalStaff)
```

In this equation, the term `LevelOfEmployee(GeneralStaff)` does not appear, due to the fact that the first level is the reference group by default. On the contrary, the first-order terms for `YearsExperience` and `LevelOfEmployee`, and all interactions were considered.

It is easy to understand that only one equation for the whole system does not allow us to get an adequate estimate of wages. We need to distinguish three models, one for each category of employees, thus obtaining the following three equations:

```
LevelOfEmployee(GeneralStaff):
Salary = 20.2 + 0.25 * YearsExperience

LevelOfEmployee(TechnicalStaff):
Salary = (20.2 + 10.4) + (0.25 + 0.24) * YearsExperience

LevelOfEmployee(Management)
Salary = (20.2 + 30.2) + (0.25 + 0.49) * YearsExperience
```

To better understand what we have done so far, we add those lines to the scatter plot already proposed:

```
>> Xvalues =
linspace(min(EmployeesSalary.YearsExperience),max(EmployeesSalary.YearsExpe
rience));
>> figure()
>> gscatter(EmployeesSalary.YearsExperience, EmployeesSalary.Salary,
EmployeesSalary.LevelOfEmployee,'bgr','x.o')
>> title('Salary of  Employees versus Years of the Experience, Grouped by
Level of Employee')
>>
line(Xvalues,feval(LMcat,Xvalues,'GeneralStaff'),'Color','b','LineWidth',2)
>>
line(Xvalues,feval(LMcat,Xvalues,'TechnicalStaff'),'Color','r','LineWidth',
2)
>>
line(Xvalues,feval(LMcat,Xvalues,'Management'),'Color','g','LineWidth',2)
```

In the code just proposed, we first generated a linearly spaced vector between the min and max values of the `YearsExperience` variable, by using the `linspace()` function. After that, we drew a scatter plot of the salary of employees (`Salary`) versus years of the experience (`YearsExperience`), grouped by level of employee (`LevelOfEmployee`). Finally, we added the three lines relative to their respective trends. To do this, we used the `feval()` function, evaluating the model at the points specified in the `Xvalues` variable. Now, it is clear that the three straight lines, representing the three equations, are distinguished by both intercepts and slopes, as shown in the following figure:

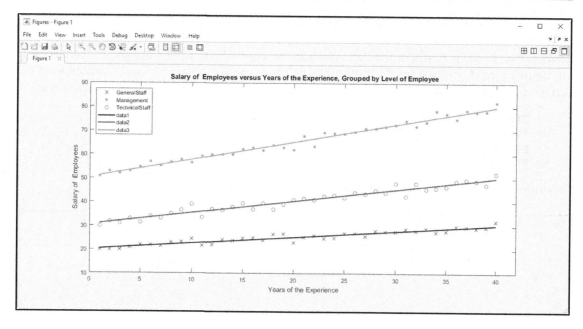

Figure 4.13: Scatter plot with three straight lines that fit three data groups

Polynomial regression

The linear model also includes polynomial regression, in which some predictors appear in degrees equal to or greater than 2. The model continues to be linear in the parameters. For example, a second-degree parabolic regression model looks like this:

$$y = \beta_0 + \beta_1 \times x + \beta_2 \times x^2$$

This model can easily be estimated by introducing the second-degree term in the regression model. The difference is that in polynomial regression, the equation produces a curved line, not a straight line. Polynomial regression is usually used when the relationship between the variables looks curved. A simple curve can sometimes be straightened out by transforming one or both of the variables. A more complicated curve, however, is best handled by polynomial regression.

More generally, a polynomial regression equation assumes the following form:

$$y = \beta_0 + \beta_1 \times x + \beta_2 \times x^2 + \beta_3 \times x^3 + ... + \beta_n \times x^n$$

In the next example, we will only deal with the case of a second-degree parabolic regression in MATLAB. Now, we'll show how to model data with a polynomial. We measured the temperature in a few hours of the day. We want to know the temperature trend even in moments of the day when we did not notice it. Those moments are, however, understood between the initial moment and the final moment in which our measurements took place:

```
>> Time = [6 8 11 14 16 18 19];
>> Temp = [4 7 10 12 11.5 9 7];
>> plot(Time,Temp,'o')
>> title('Plot of Temperature Versus Time')
```

The following figure shows the temperature in a few hours of the day:

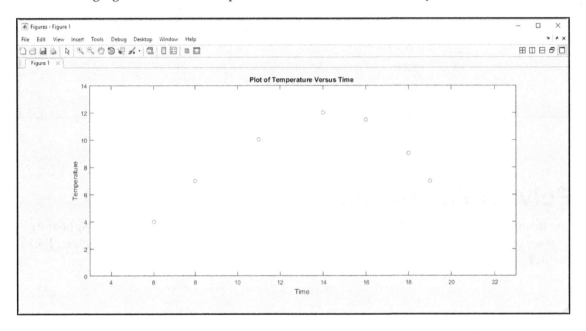

Figure 4.14: Temperature versus time

From the analysis of the figure, it is possible to note a curvilinear pattern of the data that can be modeled through a second-degree polynomial as following equation:

$$temp = \beta_0 + \beta_1 \times time + \beta_2 \times time^2$$

The unknown coefficients β_0, β_1, and β_2 are computed by minimizing the sum of the squares of the deviations of the data from the model (least squares fit). This function returns the coefficients for a polynomial of degree n (given by us) that is the best fit for the data:

 Remember, the coefficients returned by the function are in descending powers, and their length is *n+1* if *n* is the degree of the polynomial.

```
>> coeff = polyfit(Time,Temp,2)
coeff =
   -0.1408    3.8207   -14.2562
```

MATLAB calculates the polynomial coefficients in descending powers. In this case, the second-degree polynomial model of the data is given by the equation:

$$Temp = -0.1408 \times time^2 + 3.8207 \times time - 14.2562$$

After creating the model, let's verify that it actually fits our data. To do this, use the model to evaluate the polynomial at uniformly spaced times, `TimeNew`. To evaluate the model at the specified points, we can use the `polyval()` function. This function returns the value of a polynomial of degree n evaluated at the points provided by us. The input argument is a vector of length `n+1` whose elements are the coefficients in descending powers of the polynomial to be evaluated. Then, plot the original data and the model on the same plot:

```
>> TimeNew = 6:0.1:19;
>> TempNew = polyval(coeff,TimeNew);
>> figure
>> plot(Time,Temp,'o', TimeNew, TempNew)
>> title('Plot of Data (Points) and Model (Line)')
```

Analyzing the following figure, we can notice that the curve fits our data sufficiently. In any case, this model fits the data to a greater extent than a simple linear regression model.

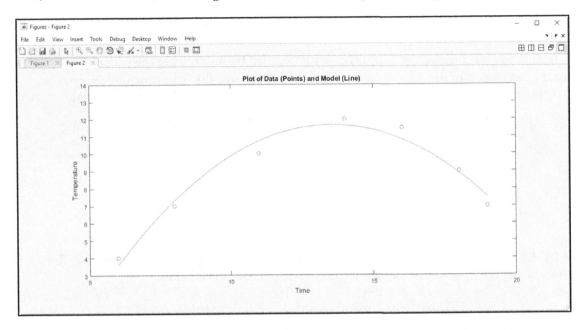

Figure 4.15: Comparison between data and simulated-data-with-polynomial model

In regression analysis, it's important to keep the order of the model as low as possible. In the first analysis, we keep the model to be of first order. If this is not satisfactory, then a second-order polynomial is tried. The use of polynomials of a higher order can lead to incorrect evaluations.

Regression Learner App

Previously, we described some MATLAB apps. They make fast and easy what is long and laborious. Some procedures that require the use of many functions are automated by a user-friendly environment. Additionally, we do not have to remember the names of all the functions useful to perform a specific analysis, as the graphical interface provides us with all the features available.

The Regression Learner App leads us into a step-by-step regression analysis. Through this app, import and explore data, select features, specify validation schemes, train models, and evaluate results, will be extremely simple and fast.

We can run automated training to look for the best regression model type, including linear regression models, regression trees, Gauss process regression models, vector support vehicles, and regression tree complexes. To reuse the model with new data or to perform a programmatic regression, we can export the model to the workspace or generate the MATLAB code to recreate the trained model.

To learn how to use this useful tool, we perform a regression analysis step by step.

 Initially, to get the data, we draw on the large collection of data available in the UCI Machine Learning Repository at the following link:

```
http://archive.ics.uci.edu/ml
```

We use a NASA dataset, obtained from a series of aerodynamic and acoustic tests of two and three-dimensional airfoil blade sections conducted in an anechoic wind tunnel. This dataset contains the following fields:

- Frequency, in hertz (named `FreqH`)
- Angle of attack, in degrees (named `AngleD`)
- Chord length, in meters (named `ChLenM`)
- Free-stream velocity, in meters per second (named `FStVelMs`)
- Suction side displacement thickness, in meters (named `SucSDTM`)
- Scaled sound pressure level, in decibels (named `SPLdB`)

To start, we download the data from the UCI Machine Learning Repository and save it in our current folder. To do this, we will use the `websave()` function; it saves content from the web service specified by url address and writes it to file. We insert the URL address to the specific dataset into a variable named `url`:

```
>> url =
'https://archive.ics.uci.edu/ml/machine-learning-databases/00291/airfoil_se
lf_noise.dat';
```

Now, we save content into a file named `AirfoilSelfNoise.csv`:

```
>> websave('AirfoilSelfNoise.csv',url);
```

We set the names of the variables in accordance with above:

```
>> varnames = {' FreqH '; 'AngleD'; 'ChLenM'; 'FStVelMs'; ' SucSDTM ';'
SPLdB'};
```

Read the data into a table and specify the variable names:

```
>> AirfoilSelfNoise = readtable('AirfoilSelfNoise.csv');
>> AirfoilSelfNoise.Properties.VariableNames = varnames;
```

So, our data is now available in the MATLAB workspace. We can start the Regression Learner App. Select the APPS tab on the MATLAB Toolstrip, and click on the Regression Lerner icon. The **Regression Lerner App** window will open, as shown in the following figure:

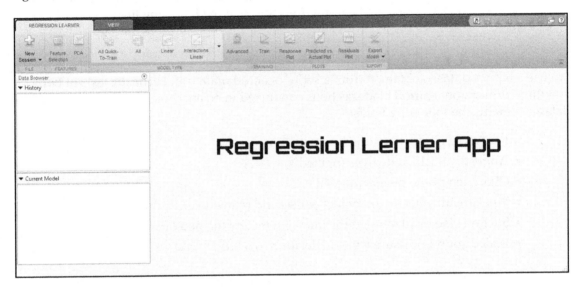

Figure 4.16: The Regression Lerner App window

To import data contained in the MATLAB workspace into the **App**, click on **New Session** on the **Regression Learner** tab, in the **File** section. The **New Session** dialog box will open, with three sections (*Figure 4.17*):

- **Step 1**: **Select a table or matrix**. In this section, we can select the origin of the data
- **Step 2**: **Select predictors and response**. In this section, we can set the variables type
- **Step 3**: **Define validation method**. In this section, we can choose the type of validation method

Validation methods allow us to examine the predictive accuracy of the fitted models. This tool helps us to choose the best model based on estimates of model performance on new data.

The following figure shows the **New Session** dialog box with the three sections we just described:

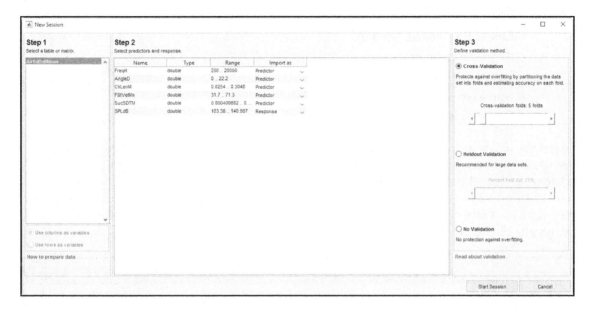

Figure 4.17: New Session dialog box for the Regression Lerner App

In the **Step 1** section of the **New Session** dialog box (*Figure 4.17*), select a table named AirfoilSelfNoise from the workspace variables. After doing this, in the **Step 2** section are shown all the variables in the table, as we can see in *Figure 4.17*. Additionally, the first labeling of variables is performed by default (Predictor and Response). If necessary, we can change that choice. After selecting the validation method, we can click on **Start Session** to finish importing the data.

Remember: a cross validation selects the number of folds to partition the dataset using the slider control. A holdout validation selects a percentage of the data to use as a validation set using the slider control. Finally, with the No Validation option, no protection against overfitting is provided.

Now we perform supervised machine learning by supplying a known set of observations of input data (predictors) and known responses. To do this, the app uses a set of the observations to train a model that generates predicted responses for new input data.

To choose the type of the model, simply click on the arrow present in the **Model Type** section of the Regression Lerner App, to expand the list of regression models. There are many algorithms to choose from:

- **Linear Regression Models**
- **Regression Trees**
- **Support Vector Machines**
- **Gaussian Process Regression Models**
- **Ensembles of Trees**

To get started, select **All Quick-To-Train**. This option trains all the model presets that are fast to fit. Click on the **Train** icon (*Figure 4.18*). A selection of model types appears in the **History** section. When the models finish training, the best RMSE score is highlighted in a box. To improve the model performance, try with all algorithms available, click on **All**, and then click on **Train**. The following figure shows the **Regression Lerner** App window with the results obtained:

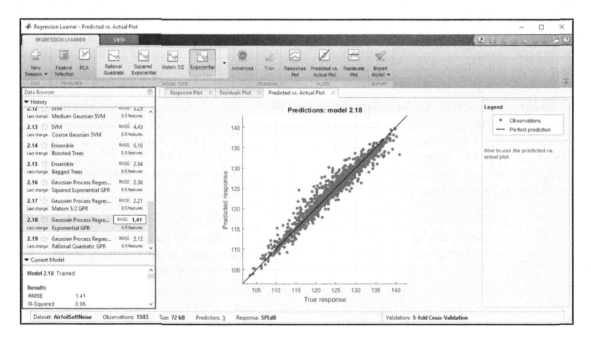

Figure 4.18: Regression Lerner App window with results obtained by the several methods available

To get an idea of the improvements obtained, it will be enough to compare the two extreme models, that is, those with the lower/higher root mean square deviation (RMSE). In the **History** section, we can notice that the lower RMSE score was obtained by **Gaussian Process Regression (RMSE=1.41)** and the higher RMSE score was obtained by **Boosted Trees model (RMSE=6.15)**.

Now, we will compare the two models that recorded extreme results. As can be seen in the following figure, in the model with the lowest RMSE (to the right of the *Figure 4.18*), the data approaches the line more closely, indicating that the predicted data is very close to the actual data:

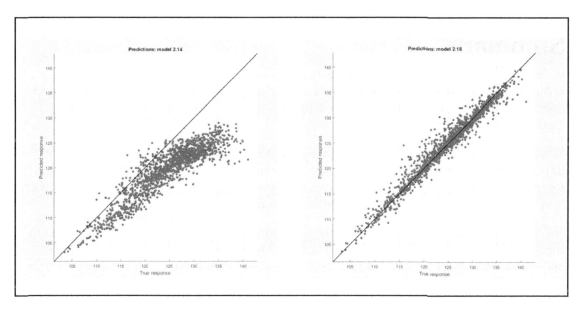

Figure 4.19: Predicted versus actual plot (worst RMSE to the left, best RMSE to the right)

The best regression model has been identified; in order to make predictions with new data, we can export this model to the workspace. To do this, simply select the best model in the **History** list.

Remember: the best model with the lower RMSE score is highlighted in a box.

On the **Regression Learner** tab, in the **Export** section (to the right of the toolstrip), three options are available:

- **Export Model**: To include the data used for training the model. A structure containing a regression model object is exported to the workspace.
- **Export Compact Model**: To exclude the training data. Unnecessary data is removed wherever possible.
- **Generate MATLAB Code**: To generate MATLAB code for our best model. This code can be used to train the model with new data.

Summary

In this chapter, we learned how to perform an accurate regression analysis in a MATLAB environment. First, we explored simple linear regression, how to define it, and how to get an OLS estimation. Then, we looked at several methods of measuring the intercept and slope of a straight line.

Next, we discovered the linear regression model builder; it creates an object inclusive of training data, model description, diagnostic information, and fitted coefficients for a linear regression. Then, we understood how to correctly interpret the results of the simulation and how to reduce outlier effects with robust regression.

So, we explored multiple linear regression techniques; several functions were analyzed to compare the relative results. We learned how to create models with response variables that depend on more than one predictor. Thus, we resolved a multiple linear regression with a categorical predictor example.

With polynomial regression, we approached a model in which some predictors appear in degrees equal to or greater than 2, to fit data with a curved line. Polynomial regression is usually used when the relationship between the variables looks curved.

Finally, we analyzed the Regression Learner App and how to it leads us into a step-by-step regression analysis. It will now be extremely simple and fast to import and explore data, select features, specify validation schemes, train models, and evaluate results.

In the next chapter, we will learn the different types of classification techniques, understand the basic concepts of classification methods and how to implement them in the MATLAB environment, prepare data for classification analysis, and learn how to perform a KNN analysis. We will also cover the Naive Bayes algorithm, decision tree, and rules learners.

5
Pattern Recognition through Classification Algorithms

Classification algorithms study how to automatically learn to make accurate predictions based on observations. Starting from a set of predefined class labels, the algorithm gives each piece of data input a class label in accordance with the training model. If there are just two distinction classes, we talk about binary classification; otherwise, we go for multi-class classification. In more detail, each category corresponds to a different label; the algorithm attaches a label to each instance, which simply indicates which class the data belongs to. A procedure that can perform this function is commonly called a **classifier**.

Classification has some analogy with regression, which we studied in `Chapter 4`, *Finding Relationships between Variables - Regression Techniques*. As well as regression, classification uses known labels of a training dataset to predict the response of the new test dataset. The main difference between regression and classification is that regression is used to predict continuous values, whereas classification works with categorical data.

For example, regression can be used to predict the future price of oil based on prices over the last 10 years. However, we should use the classification method to predict whether the price of oil will grow or decrease in the near future. In the first case, we use continuous data as a prediction and choose a continuous data response (the precise price of oil). In the second case, starting with continuous values (the price of oil over the last 10 years), we begin by classifying the various phases where a growth/diminution of price has been recorded, and then we use that classification to predict a relative trend in the near future.

This chapter shows how to classify an object using several algorithms such as nearest neighbors, discriminant analysis, decision trees, and Naive Bayes. You'll understand how to use the principles of probability for classification. We'll also cover classification techniques using decision trees.

So, we will cover the following topics:

- Decision trees
- Naive Bayes algorithms
- Discriminant analysis
- **k-Nearest Neighbors (KNN)**

At the end of the chapter, we will be able to perform different types of classification techniques, understand the basic concepts of classification methods, and how to implement them in the MATLAB environment. We'll see how to prepare data for classification analyses and how to perform a KNN analysis. We'll understand the Naive Bayes algorithm and decision tree learners.

Predicting a response by decision trees

A decision tree is the graphic demonstration of a choice made or proposed. What seems most interesting is not always useful, and not always are things so clear that you can choose between two solutions immediately. Often, a decision is determined by a series of waterfall conditions. Expressing this concept with tables and numbers is difficult, and even if a table formally represents the phenomenon, it can confuse the reader because the justification of the choice is not immediately apparent.

A tree structure helps us extract the same information with greater readability by putting the right emphasis on the branch we have entered to determine the choice or evaluation. Decision tree technology is useful in identifying a strategy or pursuing a goal by creating a model with probable results. The decision tree graph immediately orients the reading of the result. A plot is much more eloquent than a table full of numbers. The human mind prefers to see the solution first and then go back to understand the justification of the solution, instead of a series of algebraic descriptions, percentages, and data to describe a result.

A decision tree consists of:

- Nodes containing the names of independent variables
- Branches labeled with the possible values of independent variables
- Leaf nodes representing the classes, that is, collections of observations grouped according to the values of one independent variable and joined to nodes via branches

Through these tools, we assign a label to our data and classes to represent the confidence level of the classification itself. The tree thus provides the class's probability, that is, the level of belonging to the class. The following figure shows an example of a decision tree:

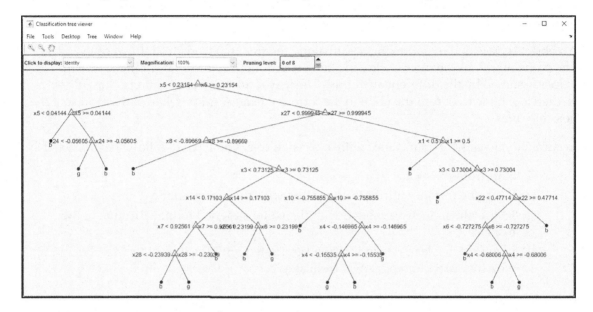

Figure 5.1: An example of a decision tree

Starting from already classified sets of data (training set), we try to define some rules that characterize the various classes. After testing the model with a test set, the resulting descriptions (classes) are generalized (inference or induction) and used to classify records whose membership class is unknown.

Decision trees are the simplest way of classifying objects into a finite number of classes. They are constructed by repeatedly dividing records into homogeneous subsets with respect to the target attribute, which must be categorical.

There are cases where classification rules are univariate, in the sense that they consider a single predictor (target attribute) at a time. However, there are multivariate algorithms too, in which the predictor is represented by a linear combination of variables.

The subdivision produces a hierarchy tree, where the subsets are called **nodes**, and the final or terminal are called **leaf nodes**. Specifically, nodes are labeled with the attribute name, branches are labeled with the possible values of the above attribute, and leaf nodes are labeled with the different values of the target attribute. I mean, the values that describe the membership classes.

An object is classified by following a path along the tree that leads from the root to a leaf. The paths represent the rules of classification or production rules. The branches are the values assumed by the different attributes. The leaves are the classifications. The rule is written along the tree from the node to the different leaves. All possible paths represent the possible rules.

In summary, to classify an instance with a decision tree, you have to follow the given steps:

1. Start from the root.
2. Select the instance attribute associated with the current node.
3. Follow the branch associated with the value assigned to that attribute in the instance.
4. If you reach a leaf, return the label associated with the leaf; otherwise, beginning with the current node, repeat from step 2.

To understand these processes, analyze a simple classification tree (*Figure 5.2*). This tree predicts classifications based on two predictors, x1 and x2. We will classify a predictor as true when x1 < 0.3 and x2 > 0.6, and false otherwise. To predict, start at the top node, represented by a triangle (Δ). The first check affects the variable x2; so, depending on whether x2 is greater than 0.6, the right branch is taken. In this way, the tree classifies the data as a true type. If x1 is smaller than 0.6, we will follow the left branch toward the lower-right triangle node. Here the tree asks whether x1 is smaller than 0.3. If so, we follow the left branch to see that the tree classifies the data as a true type. If not, we follow the right branch to see that the tree classifies the data as a false type. To do this, we simply type:

```
>> X=rand(100,2);
>> Y=(X(:,1)<0.3 | X(:,2)>0.6);
>> SimpleTree=fitctree(X,Y)
SimpleTree =
  ClassificationTree
             ResponseName: 'Y'
    CategoricalPredictors: []
               ClassNames: [0 1]
           ScoreTransform: 'none'
          NumObservations: 100
```

```
>> view(SimpleTree)
Decision tree for classification
1  if x2<0.590843 then node 2 elseif x2>=0.590843 then node 3 else true
2  if x1<0.301469 then node 4 elseif x1>=0.301469 then node 5 else false
3  class = true
4  class = true
5  class = false

>> view(SimpleTree, 'mode', 'graph')
```

Do not worry about the functions we used to create the tree; we'll look at them in detail in the next example. The following figure shows the decision tree created through the proposed procedure:

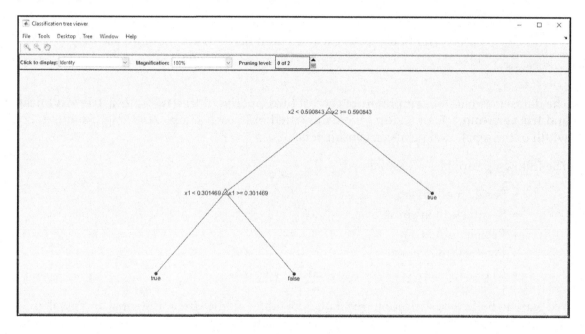

Figure 5.2: A simple decision tree

This procedure will be very familiar to those who know the basics of programming. In fact, in following the different steps, we used some typical controls of procedural programming. These are typical control structures, without which no code is able to automate a procedure. In describing the steps to follow in the classification process through a decision tree, we often use the term *if*. As we know, it represents the keyword of the *if* cycle, the fundamental structure of conditional cycles.

In the classification process, when we reach a leaf, the conditions that must be satisfied appear along the path from the root to the leaf. Therefore, any tree can be easily transformed into a collection of rules. Each rule corresponds to the path from the root to a leaf, and there are as many rules as leaves. This process generates a set of rules with the same complexity as the decision tree.

Let's see how to deal with this topic in the MATLAB environment. The Statistics and Machine Learning toolbox has all the tools needed to build a classification tree from raw data. To understand how this works, we will address a simple example dealt with in all machine learning books. I'm referring to the iris flower dataset, a multivariate dataset introduced by British statistician and biologist Ronald Fisher in his 1936 paper *The use of multiple measurements in taxonomic problems* as an example of linear discriminant analysis.

 To download the dataset and a short summary of the variables contained, please refer to the UCI Machine Learning Repository at the following link: https://archive.ics.uci.edu/ml/datasets/iris.

The dataset contains *50* samples from each of three species of Iris (**Iris setosa**, **Iris virginica**, and **Iris versicolor**). Four features were measured from each sample: the length and the width of the sepals and petals, in centimeters.

The following variables are contained:

- Sepal length in cm
- Sepal width in cm
- Petal length in cm
- Petal width in cm
- Class: `Setosa`, `Versicolour`, and `Virginica`

We want to build a classification tree that, depending on the size of the sepal and petal, is able to classify the flower species. To upload the data to MATLAB's workspace, you do not have to connect to the archive that we have previously proposed--at least not this time. This is because MATLAB has the data in a file already contained in the software distribution. So, to import the data, simply type:

```
>> load fisheriris
```

Two variables are imported into MATLAB: `meas` and `species`. The first contains the data for the length and width of the sepal and petal (`150x4 double`). The second covers the classification (`150x1 cell`). Let's see how the three species, are distributed in that variable:

```
>> tabulate(species)
      Value    Count    Percent
     setosa       50     33.33%
 versicolor       50     33.33%
  virginica       50     33.33%
```

We have thus verified that the sample is equally distributed among the three species. To have an overview of the features of the floral species just listed, we need a scatter plot matrix. The scatter plot matrix shows all the scatter plots of the species features in matrix format.

We already learned to use it in `Chapter 3`, *From Data Knowledge to Discovery*, but this time, we need an additional feature. Graphs need to show the characteristics of the species in pairs by separating the observations for groups. To get this, we can use the `gplotmatrix()` function, which creates a matrix of scatter plots. The standard syntax of the function is as follows:

```
>> gplotmatrix(a,b,group)
```

Here, `a` and `b` are matrices containing the observations of the variables. Each individual set of axes in the resulting figure contains a scatter plot of a column of `a` against a column of `b`. All plots are grouped by the grouping variable group. In our case, the variables we want to compare in pairs are contained in the meas variable, while the groups are contained in the species variable. We will write:

```
>> gplotmatrix(meas, meas, species);
```

The following figure shows the scatter plot of floral features of the three iris species:

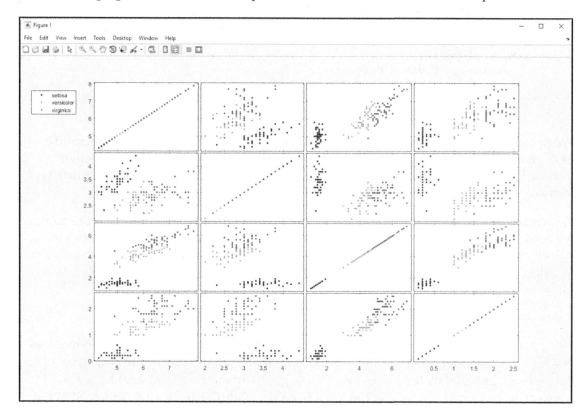

Figure 5.3: Matrix of scatter plots grouped by species

From a quick analysis of *Figure 5.3*, it is possible to note that the values of the **setosa** species are clearly separated from the other two species. In contrast, the values of the other two species overlap in all the plots.

Let's start looking at how the petal measurements differ between species. For this, we can use the two columns containing petal measurements, which we remember are the third and fourth. To represent on a plot how these measures are distributed by species, we can use a variant of the classic scatter plot that we used before. I refer to the gscatter() function, which creates a scatter plot grouped by group. Two vectors of the same size are needed as arguments. A grouping variable must be in the form of a categorical variable, vector, character array, or cell array of character vectors:

```
>> gscatter(meas(:,3), meas(:,4), species, 'rgb', 'osd');
>> xlabel('Petal length');
>> ylabel('Petal width');
```

The following figure clearly distinguishes the three floral species, which are distributed in different areas of the plot:

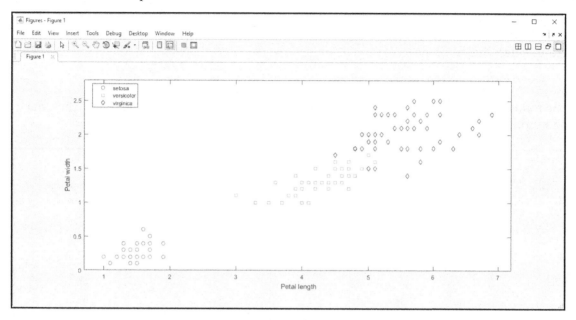

Figure 5.4: Scatter plot grouped by species

All of this would suggest that a classification based on the characteristics of the petals is possible. To create a classification tree, use the `fitctree()` function; it returns a fitted binary decision tree based on the input and output variables respectively:

```
>> ClassTree= fitctree(meas,species);
```

The returned binary tree splits branching nodes based on the values of a column of the matrix meas. Now we can see the tree created using the `view()` function. There are two ways to use this function. The `view(ClassTree)` command returns a text description, while the `view(ClassTree,'mode','graph')` command returns a graphic description of the tree. Let's see them both:

```
>> view(ClassTree)
Decision tree for classification
1  if x3<2.45 then node 2 elseif x3>=2.45 then node 3 else setosa
2  class = setosa
3  if x4<1.75 then node 4 elseif x4>=1.75 then node 5 else versicolor
4  if x3<4.95 then node 6 elseif x3>=4.95 then node 7 else versicolor
5  class = virginica
6  if x4<1.65 then node 8 elseif x4>=1.65 then node 9 else versicolor
7  class = virginica
```

```
8    class = versicolor
9    class = virginica
```

As we can see in the code just proposed, only two input variables are used for the classification: x3 and x4. These are the length and width of the petals. Now, let's see a graphic description of the tree:

```
>> view(ClassTree,'mode','graph')
```

The following figure shows a graphic description of the tree with leaves and branches. Each node contains the conditions that must be satisfied to take a specific branch:

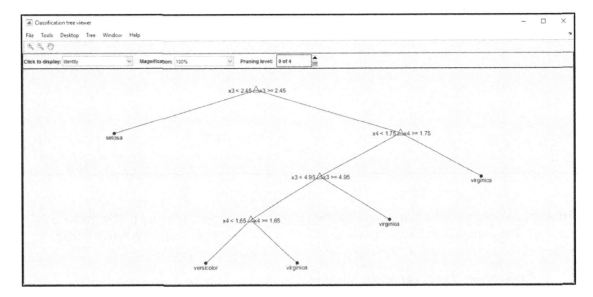

Figure 5.5: Graphic description of the tree

Figure 5.5 gives us useful information on the classification of the three floral species immediately. In most cases, the building of the decision tree is aimed at predicting class labels or responses. Indeed, after creating a tree, we can easily predict responses for new data. Suppose a new combination of four data items that represent the length and width of sepals and petals of a specific class of floral species has been detected:

```
>> MeasNew= [5.9 3.2 1.3 0.25];
```

To predict the classification based on the tree named `ClassTree`, previously created and trained, for new data, enter this:

```
>> predict(ClassTree,measNew)
ans =
  cell
    'setosa'
```

The `predict()` function returns a vector of predicted class labels for the predictor data in the table or matrix based on the trained classification tree. In this case, there is a single prediction because the variable passed to the function contained only one record. In the case of a data matrix containing multiple observations, we would have obtained a series of results equal to the number of rows of the data matrix.

So far, we have learned to build a classification tree from our data. Now we need to test the model's performance in predicting new observations. But what tools are available to measure the tree's quality?

To begin, we can calculate the resubstitution error; this is the difference between the response training data and the predictions the tree makes of the response based on the input training data. It represents an initial estimate of the performance of the model, and it works only in one direction, in the sense a high value for the resubstitution error indicates that the predictions of the tree will not be good. On the contrary, having a low resubstitution error does not guarantee good predictions for new data, so it tells us nothing about it.

To calculate the resubstitution error, simply type:

```
>> resuberror = resubLoss(ClassTree)
resuberror =
    0.0200
```

The calculated low value suggests that the tree classifies nearly all of the data correctly. To improve the measure of the predictive accuracy of our tree, we perform cross-validation of the tree. By default, cross-validation splits the training data into 10 parts at random. It trains 10 new trees, each one on nine parts of the data. It then examines the predictive accuracy of each new tree on the data not included in training that tree. As opposed to the resubstitution error, this method provides a good estimate of the predictive accuracy of the resulting tree, since it tests new trees on new data:

```
>> cvrtree = crossval(ClassTree)
cvrtree =
  classreg.learning.partition.ClassificationPartitionedModel
    CrossValidatedModel: 'Tree'
        PredictorNames: {'x1'  'x2'  'x3'  'x4'}
```

```
         ResponseName: 'Y'
      NumObservations: 150
                KFold: 10
            Partition: [1×1 cvpartition]
           ClassNames: {'setosa'  'versicolor'  'virginica'}
       ScoreTransform: 'none'
  Properties, Methods
>> cvloss = kfoldLoss(cvrtree)
cvloss =
     0.0733
```

At first, we used the `crossval()` function; it performs a loss estimate using cross-validation. A cross-validated classification model was returned. A number of properties were then available in MATLAB's workspace. Later, we calculated the classification loss for observations not used for training by using the `kfoldLoss()` function. The low calculated value confirms the quality of the model.

Probabilistic classification algorithms - Naive Bayes

Bayesian classification is a statistical technique that determines the probability that an element belongs to a particular class. For example, this technique can be used to estimate the probability of a customer belonging to the class of sports car buyers, given some customer attributes such as type of work performed, age, income, civil status, sports practiced, and so on.

The technique is based on the theorem of Bayes, a mathematician and British Presbyterian minister of the eighteenth century. The theorem defines the posterior probability of an event with respect to another. Posterior, in this context, means after taking into account the events relevant to the particular case being examined as if they have already happened.

The Bayesian classifier algorithm assumes that the effect of an event on a given class is independent of the values of other events. This assumption, called the conditional independence of the classes, is intended to simplify calculations, and for this reason the algorithm is named naive. When this assumption is true in reality, the accuracy of the algorithm is comparable to others.

Basic concepts of probability

Let's spend a few minutes talking about the basic concepts of probability. If you are already familiar with these concepts, you may want to skip this section. Otherwise, it will be interesting to deepen the basic knowledge needed to understand how probabilistic classification algorithms work.

In a bag, there are 7 white balls and 3 black balls. Except in color, the balls are identical; they are made of the same material, they are the same size, they are perfectly spherical, and so on. I'll put a hand in the bag without looking inside, pulling out a random ball. What is the probability that the pulled out ball is black?

- The balls in all are *7 + 3 = 10*. By pulling out a ball, I have *10* possible cases. I have no reason to think that some balls are more privileged than others, that is, they are more likely to be pulled out. Therefore, the 10 possible cases are equally probable.
- Of these *10* possible cases, there are only *3* cases in which the ball pulled out is black. These are the cases favorable to the expected event.

The *black ball pulled out* event therefore has 3 out of 10 possible occurrences. I define its probability as the ratio between the favorable and the possible cases, and I get:

```
Probability (black ball) = 3/10 = 0.3 = 30%
```

As we have shown in the example, the probability of an event can be expressed:

- As a fraction, for example, `3/10`
- As a decimal number, for example, `3/10 = 3: 10 = 0.30`
- As a percentage, for example, `0.30 = 30%`

Resolving this problem gives us an opportunity to give a chance definition of an event.

The probability (a priori) that a given event (*E*) occurs is the ratio between the number (*s*) of favorable cases of the event itself and the total number (*n*) of the possible cases, provided all considered cases are equally probable:

$$P = P(E) = \frac{number\ of\ favorable\ cases}{total\ number\ of\ possible\ cases} = \frac{s}{n}$$

Let's look at two simple examples:

- By throwing a coin, what is the probability that it shows a head? The possible cases are 2, heads and tails {H, T}, the favorable cases are 1{H}. So P(head) = 1/2 = 0.5 = 50%.
- By throwing a dice, what is the probability that 5 is out?
  The possible cases are 6, {1, 2, 3, 4, 5, 6}, and the favorable cases are 1{5}. So P(5) = 1/6 = 0.166 = 16.6%.

To define probability, use the concept of equally likely events. It is therefore necessary to clarify what is meant by equally likely events. To this end, the concept of the principle of insufficient reason (or principle of indifference) can be introduced, which states that:

Given a group of events, if there are no valid reasons to think that some event occurs more or less easily than others, then all group events must be considered equally likely.

To calculate the number of possible and favorable cases, in many cases, combinatorial calculations are required.

Previously, we have defined probability as the ratio between the number of favorable cases and the number of possible cases. But what values can it take? The probability of an event P(E) is always a number between 0 and 1:

$$0 \leq P(E) \leq 1$$

- An event that has probability 0 is called an impossible event. Suppose we have six red balls in a bag, what is the probability of picking a black ball? The possible cases are 6; the favorable cases are 0 because there are no black balls in the bag. P(E) = 0/6 = 0.
- An event that has probability 1 is called a certain event. Suppose we have six red balls in a bag, what is the probability of picking a red ball? The possible cases are 6; the favorable cases are 6 because there are only red balls in the bag. P(E) = 6/6 = 1.

The classical definition of probability, based on a discrete and finite number of events, is hardly extendable to the case of continuous variables. The ideal condition of perfect uniformity, where all possible outcomes (the space of events) are previously known and all are equally probable, is a weak element of that definition. The latter condition is also imposed before defining the notion of probability, resulting in circularity in the definition.

An important advance compared to the classic concept in which probability is established a priori, before looking at the data, is contained in the frequentist definition of the probability; this is instead obtained later, after examining the data. According to this concept, the probability of an event is the limit to which the relative frequency of the event tends when the number of trials tends to infinity. This definition can also be applied without prior knowledge of the space of events and without assuming the condition of equally likely events. However, it is assumed that the experiment is repeatable several times, ideally infinitely, under the same conditions.

We can then say that, in a series of repeated tests a great many times under the same conditions, each of the possible events is manifested with a relative frequency that is close to its probability:

$$relative \; frequency \approx probability$$

In the Bayesian approach, probability is a measure of the degree of credibility of one proposition. This definition applies to any event. Bayesian probability is an inverse probability; we switch from observed frequencies to probability. In the Bayesian approach, the probability of a given event is determined before making the experiment, based on personal considerations. The a priori probability is therefore tied to the degree of credibility of the event, set in a subjective way. With the Bayes theorem, on the basis of the frequencies observed, we can adjust the probability a priori to reach the probability a posteriori. Then, by using this approach, an estimate of the degree of credibility of a given hypothesis before observation of data is used in order to associate a numerical value with the degree of credibility of that hypothesis after data observation.

So far, we've talked about the likelihood of an event, but what happens when the possible events are more than one? Two random events, *A* and *B*, are independent if the probability of the occurrence of event *A* is not dependent on whether event B has occurred, and vice versa. For example, if we have two *52* decks of French playing cards. When extracting a card from each deck, the following two events are independent:

- *E1* = The card extracted from the first deck is an ace
- *E2* = The card extracted from the second deck is a clubs card

The two events are independent; each can happen with the same probability independently of the other's occurrence.

Conversely, a random event, *A*, is dependent on another event, *B*, if the probability of event *A* depends on whether event *B* has occurred or not. Suppose we have a deck of *52* cards. By extracting two cards in succession without put the first card back in the deck, the following two events are dependent:

- *E1* = The first extracted card is an ace
- *E2* = The second extracted card is an ace

To be precise, the probability of *E2* depends on whether or not *E1* occurs. Indeed:

- The probability of *E1* is *4/52*
- The probability of *E2* if the first card was an ace is *3/51*
- The probability of *E2* if the first card was not an ace is *4/51*

Let us now deal with other cases of mutual interaction between events. Accidental events that cannot occur simultaneously on a given trial are considered mutually exclusive or disjoint. By extracting a card from a deck of *52*, the following two events are mutually exclusive:

- *E1* = The ace of hearts comes out
- *E2* = One face card comes out

Indeed, the two events just mentioned cannot occur simultaneously, meaning that an ace cannot be a figure. Two events are, however, exhaustive or jointly if at least one of them must occur at a given trial. By extracting a card from a deck of *52*, the following two events are exhaustive:

- *E1* = One face card comes out
- *E2* = One number card comes out

These events are exhaustive because their union includes all possible events. Let us now deal with the case of joint probability, both independent and dependent. Given two events, *A* and *B*, if the two events are independent (I mean the occurrence of one does not affect the probability of the other), the joint probability of the event is equal to the product of the probabilities of *A* and *B*:

$$P(A \cap B) = P(A) \times P(B)$$

Let's take an example. We have two decks of 52 cards. By extracting a card from each deck, let's consider the two independent events:

- A = The card extracted from the first deck is an ace
- B = The card extracted from the second deck is a clubs card

What is the probability that both of them occur?

- $P(A) = 4/52$
- $P(B) = 13/52$
- $P(A \cap B) = 4/52 \cdot 13/52 = 52 /(52 * 52) = 1/52$

If the two events are dependent (that is, the occurrence of one affects the probability of the other), then the same rule may apply, provided $P(B|A)$ is the probability of event A given that event B has occurred. This condition introduces conditional probability, which we are going to dive into:

$$P(A \cap B) = P(A) \times P(B|A)$$

A bag contains 2 white balls and 3 red balls. Two balls are pulled out from the bag in two successive extractions without reintroducing the first ball pulled out into the bag.

Calculate the probability that the two balls extracted are both white:

- The probability that the first ball is white is 2/5
- The probability that the second ball is white, provided that the first ball is white, is 1/4

The probability of having two white balls is as follows:

- $P(two \; white) = 2/5 \cdot 1/4 = 2/20 = 1/10$

As promised, it is now time to introduce the concept of conditional probability. The probability that event A occurs, calculated on the condition that event B occurred, is called conditional probability and is indicated by the symbol $P(A \mid B)$. It is calculated using the following formula:

$$P(B|A) = \frac{P(A \cap B)}{P(A)}$$

Conditional probability usually applies when A depends on B, that is, events are dependent on each other. In the case where A and B are independent, the formula becomes:

$$P(A|B) = P(A)$$

In fact, now the occurrence of B does not affect the probability $P(A)$.

Let's take an example. What is the probability that by extracting two cards from a deck of 52, the second one is a diamond? Note the information that the first was a diamond too.

$P(diamonds \cap diamonds) = 13/52 \cdot 12/51$

Then:

$P(diamonds \mid diamonds) = (13/52 \cdot 12/51) / 13/52 = 12/51$

As a further example, you can calculate the probability that you get the number 1 by throwing a dice, given that the result is an odd number. The conditional probability we want to calculate is that of the event $B|A$; that is, *get number 1 knowing that there will be an odd number*, where A is the *get an odd number* event and B is the *get the number one* event.

The intersection event $A \cap B$ corresponds to the event *get the number 1 and an odd number* (which is equivalent to the *get the number 1* event, since 1 is odd). Therefore, the probability of getting an odd number is equal to:

$P(A) = 3/6 = 1/2$

While the probability of getting the number 1 is:

$P(A \cap B) = 1/6$

Therefore, it is possible to calculate the conditional probability of event B with respect to event A using the following formula:

$$P(B|A) = \frac{P(A \cap B)}{P(A)} = \frac{\frac{1}{6}}{\frac{1}{2}} = \frac{1}{3} \approx 0.333$$

Let us remember in this regard that playing dice is always a loss-making activity, even for a statistician.

Classifying with Naive Bayes

In the previous section, we learned to calculate many types of probabilities; it is time to benefit from the acquired skills. We will do this by defining Bayes, theorem as follows.

Let A and B be two dependent events. Previously, we said that the joint probability between the two events is calculated using the following formula:

$$P(A \cap B) = P(A) \times P(B|A)$$

Or, similarly, using the following formula:

$$P(A \cap B) = P(B) \times P(A|B)$$

By analyzing the two proposed formulas, it is clear that they have the first equal member. This implies that even the second members are equal, so we can write:

$$P(A) \times P(B|A) = P(B) \times P(A|B)$$

By solving these equations for conditional probability, we get:

$$P(B|A) = \frac{P(B) \times P(A|B)}{P(A)}$$

Or:

$$P(A|B) = \frac{P(A) \times P(B|A)}{P(B)}$$

The proposed formulas represent the mathematical statement of Bayes' theorem. The use of one or the other depends on what we are looking for.

Let's take an example. Suppose you are given two coins. The first coin is fair (heads and tails) and the second coin is wrong (heads on both sides).You randomly choose a coin and toss it, getting heads as a result. What is the likelihood of it being the second coin (wrong coin)?

Let's start by distinguishing the various events that come into play. Let's identify these events:

- *A*: The first coin was chosen
- *B*: The second coin was chosen
- *C*: After the toss comes a head

To avoid making mistakes, let us see what we need to calculate. The question made by the problem is simple. It asks us to calculate the likelihood of choosing the second coin, knowing that after the launch we got heads. In symbols, we have to calculate *P(B|C)*.

According to Bayes' theorem, we can write:

$$P(B|C) = \frac{P(B) \times P(C|B)}{P(C)}$$

Now calculate the three probabilities that appear in the previous equation. Remember that *P(B|C)* is called posterior probability and that is what we want to calculate. *P(B)* is called prior probability, linked to the second event (*B*), and is equal to 1/2, since we have two possible choices (two coins are available).

$$P(B) = \frac{1}{2}$$

P(C|B) is called likelihood and is equal to *1*, as it gives the chances of heads knowing that you have chosen the second coin (which has two heads and so is a certain event). Therefore:

$$P(C|B) = 1$$

Finally, *P(C)* is called marginal likelihood and is equal to ¾, as the coins have *4* faces (possible cases) of which three have heads (favorable cases).

$$P(C) = \frac{3}{4}$$

At this point, we can enter the calculated probabilities in the Bayes formula to get the result:

$$P(B|C) = \frac{P(B) \times P(C|B)}{P(C)} = \frac{\frac{1}{2} \times 1}{\frac{3}{4}} = \frac{2}{3}$$

Bayesian methodologies in MATLAB

As anticipated at the beginning of the topic, the Bayesian classifier algorithm assumes that the effect of an event on a given class is independent of the values of other events. This assumption, called the conditional independence of classes, is intended to simplify calculations, and for this reason the algorithm is named naive. It has been noted that the Naive Bayes classifier works well even when that independence assumption is not valid.

In MATLAB, the Naive Bayes classifier works with data in two steps:

- **First step of training**: Using a set of data, preventively classified, the algorithm estimates the parameters of a probability distribution according to the assumption that predictors are conditionally independent given the class.
- **Second step of prediction**: For a new set of data, the posterior probability of that sample belonging to each class is computed. In this way, new data is classified according to the largest posterior probability.

To date, understanding the mechanisms of classification algorithms has been easy thanks to the example provided by Fisher on the three different types of the iris flower. Given its extreme simplicity, we will continue to refer to the same dataset; in particular, we will try to classify the types of iris based on the characteristics of its petals, this time using a Bayesian classifier.

To train a Naive Bayes classifier, we can use the `fitcnb()` function; it returns a multiclass Naive Bayes model trained by the predictors provided. It is good practice to specify the class order. In this way, we can classify data with more than two classes. In this case, the predictors are the petal length and petal width, while the classes are `setosa`, `versicolor`, and `virginica`.

To import such data, simply type:

```
>> load fisheriris
```

First, we extract the third and fourth columns of the meas variable, which correspond to petal length and petal width respectively. Then, we create a table with these variables to include in the model the names of the predictors:

```
>> PetalLength = meas(:,3);
>> PetalWidth = meas(:,4);
>> PetalTable = table(PetalLength,PetalWidth);
```

To train a Naive Bayes classifier, type:

```
>> NaiveModelPetal =
fitcnb(PetalTable,species,'ClassNames',{'setosa','versicolor','virginica'})
NaiveModelPetal =
  ClassificationNaiveBayes
            PredictorNames: {'PetalLength'  'PetalWidth'}
             ResponseName: 'Y'
     CategoricalPredictors: []
                ClassNames: {'setosa'  'versicolor'  'virginica'}
            ScoreTransform: 'none'
           NumObservations: 150
         DistributionNames: {'normal'  'normal'}
    DistributionParameters: {3×2 cell}
```

A ClassificationNaiveBayes object is created with several properties and methods. To access one of these, we can use dot notation; for example, to display the mean and standard deviation of a particular Gaussian fit, type this:

```
>> NaiveModelPetal.DistributionParameters
ans =
  3×2 cell array
    [2×1 double]    [2×1 double]
    [2×1 double]    [2×1 double]
    [2×1 double]    [2×1 double]
```

This command returns a 3×2 cell array that contains the mean and standard deviation for each species and each feature (petal length and petal width). Each row contains species data (setosa, versicolor, and virginica respectively), and each column contains feature data (petal length and petal width). Thus, to access the mean and standard deviation of the versicolor species related to the petal length, type:

```
>> NaiveModelPetal.DistributionParameters{2,1}
ans =
    4.2600
    0.4699
```

To access the mean and standard deviation of the setosa species related to the petal width, type this:

```
>> NaiveModelPetal.DistributionParameters{1,2}
ans =
    0.2460
    0.1054
```

The first value is the mean; the second is the standard deviation. To test the performance of the model, compute the resubstitution error, which is the misclassification error or the proportion of misclassified observations on the training set. The resubstitution error rate indicates only how good/bad our results are; it provides us with some knowledge about the algorithm used (usually, it indicates the performance measure):

```
>> NaiveModelPetalResubErr = resubLoss(NaiveModelPetal)
NaiveModelPetalResubErr =
      0.0400
```

The result indicates that 4 percent of the observations are misclassified by the Naive Bayes algorithm. This simple calculation of the classification error does not allow us to understand the types of errors committed by our system. In particular, we cannot answer questions such as:

- Are the errors equally distributed across all classes?
- Does the system confuse just a few classes while classifying the others correctly?

To understand how these errors are distributed, we can compute the confusion matrix. A confusion matrix contains information about actual and predicted classifications made by a model. The performance of such systems is commonly evaluated by using the data in the matrix. The following table shows the confusion matrix for a two-class classifier:

	Predicted Positive	**Predicted Negative**
Actual TRUE	*TP*	*FN*
Actual FALSE	*FP*	*TN*

The entries in the confusion matrix have the following meanings:

- *TP* is the number of correct predictions that an instance is positive
- *FN* is the number of incorrect predictions that an instance is negative
- *FP* is the number of incorrect predictions that an instance is positive
- *TN* is the number of correct predictions that an instance is negative

It is clear that the values on the main diagonal represent the correct predictions; all the others are errors. In MATLAB, to compute a confusion matrix, we can use the `confusionmat()` function; it returns the confusion matrix determined by the known and predicted groups provided. Before using the function, we collect the model predictions for available data, and then we compute the confusion matrix:

```
>> PredictedValue = predict(NaiveModelPetal,meas(:,3:4));
>> ConfMat = confusionmat(species,PredictedValue)
ConfMat =
      50     0     0
       0    47     3
       0     3    47
```

As expected, there are only six errors (four percent of the available values) and they refer to the two `versicolor` and `virginica` species. To understand how the classifier distributes the predicted values, we can visualize them in the plan identified by the two coordinates: petal length and petal width. One way to visualize these values is by creating a grid of *(x,y)* values and applying the classification function to that grid. First of all, we estimate the grid extremes, calculating the min and max of the predictors:

```
>> min(meas(:,3:4))
ans =
      1.0000      0.1000
>> max(meas(:,3:4))
ans =
      6.9000      2.5000
```

Now we can create the grid:

```
>> [x,y] = meshgrid(1:.1:6.9,0.1:.1:2.5);
```

Predict responses using the model created above in the grid points:

```
>> PredictedGrid = predict(NaiveModelPetal, [x y]);
```

Now we can plot the distribution of predicted values onto the plan:

```
>> gscatter(x,y,PredictedGrid,'grb','sod')
>> xlabel('Petal Length')
>> ylabel('Petal Width')
>> title('{\bf Classification by Naïve Bayes Method}')
```

To make the figure as straightforward as possible, we've completed adding the axis labels and a title to the chart. The following figure shows the distribution of predicted values into the plan identified by the two coordinate's **Petal Length** and **Petal Width**.

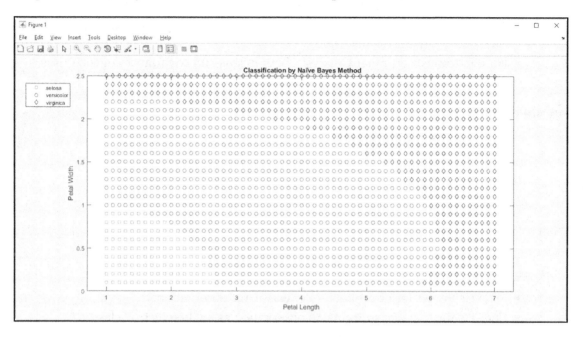

Figure 5.6: Distribution of predicted values

Describing differences by discriminant analysis

Discriminant analysis is a statistical analysis dating back to Fisher (1936 - **Linear Discriminant Analysis (LDA)**), as we have already mentioned earlier. It is a method for describing, through a one-dimensional function, the difference between two or more groups and allocating each observation to the group of origin. This is a classification problem, where the groups are known a priori and one or more new observations are classified into one of the known groups based on the measured characteristics. Each observation must have a score on one or more quantitative predictor measures, and a score on a group measure. Discriminant analysis is useful in determining whether a set of variables is effective in predicting category membership.

In MATLAB, the discriminant analysis model is created on the following assumptions:

- Each class generates data using a multivariate normal distribution. That is, the model assumes that data generated has a Gaussian mixture distribution.
- For linear discriminant analysis, the model has the same covariance matrix for each class, only the means vary.
- For quadratic discriminant analysis, both means and covariances of each class vary.

The discriminant analysis model is created to minimize the expected classification cost. Based on these assumptions, the model equation assumes the following form:

$$Y = \underset{y=1,..k}{\arg\min} \sum_{k=1}^{K} P(k|x)C(y|k)$$

Where:

- Y is the predicted classification
- K is the number of classes
- $P(k|x)$ is the posterior probability of class k for observation x
- $C(y|k)$ is the cost of classifying an observation as y when its true class is k

In the previous paragraph, we used the data in the `fisheriris` dataset, already available in MATLAB, which was used by Fisher as an example of LDA. Why change right now? So we will refer to the same dataset in the next example. Remember, to import the data, simply type:

```
>> load fisheriris
```

To perform a discriminant analysis in the MATLAB environment, we can use the `fitcdiscr()` function, that returns a fitted discriminant analysis model based on the input and output variables provided. The model estimates the parameters of a Gaussian distribution for each class. Train a discriminant analysis model using the entire dataset:

```
>> DiscrModel = fitcdiscr(meas,species)
DiscrModel =
  ClassificationDiscriminant
            ResponseName: 'Y'
   CategoricalPredictors: []
              ClassNames: {'setosa'    'versicolor'    'virginica'}
          ScoreTransform: 'none'
         NumObservations: 150
```

```
      DiscrimType: 'linear'
               Mu: [3×4 double]
           Coeffs: [3×3 struct]
```

To access the model properties, use dot notation. In the summary printed on the command-line interface, we can notice, at the second-last row, the `Mu` variable. It represents the group means for each feature (height and width for sepal and petal) for each predictor. To display it onscreen, simply type:

```
>> DiscrModel.Mu
ans =
      5.0060    3.4280    1.4620    0.2460
      5.9360    2.7700    4.2600    1.3260
      6.5880    2.9740    5.5520    2.0260
```

Each value represent, the mean of the variables for each class, the first row for `setosa` species, the second row for `versicolor`, and the last row for `virginica`. In the last row of the summary shown by the `fitcdiscr()` function, there is the `Coeffs` variable. What is this? Let's visualize the content:

```
>> DiscrModel.Coeffs
ans =
  3×3 struct array with fields:
    DiscrimType
    Const
    Linear
    Class1
    Class2
```

This is an *n-by-n* structured array, where *n* is the number of classes. In our case, a *3-by-3* structured array, because there are *3* classes. Each structured array contains coefficients of the linear boundaries between two classes. Why are we now talking about boundaries? This is simple; the model divides the n-dimensional space into areas belonging to a specific class. The boundaries just delimit those zones. If a new item falls into a specific area, identified by such boundaries, it will be attributed to that class.

So `Coeffs(i,j)` contains boundaries data between class `i` and class `j`. The equation of the boundary between these classes is:

```
Const + Linear * x = 0
```

Where x is a vector containing the features of the distribution. In this regard, we only use the petals features to construct the model, so that we can represent everything on a two-dimensional space.

```
>> X = [meas(:,3) meas(:,4)];
```

Train a discriminant analysis model using only the petals features:

```
>> DiscrModelPetal = fitcdiscr(X,species)
DiscrModelPetal =
  ClassificationDiscriminant
            ResponseName: 'Y'
   CategoricalPredictors: []
              ClassNames: {'setosa'  'versicolor'  'virginica'}
          ScoreTransform: 'none'
         NumObservations: 150
             DiscrimType: 'linear'
                      Mu: [3×2 double]
                  Coeffs: [3×3 struct]
```

Display the species distribution on the scatter plot:

```
>> gscatter(meas(:,3), meas(:,4), species,'rgb','osd');
```

Retrieve the coefficients for the linear boundary between the setosa and the versicolor classes (first and second class in the order).

```
>> Const12 = DiscrModelPetal.Coeffs(1,2).Const;
>> Linear12 = DiscrModelPetal.Coeffs(1,2).Linear;
```

Plot the curve that separates the first and second classes:

```
>> hold on
>> Bound12 = @(x1,x2) Const12 + Linear12(1)*x1 + Linear12(2)*x2;
>> B12 = ezplot(Bound12,[0 7.2 0 2.8]);
>> B12.Color = 'r';
>> B12.LineWidth = 2;
```

Retrieve the coefficients for the linear boundary between the versicolor and the verginica classes (second and third class in the order).

```
>> Const23 = DiscrModelPetal.Coeffs(2,3).Const;
>> Linear23 = DiscrModelPetal.Coeffs(2,3).Linear;
```

Plot the curve that separates the first and second classes:

```
>> Bound23 = @(x1,x2) Const23 + Linear23 (1)*x1 + Linear23 (2)*x2;
>> B23 = ezplot(Bound23,[0 7.2 0 2.8]);
>> B23.Color = 'b';
>> B23.LineWidth = 2;
```

Finally, set the axis label and title:

```
>> xlabel('Petal Length')
>> ylabel('Petal Width')
>> title('{\bf Linear Classification by Discriminant Analysis}')
```

The following figure shows a scatter plot of the Fisher Iris distribution with the boundaries between the species.

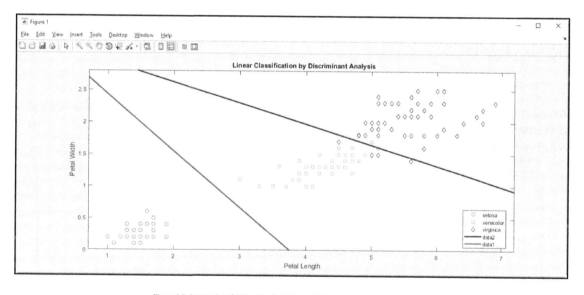

Figure 5.7: Scatter plot of Fisher Iris distribution with the boundaries between the species

We now check the correct functioning of the algorithm by classifying three new points that, as shown in *Figure 5.8*, fall in the three floral typology areas. These points are:

- *P1: Petal Length = 2 cm; Petal Width = 0.5 cm*
- *P2: Petal Length = 5 cm; Petal Width = 1.5 cm*
- *P3: Petal Length = 6 cm; Petal Width = 2 cm*

Let's first create two vectors containing the petal length and petal width of the new data respectively.

```
>> NewPointsX=[2 5 6];
>> NewPointsY=[0.5 1.5 2];
```

To predict the classes of the new data, we can use the `predict()` function, which returns a vector of predicted class labels for the predictor data provided, based on the trained discriminant analysis classification model.

```
>> LabelsNewPoints = predict(DiscrModelPetal,[NewPointsX' NewPointsY'])
LabelsNewPoints =
   3x1 cell array
     'setosa'
     'versicolor'
     'virginica'
```

Now, we plot the three points in the scatter plot with boundaries to verify correct classification:

```
>> plot(NewPointsX,NewPointsY,'*')
```

In the following figure, the new data points in the scatter plot, with boundaries, are shown. It is easy to check that the classification offered by the `predict()` function coincides with what we can do visually:

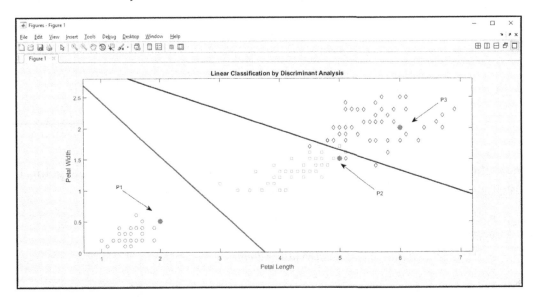

Figure 5.8: Scatter plot with the boundaries between the species and new data points

As can be seen in *Figure 5.8*, the classification performed by the discriminant analysis is very good, except for some values that fall around the boundaries between the `versicolor` and `virginica` species. To improve the results, if possible, set the `DiscrimType` name-value pair to `pseudoLinear` or `pseudoQuadratic`.

To test the performance of the model, compute the resubstitution error.

```
>> DiscrModelResubErr = resubLoss(DiscrModel)
DiscrModelResubErr =
    0.0200
```

The result indicates that 2 percent of the observations are misclassified by the linear discriminant function. To understand how these errors are distributed, we can compute the confusion matrix. Before computing the confusion matrix, we collect the model predictions for available data, and then compute the confusion matrix.

```
>> PredictedValue = predict(DiscrModel,meas);
>> ConfMat = confusionmat(species,PredictedValue)
ConfMat =
    50     0     0
     0    48     2
     0     1    49
```

As expected, there are only three errors (two percent of the available values) and they refer to the two `versicolor` and `virginica` species. We can see which ones they are by drawing *X* through the misclassified points:

```
>> Err = ~strcmp(PredictedValue,species);
>> gscatter(meas(:,3), meas(:,4), species,'rgb','osd');
>> hold on
>> plot(meas(Err,3), meas(Err,4), 'kx');
>> xlabel('Petal length');
>> ylabel('Petal width');
```

Let's analyze the code just written down. We first found incorrect values using the `strcmp()` function, which compares two strings and returns 1 (true) if the two are identical and 0 (false) otherwise. Subsequently, we traced a scatter plot grouped by species, using the two `Petal length` and `Petal width` features. Then, we added the indicators at the wrong values, and finally we added axis labels.

The following figure shows a scatter plot grouped by species with incorrect values indicated:

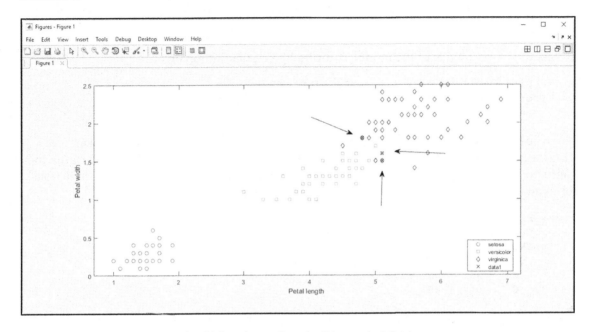

Figure 5.9: Scatter plot grouped by species with incorrect values indicated

As expected, the three errors are located on the boundary between the two species versicolor and virginica.

Find similarities using nearest neighbor classifiers

In the classification analysis, the objective is to verify the existence of differences between classes according to the variables considered. This leads to the formulation of a model that can assign each sample to the class to which it belongs. If the model is obtained from a set whose classes are known (training set), the predictive power of the model itself can be verified by using another set of data (evaluation set) also with a known class. Those samples are classified according to the previously elaborated model.

Among the different types of existing classifiers, we also find the *nearest neighbor*, which identifies the class of belonging to a tested sample based on the distance of this from stored and classified objects. In most cases, the distance is defined as *Euclidean distance between two points*, calculated according to the following formula:

$$Distance = \sqrt{\sum_{i=0}^{n}(x_i - y_i)^2}$$

On a bidimensional plane, the Euclidean distance represents the minimum distance between two points, so the straight line connecting two points. This distance is calculated as the square root of the sum of the squared difference between the elements of two vectors, as indicated in the previous formula.

An object is assigned to the class based on the majority vote of its neighbors, the most common among its KNN is chosen (k is a positive integer, typically small). If $k = 1$, then the object is simply assigned to the class of that single nearest neighbor. This type of classifier, however, is not very sensitive, because it is subject to frequent errors (since it ranks based on only one stored object).

Therefore, you usually choose a larger K (between *1* and *10*) and assignment of an object to a given class is based on a simple majority criterion. Choosing the optimal value for K is best done by first inspecting the data. In general, a large K value is more precise, as it reduces the overall noise, but there is no guarantee. In most cases, an odd K is chosen to avoid parity situations; otherwise the classification may also take into account the distances of the K objects from the sample to be graded.

A great advantage of this method is to be able to classify objects whose classes are not linearly separable. It is also a very stable classifier, as small perturbations in training data do not significantly affect the results obtained.

The most obvious disadvantage, however, is that it does not provide a true mathematical model, but each new classification must be made by adding the new datum to the initial set and repeating the calculation procedure for the selected K value. It also needs a fairly large amount of data to make realistic predictions and is sensitive to the noise of the data being analyzed.

In MATLAB, the KNN classifier is constructed through the `fitcknn()` function, which returns a KNN classification model based on the predictors and the response provided. Again, we will use the `fisheriris` dataset to compare the different classification algorithms proposed in this chapter:

```
>> load fisheriris
```

This command creates two variables: `meas` and `species`. The first contains the data for the length and width of the sepal and petal (`150x4 double`). The second covers the classification (`150x1 cell`). To construct a KNN classifier for this data with *k*, the number of nearest neighbors in the predictors, equal to 3, simply type:

```
>> KnnModel = fitcknn(meas,species,'NumNeighbors',3)
KnnModel =
  ClassificationKNN
            ResponseName: 'Y'
    CategoricalPredictors: []
              ClassNames: {'setosa'  'versicolor'  'virginica'}
          ScoreTransform: 'none'
         NumObservations: 150
                Distance: 'euclidean'
            NumNeighbors: 3
```

The `fitcknn()` function returns a nearest neighbor classification object named `KnnModel`, where both distance metric (nearest) and number of neighbors can be altered.

Remember, we can examine the properties of classification objects by double-clicking `KnnModel` in the **Workspace** window.

This opens the **VARIABLE** editor, in which a long list of properties is shown. To examine a single one, just double-click on the relative icon; in this way, a new variable window is opened and its content is shown. The following figure shows model properties in the **VARIABLE** editor window.

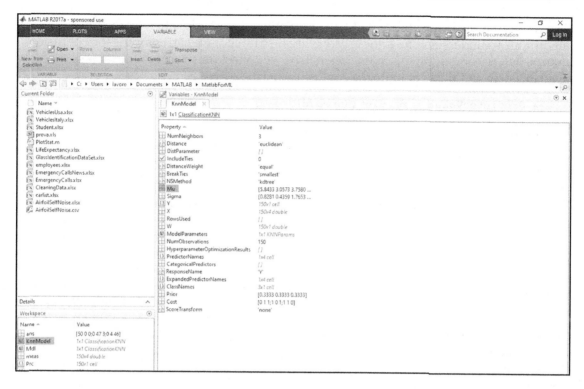

Figure 5.10: Variable editor window

To access the properties of the model just created, use dot notation. For example, to access the name of the response variable, simply type:

```
>> KnnModel.ClassNames
ans =
  3×1 cell array
    'setosa'
    'versicolor'
    'virginica'
```

To test the performances of the model, compute the resubstitution error.

```
>> Knn3ResubErr = resubLoss(KnnModel)
Knn3ResubErr =
    0.0400
```

The result indicates that *4* percent of the observations are misclassified by the KNN algorithm. To understand how these errors are distributed, we can compute the confusion matrix. Before computing the confusion matrix, we collect the model predictions for available data and then compute the confusion matrix:

```
>> PredictedValue = predict(KnnModel,meas);
>> ConfMat = confusionmat(species,PredictedValue)
ConfMat =
    50     0     0
     0    47     3
     0     3    47
```

As expected, there are only seven errors (four percent of the available values) and they refer to the two `versicolor` and `virginica` species. Previously, we said that the simple calculation of the classification error does not allow us to understand the type of errors committed by our system. In that case, the confusion matrix comes to our rescue, because it allows you to evaluate how errors and correct decisions made by our classifier are distributed. But, to make a proper estimate of the performance of our classifier, we have to do something more.

Since performance estimates depend on the data used, simply dividing random data between training and test sets does not guarantee that results are statistically significant. The repetition of the evaluation on different random divisions and the calculation of performance in terms of the mean and standard deviation of individual ratings make it possible to have a more reliable estimate. However, repetition of evaluations across random divisions may also prevent the most complex data being graded when evaluating (or training). The solution to these problems is offered by cross-validation.

In cross-validation, all available data is used, in fixed-size groups or, alternatively, as a test set and a training set. Therefore, each pattern is classified (at least once) and used for training. In practice, the sample is subdivided into groups of equal number; one group at a time is excluded and tries to predict it with non-excluded groups. This process is repeated *k* times, such that each subset is used exactly once for validation. This is to verify the quality of the prediction model used.

In MATLAB, cross-validation is performed by the `crossval()` function, which creates a partitioned model from a fitted KNN classification model. By default, this function uses *10*-fold cross-validation on the training data to create the model:

```
>> CVModel = crossval(KnnModel)
CVModel =
  classreg.learning.partition.ClassificationPartitionedModel
    CrossValidatedModel: 'KNN'
         PredictorNames: {'x1'   'x2'   'x3'   'x4'}
```

```
        ResponseName: 'Y'
    NumObservations: 150
              KFold: 10
          Partition: [1x1 cvpartition]
         ClassNames: {'setosa'  'versicolor'  'virginica'}
     ScoreTransform: 'none'
```

A `ClassificationPartitionedModel` object is created with several properties and methods. A brief summary of these are shown in the code just proposed.

Remember, we can examine the properties of the `ClassificationPartitionedModel` object by double-clicking `CVModel` in the **Workspace** window.

Now, we will visualize the cross-validation loss, which is the average loss of each cross-validation model when prediction is executed on data that is not used for training.

```
>> KLossModel = kfoldLoss(CVModel)
KLossModel =
    0.0333
```

In this case, the cross-validated classification accuracy is very close to the resubstitution accuracy. Therefore, you can expect the classification model to misclassify approximately four percent of the new data, assuming that the new data has about the same distribution as the training data.

Previously, we said that choosing the optimal value for *K* is very important in order to create the best classification model. So, we try to change the value of *k* and see what happens. To change the *k* value simply modifies the `NumNeighbors` property of the model. Let's see what happens by fixing `k = 5`:

```
>> KnnModel.NumNeighbors = 5
KnnModel =
  ClassificationKNN
            ResponseName: 'Y'
    CategoricalPredictors: []
              ClassNames: {'setosa'  'versicolor'  'virginica'}
          ScoreTransform: 'none'
         NumObservations: 150
                Distance: 'euclidean'
            NumNeighbors: 5
```

The model is newly fitted and a brief summary are listed on the command window. To see if there was an improvement in performance, compare the resubstitution predictions and cross-validation loss with the new number of neighbors.

```
>> Knn5ResubErr = resubLoss(KnnModel)
Knn5ResubErr =
    0.0333
```

We run cross-validation again and display the cross-validation loss.

```
>> CVModel = crossval(KnnModel);
>> K5LossModel = kfoldLoss(CVModel)
K5LossModel =
    0.0267
```

As can be seen from the comparison of the results obtained by the two models, the choice of $k = 5$ improved the performance of the model. In this regard, we recalculate the matrix of confusion:

```
>> PredictedValue = predict(KnnModel,meas);
>> ConfMat = confusionmat(species,PredictedValue)
ConfMat =
    50     0     0
     0    47     3
     0     2    48
```

By modifying the classifier, we have reduced the number of misclassification errors, which are now only 5.

We continue in our work to improve model performance. At the beginning of the section, we saw that the fitcknn() function uses Euclidean distance by default to evaluate the nearest neighbor. But what if we change that setting?

To set the distance metric, we need to specify the comma-separated pair consisting of Distance and a valid distance metric name or function handle. For example, we now modify the model to use cosine distance instead of the default. To use cosine distance, you must recreate the model using the exhaustive search method:

```
>> KnnModel2 =
fitcknn(meas,species,'NSMethod','exhaustive','Distance','cosine','NumNeighb
ors',5);
```

Compute the resubstitution error:

```
>> Knn5ResubErr2 = resubLoss(KnnModel2)
Knn5ResubErr2 =
    0.0200
```

Now, collect the model predictions for the available data, and then compute the confusion matrix for the new model:

```
>> PredictedValue = predict(KnnModel2,meas);
>> ConfMat = confusionmat(species,PredictedValue)
ConfMat =
    50    0    0
     0   48    2
     0    1   49
```

By modifying the distance metric of the classifier, we have reduced the number of misclassification errors, which are now only 3.

Classification Learner app

In the preceding paragraphs, we have faced several classification problems using some of the algorithms available in the MATLAB environment. We did it in programming mode, deliberately in order to understand in detail the different procedures. Now that we have fully understood these concepts, we can relax and explore the tools MATLAB offers us to perform interactive classification with the use of the Classification Learner app.

Using this app, we can classify our data using various algorithms and compare the results in the same environment. Select features, specify validation schemes, train models, and assess results becomes extremely simple and automatic with this app. The classification models available are: decision trees, discriminant analysis, **Support Vector Machines (SVM)**, logistic regression, nearest neighbors, and ensemble classification.

The Classification Learner app performs supervised machine learning, starting from a known set of input data and known responses to the data. Use the data to train a model that generates predictions for the response to new data. The model created can be used to predict new data by exporting it to the workspace or generating MATLAB code to recreate the trained model.

We start importing data into MATLAB's workspace:

```
>> load fisheriris
```

Before proceeding, we create a table with the data we need; subsequently, we will understand why:

```
>> IrisTable = table(meas(:,1),meas(:,2),meas(:,3),meas(:,4),species);
>> varnames =
{'SetalLength','SetalWidth','PetalLength','PetalWidth','Species'};
>> IrisTable.Properties.VariableNames = varnames;
```

So, data is now available in the MATLAB workspace. We can start the Classification Learner app. Select the **APPS** tab on the MATLAB Toolstrip and click on the **Classification Learner** icon. The **Classification Learner** app window will open, as shown in the following figure:

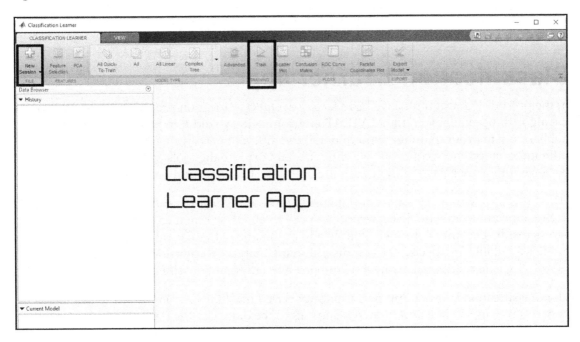

Figure 5.11: Classification Learner app window

To import in the app, data contained in the MATLAB workspace, click **New Session** on the **Classification Learner** tab in the **File** section. The **New Session** dialog box will open, with three sections (*Figure 5.12*):

- **Step 1**: **Select a table or matrix**. In this section, we can select the origin of the data
- **Step 2**: **Select predictors and response**. In this section, we can set the variables, type
- **Step 3**: **Define validation method**. In this section, we can choose the type of validation method

Validation methods allow us to examine the predictive accuracy of the fitted models. This tool helps us to choose the best model based on estimated model performance on the new data.

In the following figure, you can see the **New Session** dialog box with the three sections just described:

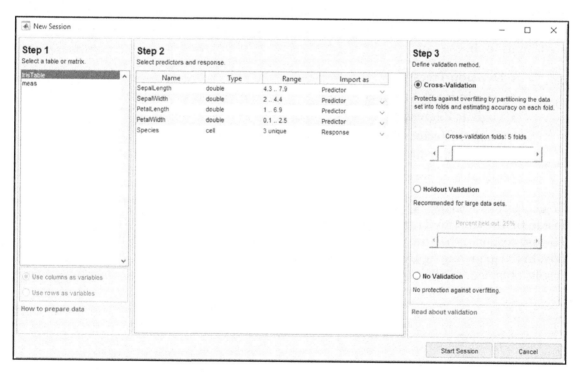

Figure 5.12: New Session dialog box for the Classification Learner app

In the **Step 1** section of the **New Session** dialog box (*Figure 5.12*), select the table named `IrisTable` from the workspace variables. After doing this, in the **Step 2** section are shown all the variables, in the table, as we can see in *Figure 5.12*. Additionally, the first labeling of variables is performed by default (**Predictor** and **Response**). If necessary, we can change that choice. After selecting the validation method, we can click **Start Session** to finish importing the data.

Remember, for **Cross-Validation**, select the number of folds to partition the data set using the slider control. For **Holdout Validation**, select a percentage of the data to use as a validation set using the slider control. Finally, with the **No Validation** option, no protection against over fitting is provided.

Now, we perform supervised machine learning by supplying a known set of observations of input data (predictors) and known responses. To do this, the app uses a set of the observations to train a model that generates predicted responses for new input data.

To choose the type of model, simply click on the arrow present in the Model Type section of the Classification Learner app to expand the list of regression models. There are many algorithms to choose from:

- **Decision Trees**
- **Discriminant Analysis**
- **Logistic Regression**
- **Support Vector Machines**
- **Nearest Neighbor Classifiers**
- **Ensemble Classifiers**

To get started, select **All Quick-To-Train**. This option trains all the model presets that are fast to fit. Click on the **Train** icon (*Figure 5.11*). A selection of model types appears in the History section. When the models finish training, the best accuracy score is highlighted in a box. In the following figure is shown the **Classification Learner** app window with the results obtained.

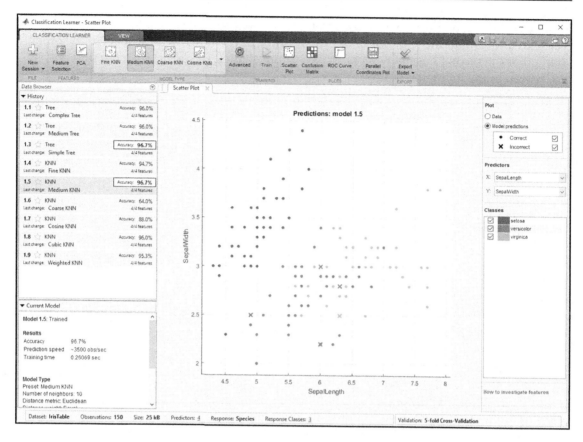

Figure 5.13: Classification Learner app window with the results obtained by the several methods available

To get an idea of the improvements obtained, it will be enough to compare the two extreme models, that is, those with the lower/higher accuracy. In the **History** section, we can notice that the lower accuracy score was obtained by **Coarse KNN** (**Accuracy = 64%**), the higher accuracy score was obtained by **Medium KNN** (**Accuracy = 96.7%**).

By simply clicking on the two templates in the window you will see classification errors. It is easy to understand the superiority of the **Medium KNN** model with respect to the other, noting that the second has many more crosses (representing the error) than the first one, as can be seen in the following figure.

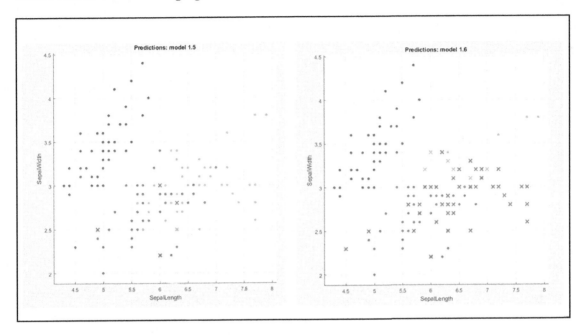

Figure 5.14: Comparison between classification models (best accuracy to the left, worst accuracy to the right)

Finally, on the **Classification Learner** tab, in the **Export** section (to the right of the toolstrip), three options are available:

- **Export Model**: to include the data used for training the model. A structure containing a regression model object is exported to the workspace.
- **Export Compact Model**: to exclude the training data; unnecessary data is removed where possible.
- **Generate MATLAB Code**: to generate MATLAB code for our best model. This code can be used to train the model with new data.

Summary

In this chapter, we learned how to perform an accurate classification in a MATLAB environment. First, we explored decision trees methods; we learned concepts like nodes, branches, and leaf nodes. We saw how to classify objects into a finite number of classes by repeatedly dividing the records into homogeneous subsets with respect to the target attribute. Then, we looked at how to predict a response with decision trees.

Next, we discovered the probabilistic classification algorithm that determines the probability that an element belongs to a particular class. We learned the basic concepts of probability theory: classical probability definition, dependent and independent events, joint probability and conditional probability, which is the basis of these methods. Then, we understood how to classify with the Naive Bayes algorithm.

We explored discriminant analysis methodologies; several examples were analyzed to compare the relative results. We learned how to create models to minimize the expected classification cost. Thus, we discovered how to test the performance of models and compute the resubstitution error.

With nearest neighbor classifiers, we learned how to identify the class of a sample based on the distance of it from other classified objects. We discovered how to fix the distance metric and how to choose the optimal value for K. So, we now understand how to improve model performance through cross-validation.

Finally, we analyzed the Classification Learner app, and how to it leads us into step-by-step classification analysis. Now, to import and explore data, select features, specify validation schemes, train models, and evaluate results, will be extremely simple and fast.

In the next chapter, we will learn different types of clustering techniques, how to apply clustering methods to our data and how the clustering algorithm works. We will get an understanding of the basic concepts that clustering methods use to group data using similarity measures, and discover how to prepare data for clustering analysis. We'll also learn topics like K-means techniques, cluster trees, and dendrograms.

6
Identifying Groups of Data Using Clustering Methods

Clustering methods are designed to find hidden patterns or groupings in a dataset. Unlike the supervised learning methods covered in previous chapters, these algorithms identify a grouping without any label to learn from through the selection of clusters based on similarities between elements.

This is an unsupervised learning technique that groups statistical units to minimize the **intragroup distance** and maximize the **intergroup distance**. The distance between the groups is quantified by means of similarity/dissimilarity measures defined between the statistical units.

To perform cluster analysis, no prior interpretative model is required. In fact, unlike other multivariate statistical techniques, this one does not make an *apriori* assumption on the existing fundamental typologies that may characterize the observed sample. This, however, occurs in the case of discriminating analysis, which makes it possible to split a set of individuals into groups predetermined from the beginning according to the different modes assumed by one or more characters. The cluster analysis technique has an exploratory role to look for existing but not-yet-identified structures in order to deduce the most likely group. This analysis is in fact a purely empirical method of classification, and as such, in the first place, it is an inductive technique.

This chapter shows you how to divide data into clusters, or groupings of similar items. You'll learn how to finding groups of data with K-means and K-medoids methods. We'll also cover grouping techniques using hierarchical clustering.

We will cover the following topics:

- Hierarchical clustering
- K-means method
- K-medoids method
- Gaussian mixture models
- Dendrograms

At the end of the chapter, we will be able to perform different types of clustering techniques. We will learn how to apply clustering methods to our data, and how the clustering algorithm works. We will understand the basic concepts that clustering methods use to group data using similarity measures. We will discover how to prepare data for clustering analysis. We'll also learn topics such as K-means and K-medoids techniques, cluster trees and dendrograms, and finally Gaussian mixture models.

Introduction to clustering

In clustering, as in classification, we are interested in finding the law that allows us to assign observations to the correct class. But unlike classification, we also have to find a plausible subdivision of our classes.

While in classification, we have some help from the target (the classification provided in the training set), in the case of clustering, we cannot rely on any additional information and we have to deduce the classes by studying spatial distribution of data.

The areas where data is thickened corresponds to similar observation groups. If we can identify observations that are similar to each other and at the same time different from those of another cluster, we can assume that these two clusters match different conditions. At this point, there are two things we need to go more deeply into:

- How to measure similarity
- How to define a grouping

The concept of distance and how to define a group are the two ingredients that describe a clustering algorithm.

Similarity and dissimilarity measures

Clustering involves identifying groupings of data. This is possible thanks to the measure of the proximity between the elements. The term **proximity** is used to refer to either similarity or dissimilarity. So, a group of data can be defined once you have chosen how to define the concept of similarity or dissimilarity. In many approaches, this proximity is conceived in terms of distance in a multidimensional space. The quality of the analysis obtained from clustering algorithms depends a lot on the choice of metric, hence, on how the distance is calculated. Clustering algorithms group elements based on their reciprocal distance, so belonging to a set depends on how close the element under consideration is to the same set. Then, one can say that some observations form a cluster if they tend to be closer to each other than those related to other sets.

What do we mean by similarity and dissimilarity? By the term **similarity between two objects**, we refer to the numeral measure of the degree to which the two objects are alike. Consequently, similarities are higher for pairs of objects that are more alike. Similarities are usually non-negative and are often between *0* (no similarity) and *1* (complete similarity).

On the contrary, by the term **dissimilarity between two objects**, we refer to the numerical measure of the degree to which two objects are different. Dissimilarity is lower for more similar pairs of objects. Frequently, the term **distance** is used as a synonym for dissimilarity. Just like similarities, dissimilarities sometimes fall in the interval *[0,1]*, but it is also common for them to range from *0* to ∞.

Dissimilarities between data objects can be measured by distance. Distances are dissimilarities with certain properties. For example, we can measure distance as the Euclidean distance, *d*, between two points, *x* and *y*, with the following formula:

$$d(x, y) = \sqrt{\sum_{k=1}^{n} (x_i - y_i)^2}$$

Remember that, on a bidimensional plane, the Euclidean distance represents the minimum distance between two points or the straight line connecting two points. This distance is calculated as the square root of the sum of the squared difference between the elements of two vectors, as indicated in the previous formula.

But distance can be measured in so many other ways, for example, with the **Minkowski distance** metric. This represents a generalization of the Euclidean distance measure:

$$d(x, y) = \left(\sum_{k=1}^{n} |x_i - y_i|^r \right)^{1/r}$$

In the previous formula, *r* is a parameter. Another possibility is to use the metric of Manhattan; it is obtained from the Minkowski distance metric just by placing *r = 1*. Let's see it in the following formula:

$$d(x, y) = \sum_{k=1}^{n} |x_i - y_i|$$

Then, there is the cosine distance, which we used in the previous chapter to improve the performance of the nearest classifier that contains the dot product scaled by the product of the Euclidean distances from the origin. It represents the angular distance of two vectors, ignoring their scale. The cosine distance is calculated according to the following formula:

$$d(x, y) = \frac{\sum\limits_{k=1}^{n} x_i y_i}{\sum\limits_{k=1}^{n} x_i^2 \sum\limits_{k=1}^{n} y_i^2}$$

Once we have chosen the metric suitable for our case, we can go further. So far, we have seen different formulas that allow us to calculate the distance between two objects. What happens if the objects to be analyzed are nominal instead of metrics?

For nominal data, which forms simple sequences called strings, you can use various distance concepts. A possible distance between two strings can be measured by counting the number of symbols that do not coincide between strings. For example, between the two strings shown in the following figure, the distance defined is *4* because there are four different characters:

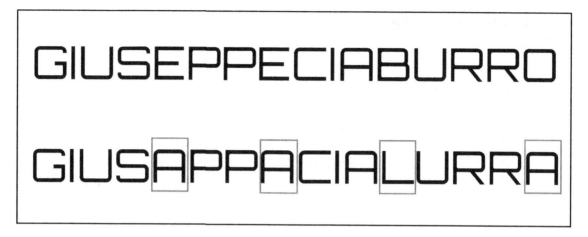

Figure 6.1: Distance measure between two strings

Another possible spacing between strings can be defined by fixing a set of possible editing operations, for example:

- Enter a symbol
- Delete a symbol
- Edit a symbol

In this way, we can say that the distance between two strings is the minimum number of operations among the predefined necessary to switch from one string to another. A distance calculated in this way is called edit distance.

Methods for grouping objects

Once you have chosen a way to calculate the distance, we have to decide how to form groups. Two main algorithm families can be identified:

- Hierarchical clustering works by doing a data hierarchy. The data is described through a taxonomic tree, similar to those used in biology.
- Partitioning clustering works by making a data space partition. The data space is divided into many sub-zones; the union of all the sub-zones gives full space, and one sub-zone is not superimposed onto other sub-zones.

Hierarchical clustering

In hierarchical clustering, clusters are constructed by recursively partitioning the instances in either a top-down or bottom-up fashion. We can divide these methods as follows:

- **Agglomerative algorithm (Bottom-up)**: The solution is obtained from individual statistical units. At each iteration, the most closely related statistical units are aggregated; the procedure ends when all units are aggregated into a single cluster.
- **Divisive algorithm (Top-down)**: In this case, all units are in the same class, and at each subsequent iteration, the unit most dissimilar to the others is assigned to a new cluster.

Both methods lead to the formation of a dendrogram, representing a nested grouping of objects and the similarity levels at which groupings change. A clustering of data objects is obtained by cutting the dendrogram at the desired similarity level. The merging or division of clusters is performed according to a similarity measure, chosen so as to optimize a criterion.

In the following figure is a recursive partitioning of instances in the formation of a dendrogram:

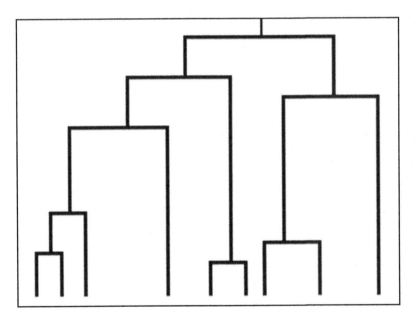

Figure 6.2: Example of a hierarchical clustering dendrogram

Partitioning clustering

Partitioning clustering decomposes a dataset into a set of disjoint clusters. Given a dataset, a partitioning method constructs several partitions of the data, with each partition representing a cluster. These methods relocate instances by moving them from one cluster to another, starting from an initial partitioning. Such methods typically require that the number of clusters be preset by the user. To achieve global optimality in partitioning-based clustering, an exhaustive enumeration process of all possible partitions is required. The following figure shows how a partitioning clustering constructs several partitions of the data:

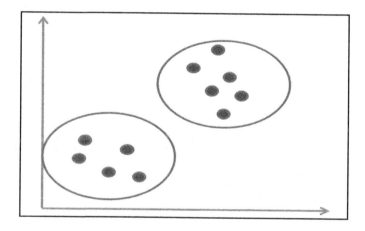

Figure 6.3: Example of partitioning clustering

In partitioning clustering, we select a set of parameters in advance. These parameters are then adjusted to optimally satisfy a chosen criterion of separation and compactness of our clusters. In this way, a hidden feature of the data can be highlighted, revealing the partitioning key. Typically, this leads to minimizing a measure of dissimilarity in the samples within each cluster, while maximizing the dissimilarity of different clusters. For example, we can use centers to represent clusters and then improve the partitioning by moving objects from group to group.

Hierarchical clustering

In MATLAB, hierarchical clustering produces a cluster tree or dendrogram by grouping data. A multilevel hierarchy is created, where clusters at one level are joined as clusters at the next level. From individual statistical units, the most closely related statistical units are aggregated at each iteration. In the Statistics and Machine Learning Toolbox, there is everything you need to do agglomerative hierarchical clustering. Using the `pdist`, `linkage`, and `cluster` functions, the `clusterdata` function performs agglomerative clustering. Finally, the dendrogram function plots the cluster tree.

As said, the procedure for forming the dendrogram requires the use of multiple functions. These functions are called by the `clusterdata` function, which represents the main function.

Analyzing the sequence of calls of these functions in detail can be particularly useful for understanding the whole process. Let's look at them sequentially:

- **Pdist**: As mentioned earlier, clustering is based on identifying possible similarities or dissimilarities between each pair of objects in the dataset. So the first thing to do is just this: measure the similarity. In fact, the `pdist` function calculates the distance between the objects. The `pdist` function supports many different ways to calculate this measure; later, we will see how to use it in a practical example.
- **Linkage**: Once you have identified any similarities, you need to group objects into a binary and hierarchical cluster tree. The `linkage` function connects pairs of objects that are close to each other. It uses the distance information generated in the previous step to determine the proximity of objects to each other. Because objects are associated with binary clusters, newly created clusters are grouped into larger clusters until a hierarchy tree is formed. This is why we talk about cluster agglomeration.
- **Cluster**: We just have to determine where to cut the cluster tree hierarchy. The `cluster` function cuts the ramifications from the bottom of the hierarchy tree and assigns all the objects below each cut to a single cluster. This creates a data partition. The `cluster` function can create these clusters by detecting natural groupings in the hierarchical tree or by cutting the hierarchy tree into an arbitrary point.

Now let's just use these functions by analyzing a simple example.

Similarity measures in hierarchical clustering

Earlier, we said that clustering involves identifying groupings of data. This is possible thanks to the measure of proximity between elements. The term proximity is used to refer to either similarity or dissimilarity. Let's see, then how this can be done in MATLAB.

In MATLAB, we can use the `pdist` function to calculate the distance between every pair of objects in a dataset. For a dataset made up of k objects, there are $k*(k-1)/2$ pairs in the dataset. The result of this computation is commonly known as a distance or dissimilarity matrix; the following figure shows an example:

```
         0
   14.1421          0
  127.2792   113.1371          0
  120.4159   106.3015    10.0000          0
   31.6228    20.0000   100.0000    94.3398          0
   70.7107    56.5685    56.5685    50.0000    44.7214          0
```

Figure 6.4: Distance matrix

The `pdist()` function computes the Euclidean distance between pairs of objects in a k-by-n data matrix. The rows of the matrix correspond to observations, and columns correspond to variables. The result is a row vector of length $k(k-1)/2$, corresponding to pairs of observations in the source matrix. The distances are arranged in the order $(2,1)$, $(3,1)$, ..., $(k,1)$, $(3,2)$, ..., $(k,2)$, ..., $(k,k-1)$. To get the distance matrix, you need to use the `squareform()` function, but we will look at that later on.

As mentioned, the `pdist()` function calculates the Euclidean distance between the objects by default, but there are many ways to calculate the distance. To do this, we can specify one of the other options provided by the function syntax. The following metrics are our choices: `euclidean`, `squaredeuclidean`, `seuclidean`, `cityblock`, `minkowski`, `chebychev`, `mahalanobis`, `cosine`, `correlation`, `spearman`, `hamming`, `jaccard`. In addition, custom distance functions can be created.

As a first example, we will use a matrix containing a series of six points on the Cartesian plane, identified by pairs of coordinates *(x, y)*:

1. *A = (100,100)*
2. *B = (90,90)*
3. *C = (10,10)*
4. *D = (10,20)*
5. *E = (90,70)*
6. *F = (50,50)*

In the following image, these points are plotted on the Cartesian plane:

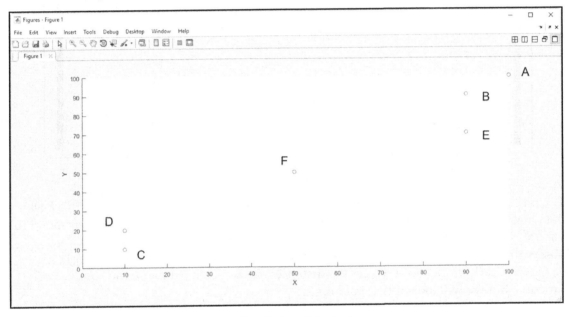

Figure 6.5: Series of points on the Cartesian plane

To insert these points in MATLAB, simply type:

```
>> DataPoints = [100 100;90 90;10 10;10 20;90 70;50 50]
DataPoints =
    100    100
     90     90
     10     10
     10     20
     90     70
     50     50
```

Let's now apply the `pdist` function. This function returns the distance information in a vector, where each element contains the distance between a pair of points:

```
>> DistanceCalc = pdist(DataPoints)
DistanceCalc =
  Columns 1 through 11
    14.1421   127.2792   120.4159    31.6228    70.7107   113.1371   106.3015
 20.0000           56.5685    10.0000   100.0000
  Columns 12 through 15
    56.5685    94.3398    50.0000    44.7214
```

The `pdist` function calculates the distance between point *A* and point *B*, point *A* and point *C*, and so on until the distances between all the pairs have been calculated. Previously, we talked about matrix distance, but what the `pdist()` function provides us with is a vector that does not make it easy to analyze the result.

To understand the relationship between the distance information, we can reformat the distance vector into a matrix using the `squareform()` function. In this matrix, element *i,j* corresponds to the distance between point *i* and point *j*. In the following matrix, element *1,1* represents the distance between point *1* and itself, which is zero of course. Element *1,2* represents the distance between point *1* and point *2*, and so on:

```
>> DistanceMatrix = squareform(DistanceCalc)
DistanceMatrix =
        0    14.1421   127.2792   120.4159    31.6228    70.7107
  14.1421         0   113.1371   106.3015    20.0000    56.5685
 127.2792   113.1371         0    10.0000   100.0000    56.5685
 120.4159   106.3015    10.0000         0    94.3398    50.0000
  31.6228    20.0000   100.0000    94.3398         0    44.7214
  70.7107    56.5685    56.5685    50.0000    44.7214         0
```

It is possible to note that the matrix is symmetric, that is, $a_{ij} = a_{ji}$. In some cases, normalizing values in the dataset before calculating distance information is particularly convenient. Why should we normalize a dataset? We recall that in raw data, variables can be measured by different scales. These differences in collected values can distort proximity calculations. At this point, the `zscore()` function converts all values in the dataset to use the same proportional scale.

Defining a grouping in hierarchical clustering

The concept of distance and how to define a group are the two ingredients that describe a clustering algorithm. We pointed this out at the beginning of the chapter. So, after calculating the proximity between the objects in the dataset, we have to determine how the dataset objects should be grouped into clusters. To do this, we will use the `linkage` function. Starting from the distance measure generated by the `pdist()` function, we will link pairs of objects that are close into binary clusters. The `linkage` function works this way: after you create the cluster of binaries, they are grouped together and other objects are added to create larger clusters until all objects in the original dataset are linked into a hierarchical tree.

Now, we apply this function to the data already calculated in the previous paragraph:

```
>> GroupsMatrix = linkage(DistanceCalc)
GroupsMatrix =
      3.0000     4.0000    10.0000
      1.0000     2.0000    14.1421
      5.0000     8.0000    20.0000
      6.0000     9.0000    44.7214
      7.0000    10.0000    50.0000
```

With this simple command, we have already done the bulk of the job, in the sense that the `linkage` function has identified possible groupings based on the measurements of the distances previously calculated. To understand how the function works, let's analyze in the results in `GroupsMatrix` in detail.

In this matrix, each row identifies a newly created cluster. Then, by analyzing such a matrix row by row, we can trace the procedure used for the construction of agglomerative clustering. The first two columns identify the points that have been linked, at least in the first lines, then the newly created clusters. We recall that the hierarchical cluster is of the agglomerative type and starts from small clusters to add more elements and generate larger clusters. The third column contains the distance between these points. In this case, the linkage function begins by grouping points 3 and 4, which correspond to C and D respectively (see the preceding numbered list of points); they have the closest proximity (measured *distance=10.0000*). The linkage function continues by grouping points 1 and 2, corresponding to A and B respectively, which have a measured distance of `14.1421`.

Initially, the function has identified two groups, but there are additional rows in the `GroupsMatrix` matrix. What do they contain? The third row indicates that the linkage function grouped points *5* and *8*. But there were only six points; what does that mean? Point *8* is the newly formed binary cluster created by the grouping of points *1* and *2*. When the linkage function groups two objects into a new cluster, it must assign the cluster a unique index value, starting with the value *k* + *1*, where *k* is the number of points in the original dataset. Values *1* through *6* are already used by the original dataset. Similarly, point *7* is the cluster formed by grouping points *3* and *4*, that is, the first cluster identified. Then, the third row indicates the cluster obtained by grouping point *E* (the fifth point in the sequence) and **Cluster 8** corresponds to the cluster identified by grouping points *C* and *D* (the first and second points in the sequence):

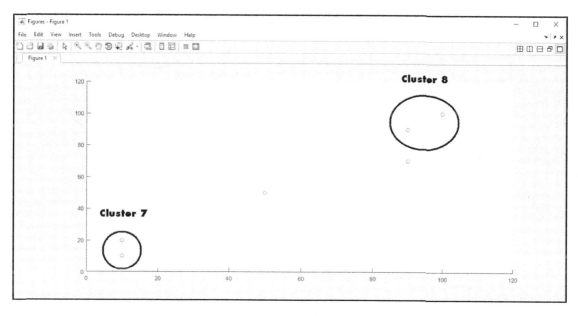

Figure 6.6: The first clusters created

The fourth row indicates the cluster obtained by grouping point *F* (the sixth point in the sequence) and **Cluster 9**, corresponding to the cluster last identified. As the final cluster, the linkage function grouped **Cluster 7**, the first cluster identified, and the newly formed cluster made up of **Cluster 9** with point 6 from the original dataset:

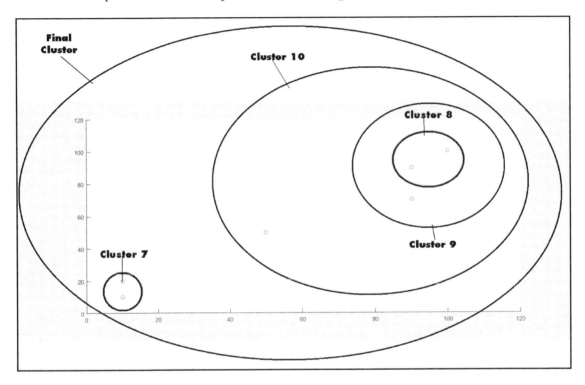

Figure 6.7: The way linkage groups points into a hierarchy of clusters (Euler Venn diagram)

The linkage function uses distances calculated by the `pdist()` function to determine the order in which the clusters are individuated. Subsequently, this function must be able to calculate the distances between newly discovered clusters. By default, the `linkage` function uses a method known as single linkage. However, there are a number of different methods available. They are: average, centroid, complete, median, single, ward, and weighted.

In the end, we only have to draw the dendrogram. To do this, we will use the `dendrogram()` function. This function generates a dendrogram plot of the hierarchical binary cluster tree. A dendrogram consists of many U-shaped lines that connect data points in a hierarchical tree. The height of each *U* represents the distance between the two data points being connected:

```
>> dendrogram(GroupsMatrix)
```

The following figure shows a dendrogram of a hierarchical cluster obtained from a series of points on the Cartesian plane:

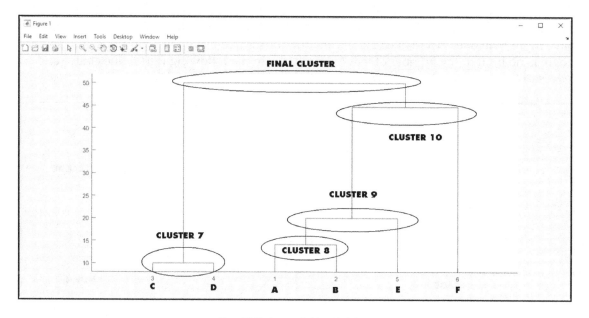

Figure 6.8: Dendrogram of a hierarchical cluster

In *Figure 6.8* is the arrangement of the clusters produced by hierarchical clustering. At first glance, we can understand the different clusters operated by the algorithm, but to better understand what has been done so far, it is necessary to go deep into the subject.

How to read a dendrogram

A dendrogram is a branching diagram that represents the relationships of similarity among a group of entities. The dendrogram shows the elements on the horizontal axis, and on the vertical axis, it returns the level of distance to which the fusion of two elements occurs. It indicates the strength of existing relationships between two elements based on the distance between the X axis and the nearest horizontal line that connects the vertical lines corresponding to the two elements considered.

To understand the relationship between two elements, draw a path from one to the other, following the tree diagrams and choosing the shortest path. The distance from the source to the most external horizontal line touched by the path represents the degree of similarity between the two elements.

Let's learn now how to define the elements of a dendrogram. Each branch (horizontal line) is called a **clade**. The terminal end of each clade is called a **leaf**. The segments that start from the clades to reach the nodes are called **chunks**. Clades can have just one leaf, in this case called **simplicifolious**. This is a term from botany which means single-leafed or they can have more than one. Two-leaved clades are bifolious, three-leaved are trifolious, and so on. There is no limit to the number of leaves in a clade. In the following figure, the clades and leaves of a dendrograms are shown:

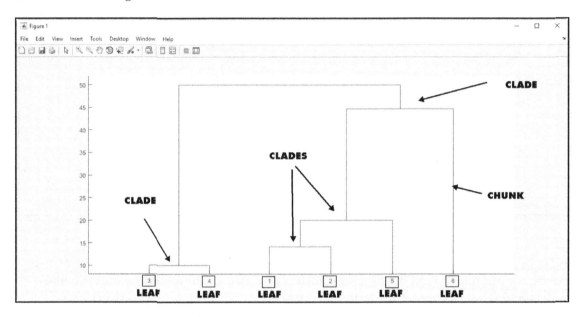

Figure 6.9: Clades and leaves of a dendrogram

The arrangement of the clades tells us which leaves are most similar to each other. The height of the branch indicates how similar or different they are from each other; the greater the height, the greater the difference. We can use a dendrogram to represent the relationships between any kinds of entities, as long as we can measure their similarity to each other. There are two ways to interpret a dendrogram:

- In terms of large-scale groups
- In terms of similarities among individual chunks

To identify large-scale groups, we start reading from the top down, finding the branch points that are at high levels in the structure. In *Figure 6.9*, we see that the first group of the tree on the left is completely separate from all the others. This is the first group identified from the linkage function. We interpret its placement as indicating that the cluster in that chunk is substantially different from the points in the remaining clusters.

Also, we can notice that the other groups on the right are more closely related. Starting from the bottom, we can locate the cluster obtained by grouping points *1* and *2*; this is the second cluster identified by the `linkage` function. As we know, point *5*, and subsequently point *6*, is added to this cluster.

Now, we will analyze the dendrogram in terms of similarities among individual chunks. Let's look at the clusters identified in a sequence from the linkage function. We will do this by analyzing clades and chunks. We usually label clades at any level of the diagram, moving from left to right and top to bottom. If we are trying to identify which individual segments are most similar to each other, we read the dendrogram from the bottom up, identifying the first clades to join together as we move from bottom to top.

The height of the vertical lines (chunks) indicates the degree of difference between branches; the longer the line, the greater the difference. Analyzing *Figure 6.9*, from left to right, the numbers along the horizontal axis represent the indices of the points in the original dataset. The links between points are represented as upside-down U-shaped lines. The height of *U* indicates the distance between the points. For example, the chunks representing the cluster containing points *3* and *4* have the smallest height (`10.0000`). These points are the closest ones. The chunks representing the cluster that groups points *1* and *2* have height equal to `14.1421`, the second in the height order. And so on. Then the height of the chunks gives us a measure of the distance between the groups.

Verifying your hierarchical clustering

In the previous section, we learned to read a dendrogram; now we have to check the work done. We can do this precisely by recalculating the distances and deepening the divisions carried out. The Statistics and Machine Learning Toolbox has all the functions required to do so, as described later.

Previously, we said that the height of the branches indicates how similar or different they are from each other; the greater the height, the greater the difference. This height is known as the **cophenetic distance** between the two objects forming the cluster. We can compare the cophenetic distances between two objects using the `cophenet()` function. This is the best way to verify the performance of the dissimilarity measurement. For example, we can compare the results of clustering the same dataset using different distance calculation methods or clustering algorithms. Let's start doing this on the calculations just made:

```
>> VerifyDistaces = cophenet(GroupsMatrix, DistanceCalc)
VerifyDistaces =
    0.8096
```

It is a measure of how well the cluster is generated. In a valid cluster tree, the linking of objects should have a strong correlation with the distances between objects in the distance measured. The `cophenet()` function computes the cophenetic correlation coefficient for the hierarchical cluster tree. The closer this value is to *1*, the more accurate hierarchical clustering is.

To improve the performance of the model, we can recalculate the distance between points by using the `pdist()` function with the same dataset, but this time specifying another type of metric:

```
>> NewDistanceCalc = pdist(DataPoints, 'cosine')
NewDistanceCalc =
  Columns 1 through 9
    0.0000    0.0000    0.0513    0.0077    0.0000    0.0000          0.0513
  0.0077    0.0000
  Columns 10 through 15
    0.0513    0.0077    0.0000    0.0979    0.0513    0.0077
```

Now, starting from the new distance measure generated by the `pdist()` function and using the `cosine` metric, we will link objects that are close into clusters, this time using a different algorithm for computing the distance between clusters. In particular, we will use the `weighted` method, which computes the weighted average distance:

```
>> NewGroupsMatrix = linkage(NewDistanceCalc,'weighted')
NewGroupsMatrix =
    3.0000    6.0000    0.0000
    1.0000    7.0000    0.0000
    2.0000    8.0000    0.0000
    5.0000    9.0000    0.0077
    4.0000   10.0000    0.0746
```

Finally, we call the `cophenet()` function to evaluate the clustering solution:

```
>> NewVerifyDistaces = cophenet(NewGroupsMatrix, NewDistanceCalc)
NewVerifyDistaces =
    0.9302
```

The result shows that using a different distance and the linkage method improves the hierarchical clustering's performance.

Partitioning-based clustering methods - K-means algorithm

K-means clustering is a partitioning method and as anticipated, this method decomposes a dataset into a set of disjoint clusters. Given a dataset, a partitioning method constructs several partitions of this data, with each partition representing a cluster. These methods relocate instances by moving them from one cluster to another, starting from an initial partitioning.

The K-means algorithm

The K-means algorithm is a clustering algorithm designed in 1967 by MacQueen which allows the dividing of groups of objects into K partitions based on their attributes. It is a variation of the **expectation-maximization (EM)** algorithm, whose goal is to determine the K data groups generated by Gaussian distributions. The K-means algorithm differs in the method used for calculating the Euclidean distance while calculating the distance between each of two data items; EM uses statistical methods.

In K-means, it is assumed that object attributes can be represented as vectors and thus form a vector space. The goal is to minimize the total intra-cluster variance (or standard deviation). Each cluster is identified by a centroid.

The algorithm follows an iterative procedure:

1. Choose the number of clusters K.
2. Initially create K partitions and assign each entry partition either randomly or using some heuristic information.
3. Calculate the centroid of each group.
4. Calculate the distance between each observation and each cluster centroid.
5. Then construct a new partition by associating each entry point with the cluster whose centroid is closer to it.
6. The centroid for new clusters is recalculated.
7. Repeat steps 4 through 6 until the algorithm converges.

The purpose of the algorithm is to locate k centroids, one for each cluster. The position of each centroid is of particular importance and different positions cause different results. The best choice is to put them as far apart as possible from each other. When this is done, you must associate each object with the nearest centroid. In this way, we will get a first grouping. After finishing the first cycle, we go to the next one by recalculating new k centroids as the cluster's barycentres resulting from the previous one. Once you locate these new k centroids, you need to make a new connection between the same datasets and the new closest centroid. At the end of these operations, a new cycle is performed. As a result of this cycle, we can note that the k centroids change their position step by step until they are modified. So, the centroid does not move anymore. In the following figure, k centroids of the data distribution are shown:

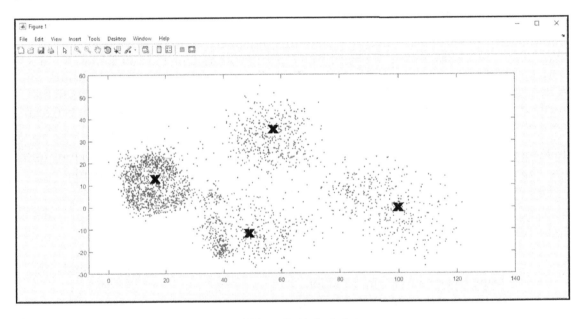

Figure 6.10: k centroids of the data distribution

The kmeans() function

In MATLAB, K-means clustering is performed by the `kmeans()` function; it partitions data into k mutually exclusive clusters and returns the index of the cluster to which it has assigned each object.

The objects and the centroid define a specific cluster in the partition. The centroid for each cluster is the point where the sum of distances from all objects in that cluster is minimized. K-means calculates the cluster centroid differently for each distance measure to minimize the sum of the specified measure. We can set different methods of calculating such distances as we can choose from different methods of minimizing such distances using different input parameters at `kmeans` function. This list summarizes the available distance measures:

- `sqeuclidean`: Squared Euclidean distance (default). Each centroid is the mean of the points in that cluster.
- `cityblock`: Sum of absolute differences; each centroid is the component-wise median of the points in that cluster.
- `cosine`: One minus the cosine of the included angle between points; each centroid is the mean of the points in that cluster after normalizing those points to unit the Euclidean length.
- `correlation`: One minus the sample correlation between points; each centroid is the component-wise mean of the points in that cluster after centering and normalizing those points to zero mean and the unit standard deviation.
- `hamming`: This measure is only suitable for binary data. It is the proportion of bits that differ. Each centroid is the component-wise median of points in that cluster.

By default, `kmeans()` uses the k-means++ algorithm for cluster center initialization and the squared Euclidean metric to determine distances.

OK, let's see the `kmeans()` function in action. Suppose we have a dataset containing the results of measurements made on some minerals extracted from different quarries. In particular, the measurements of specific weight and hardness (Mohs scale) are available. These measurements are saved in a `.xls` format file named `Minerals.xls`. Let's start by importing data into the MATLAB workspace:

```
>> Minerals = xlsread('Minerals.xls');
```

From the newly imported MATLAB matrix (*2470x7*), we only extract the first two columns:

```
>> InputData = Minerals(:,1:2);
```

Let's first look at the data by drawing a chart:

```
>> gscatter(InputData(:,1), InputData(:,2))
```

The following figure shows a distribution of the dataset under analysis:

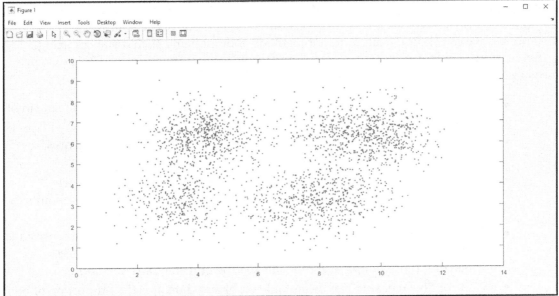

Figure 6.11: Distribution of our dataset

Analyzing *Figure 6.11*, the points seem to focus on four regions characterized by different values of the two variables. This suggests performing the cluster analysis by fixing $k = 4$. To make the result reproducible, in order to obtain the same analysis, we fix the following parameter:

```
>> rng(1);
```

The rgn() function controls random number generation, so the rand, randi, and randn functions produce a predictable sequence of numbers. Let's then apply the kmeans() function:

```
>> [IdCluster,Centroid] = kmeans(InputData,4);
```

Two variables have been created: IdCluster, and Centroid. The first is a vector containing the predicted cluster indices corresponding to the observations in InputData. The second is a *4-by-2* matrix containing the final centroid locations. As mentioned before, this function uses the k-means++ algorithm for centroid initialization and squared Euclidean distance by default.

Now, we've added any data in the original dataset to each of the four clusters we've ever had to build. Let's see them in a scatter plot:

```
>> gscatter(InputData(:,1), InputData(:,2), IdCluster,'bgrm','x*o^')
```

The following figure shows a scatter plot of four clusters:

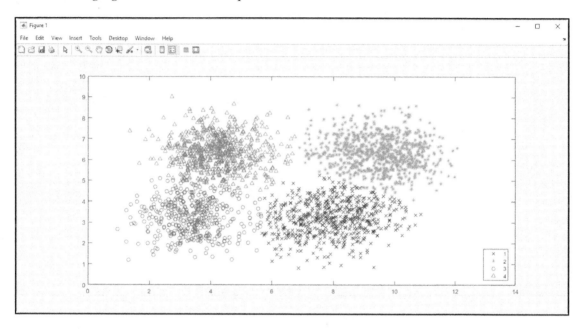

Figure 6.12: Scatter plot of clusters

From an analysis of *Figure 6.12*, the clear separation between the clusters identified by the kmeans() function is evident. Each cluster is automatically represented by a different color, which helps us locate it, in particular at the boundaries, where the data is confused with each other. Also, the marker we set on the scatter plot helps us with that.

Add the centroids of each cluster to the newly drawn figure:

```
>> hold on
>>
plot(Centroid(:,1),Centroid(:,2),'x','LineWidth',4,'MarkerEdgeColor','k','M
arkerSize',25)
```

To emphasize the position of the centroid, we have set the relevant marker appropriately. In the following figure, the scatter plot of clustering and the position of each centroid are shown. Specifically, we the **x** as the marker, the line thickness to 4, the marker color as black, and marker size to 25.

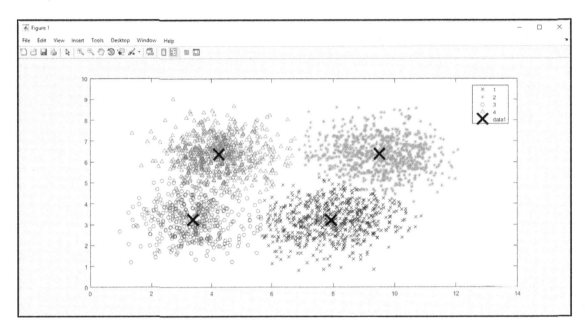

Figure 6.13: A scatter plot of clustering and the position of each centroid

From an analysis of *Figure 6.13*, the function of the centroid is clear as the center of mass of a cluster defined by the points. As noted before, the centroid's location minimizes the sum of squared distances from the other points.

A further look at *Figure 6.13* tells us how often, cluster boundaries are not well-defined, at least not on this type of chart. Close to the boundaries of the clusters, there are points that blend together, and it becomes difficult to identify which clusters they belong to.

The silhouette plot

To analyze exactly what is happening to the boundaries of the clusters, in order to understand how well they are separated, we can make a silhouette plot using cluster indices issued by `kmeans()`. The silhouette plot displays a measure of how close each point in one cluster is to points in neighboring clusters. The `silhouette()` function plots cluster silhouettes for the data matrix provided, with clusters defined. Rows of the input matrix correspond to points; columns correspond to coordinates.

The cluster defined can be a categorical variable, numeric vector, character matrix, or cell array of character vectors containing a cluster name for each point. The `silhouette()` function treats NaNs or empty character vectors in the cluster provided as missing values and ignores the corresponding rows of the input matrix. By default, the `silhouette()` function uses the squared Euclidean distance between the points in the input matrix:

```
>> silhouette(InputData, IdCluster)
```

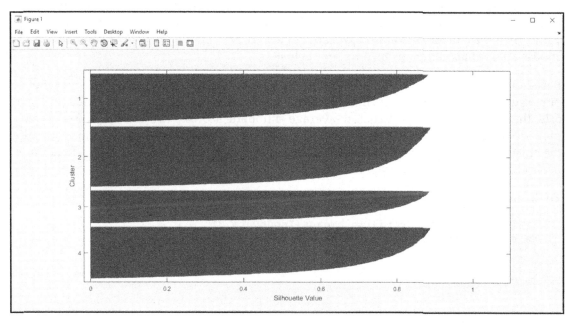

Figure 6.14: Silhouette plot for K-means clustering

On the *X* axis of *Figure 6.14* is the **Silhouette Value**. It measures ranges from *+1*, indicating points that are very distant from neighboring clusters, through *0*, indicating points that are not distinctly in one cluster or another, to *-1*, indicating points that are probably assigned to the wrong cluster. This plot returns these values in its first output.

 Remember: the silhouette value for each point is a measure of how similar that point is to points in its own cluster when compared to points in other clusters.

A silhouette plot can be used to verify the separation distance between the resulting clusters. This plot displays a measure of how close each point in one cluster is to points in neighboring clusters and thus provides a way to visually assess parameters such as number of clusters.

High values in the silhouette plot identify the points correctly represented by the cluster and nothing connected to neighboring clusters. If most points have a high silhouette value, then the clustering solution is appropriate. If many points have a low or negative silhouette value, then the clustering solution must be reviewed. So, silhouette analysis can be used to choose an optimal value for the number of clusters.

Based on what has been said and from the analysis of *Figure 6.14*, we try to find out whether our assumption of *k* = 4 in applying the K-means algorithm has given good results. In *Figure 6.14*, there are no clusters with below-average silhouette scores. Furthermore, the silhouette plots do not present wide fluctuations in size. Also, from the thickness of the silhouette plot, the cluster size can be verified. All the plots are more or less of similar thickness, hence are of similar sizes. All this confirms that our choice of number of clusters is right.

To do an additional check, we see what happens if we fix *k* = 3:

```
>> [IdCluster3,Centroid3] = kmeans(InputData,3);
>> silhouette(InputData, IdCluster3)
```

The following figure shows a silhouette plot for K-means clustering with $k=3$:

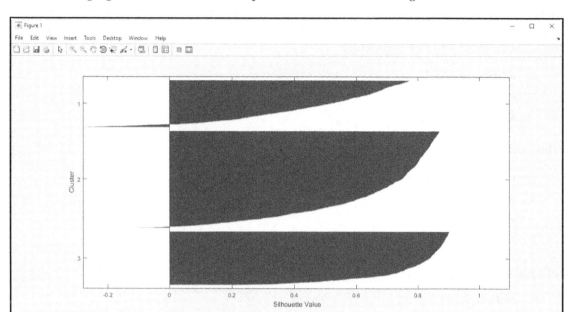

Figure 6.15: Silhouette plot for K-means clustering (k=3)

By comparing the two silhouette plots (*Figure 6.14* and *Figure 6.15*), it is clear that the choice of $k = 3$ is incorrect. In fact, by analyzing *Figure 6.15*, we notice several problems. Unlike what is shown in *Figure 6.14*, in the latter there are clusters with below-average silhouette scores (cluster 1 and cluster 2). Furthermore, the silhouette plots present wide fluctuations in size; in particular, plot 2 is bigger in size owing to the grouping of the two subclusters into one big cluster. Ultimately, we get confirmation that the first choice ($k = 4$) was the right one.

In this way, we have confirmed the correct choice of the number of clusters. But such control was carried out by comparing the relative silhouette plots. Is there a function that allows us to evaluate the best choice of k automatically? It is legitimate to ask such a question. Once again, the answer is affirmative. Practically all that comes to mind has already been addressed in the MATLAB environment.

To evaluate the optimal number of clusters, we can use the `evalclusters` function, which creates a clustering evaluation object containing data used to evaluate the optimal number of data clusters. Unfortunately, only some algorithms can be evaluated using this feature. Here is the list of available algorithms:

- `kmeans`
- `linkage`
- `gmdistribution`

While clustering, the evaluation criteria available are:

- `CalinskiHarabasz`
- `DaviesBouldin`
- `gap`
- `silhouette`

Let's see what we get in our case:

```
>> EvaluateK =
evalclusters(InputData,'kmeans','CalinskiHarabasz','KList',[1:6])
eva =
  CalinskiHarabaszEvaluation with properties:
    NumObservations: 2470
         InspectedK: [1 2 3 4 5 6]
    CriterionValues: [NaN 3.2944e+03 3.4436e+03 4.3187e+03 3.9313e+03
3.8437e+03]
           OptimalK: 4
```

We choose K-means as the algorithm and `CalinskiHarabasz` as the evaluation criterion. The result has confirmed that the optimal choice of k is 4, as we did from the beginning.

Partitioning around the actual center - K-medoids clustering

K-medoids is a partitioning clustering algorithm related to the K-means algorithm. Given a set of n objects and a k number that determines how many clusters you want to output, K-medoids divides the dataset into groups, trying to minimize the average quadratic error, the distance between the points of a cluster, and the point designated to be the center.

What is a medoid?

Unlike K-means, where this point is artificial (that is, the pure average of all points in the cluster also named centroid), in K-medoids, the point used is placed more centrally; so the center is one of the actual data points (medoid). A medoid can be defined as an object of a cluster whose average disparity over all objects in the cluster is minimal; thus, it will be the most central point of a given dataset. K-medoids are more robust to noise and outliers than K-means, because a mean is easily influenced by extreme values.

The kmedoids() function

In MATLAB, K-medoids clustering is performed by the kmedoids() function, which partitions the observations of a matrix into *k* clusters and returns a vector containing the cluster indices of each observation. Rows of the input matrix correspond to points, and columns correspond to variables. Similar to the kmeans function, kmedoids by default uses squared Euclidean distances and the k-means++ algorithm to choose the initial cluster medoid positions.

Now, let's see how to apply this method. A large distribution company wants to reorganize its network by optimizing the position of its offices. To make it faster and cheaper to transfer goods from sorting hubs to peripheral locations, it seeks to identify the best positions. The company has the positions of its peripheral locations and wants to find the optimal position where the hubs are to be located. The geographical coordinates have been transformed into relative coordinates for compatibility issues with the kmedoids function. This information is contained in the file named PeripheralLocations.xls. Let's start by importing data into the MATLAB workspace:

```
>> PerLoc = xlsread('PeripheralLocations.xls');
```

Now we have the newly imported MATLAB matrix named PerLoc (*2650 x 2*). Let's first look at the data by drawing a scatter plot:

```
>> gscatter(InputData (:,1), InputData (:,2))
```

The following figure shows a distribution of the dataset under analysis:

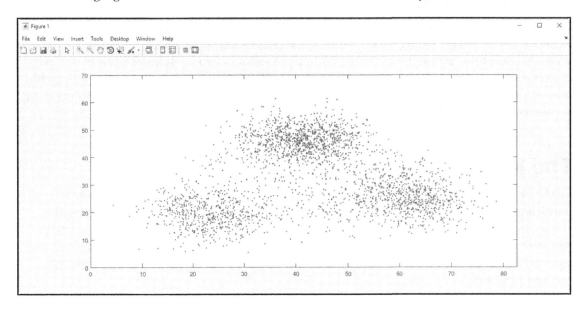

Figure 6.16: Locations of the peripheral offices

From the first visual analysis, it is possible to identify three large areas in which the peripheral offices of the company are distributed. All this suggests that we should identify three existing offices, which will become hubs from which to start the distribution of goods for peripheral locations. At this point, we will identify the positions of the three future hubs and all the sites belonging to each of them through a clustering analysis.

It is clear that the location of each hub will be the center of each cluster. Since this position is a real value (it must be an existing office), the use of the kmedoids method becomes a logical choice:

```
>> [IdCluster,Kmedoid,SumDist,Dist,IdClKm,info] = kmedoids(PerLoc,3);
```

Where:

- `IdCluster` contains the cluster indices of each observation
- `Kmedoid` contains the *k* cluster medoid locations
- `SumDist` contains the within-cluster sums of point-to-medoid distances
- `Dist` contains distances from each point to every medoid
- `IdClKm` contains the cluster indices of each medoid
- `info` contains information about the options used by the algorithm when executed

Let's take a look at the information returned by the function:

```
>> info
info =
  struct with fields:
        algorithm: 'pam'
            start: 'plus'
         distance: 'sqeuclidean'
       iterations: 3
    bestReplicate: 1
```

That command returns the algorithm type, metrics used, and number of iterations with the best performance, among others. The algorithm type is `pam`, the acronym of **Partitioning Around Medoids**. This is the classical algorithm for solving the K-medoids problem. The second parameter listed is the method that we have adopted for choosing the initial cluster medoid positions. The third is the metric adopted; in this case, squared Euclidean distance has been chosen. Finally, the number of iterations and the best iteration have been listed.

So, we can plot the clusters and the cluster medoids:

```
>> gscatter(PerLoc(:,1), PerLoc(:,2), IdCluster,'bgr','xo^')
>> hold on
>>
plot(Kmedoid(:,1),Kmedoid(:,2),'x','LineWidth',4,'MarkerEdgeColor','k','Mar
kerSize',25)
```

In the following figure, the scatter plot of clustering and the position of each medoid are shown. To emphasize the position of the medoid, we have set the relevant marker appropriately.

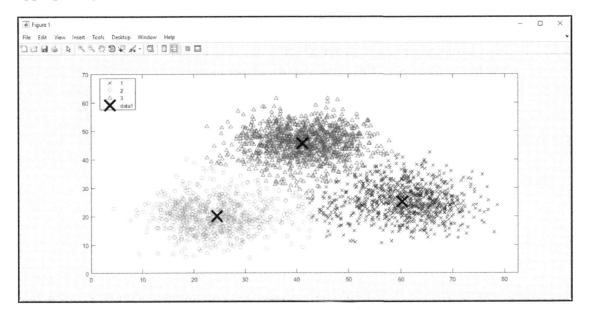

Figure 6.17: Scatter plot of clustering and the position of each medoid

From an analysis of *Figure 6.17*, it is clear that the peripheral sites are grouped into three clusters identified by the kmedoids() function. The strategic position of the hubs found is intuitive. The different colors and different markers for each cluster allow us to easily identify the affinity of each site to its cluster.

Evaluating clustering

To evaluate the clustering result, we can use the silhouette plot, as we did in the case of the k-means method. We recall in this regard that on the X axis of this plot, the silhouette values are reported. The silhouette value for each point is a measure of how similar that point is to points in its own cluster when compared to points in other clusters. On the Y axis, the different clusters are reported:

```
>> silhouette(PerLoc, IdCluster)
```

Remember: the **Silhouette Value** ranges from *+1*, indicating points that are very distant from neighboring clusters, through *0*, indicating points that are not distinctly in one cluster or another, to *-1*, indicating points that are probably assigned to the wrong cluster.

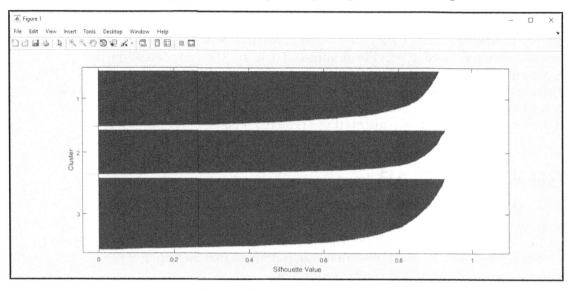

Figure 6.18: Silhouette plot for K-medoids clustering

In *Figure 6.18*, there are only two clusters with below-average silhouette scores, and these values are very limited. Furthermore, the silhouette plots do not present wide fluctuations in size. All the plots are more or less of similar thickness, hence are of similar sizes. All this confirms that our choice on the number of clusters is right.

Clustering using Gaussian mixture models

So far, we have addressed clustering issues through different approaches. Another way of dealing with these problems is the model-based approach. In this case, we will use certain models for clusters and attempt to optimize the fit between the data and the model. In other words, each cluster can be mathematically represented by a parametric distribution, such as Gaussian (continuous) or Poisson (discrete).

Gaussian distribution

Gaussian distribution has some limitations when modeling real-world datasets. Very complex densities can be modeled with a linear combination of Gaussian weights weighed appropriately. A mixture model is a type of density model that is packed with a number of density functions, usually Gaussian (**Gaussian Mixture Models (GMM)**), and these functions are combined to provide multimodal density. These models allow the representation of probability distributions in the presence of subpopulations, where the mixture components are the densities on the subpopulations and the weights are the proportions of each subpopulation in the overall population. In GMM, we can actually consider clusters as Gaussian distributions centered on their barycentres.

GMM in MATLAB

In MATLAB, we can fit GMM using the `fitgmdist()` function; it returns a Gaussian mixture distribution model named `GMMModel` with k components (fixed by the user) fitted to the input dataset. These models are composed of k (positive integer) multivariate normal density components. Each component has an n-dimensional mean (n is a positive integer), *n-by-n* covariance matrix, and mixing proportion.

This function fits models to data using the iterative EM algorithm. By using initial values for component means, covariance matrices, and mixing proportions, the EM algorithm proceeds through the following steps:

1. **Expectation step**: For each observation, the algorithm computes posterior probabilities of component memberships. The result is an *n-by-k* matrix, and it contains the posterior probability.
2. **Maximization step:** Using the posterior probability matrix elements as weights, the algorithm estimates the component means, covariance matrices, and mixing proportions by applying maximum likelihood.

The algorithm iterates over these steps until convergence. The likelihood surface is complex, and the algorithm might converge to a local optimum. Also, the resulting local optimum might depend on the initial conditions. A fitted `gmdistribution` model object is returned. This object contains properties that store the estimation results, which include the estimated parameters, convergence information, and information criteria. To access these properties, dot notation can be used.

Now, let's see how to apply this method. Suppose we have a distribution deriving from several measurements of two physical quantities collected in different locations around the world. Our aim is to group these measures into clusters of different climatic zones. This information is contained in the file named `ClimaticData.xls`. Let's start by importing data into the MATLAB workspace:

```
>> Data = xlsread('ClimaticData.xls');
```

Now we have the newly imported MATLAB matrix named `Data` (*1570 x 2*). Let's first look at the data by drawing a scatter plot:

```
>> gscatter(Data(:,1),Data(:,2))
```

The following figure shows a distribution of the dataset under analysis:

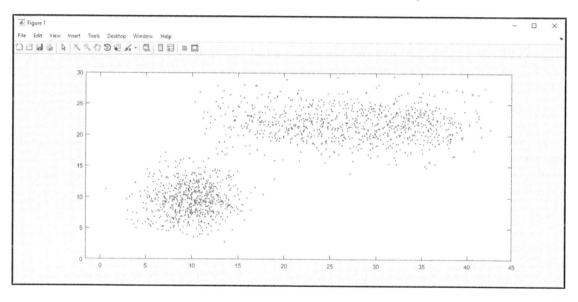

Figure 6.19: Distribution of a dataset

Analyzing *Figure 6.19*, the points seem to focus on two regions characterized by different values of the two physical quantities (two climatic zones). This suggests performing the cluster analysis by fixing $k = 2$. All this is fairly clear and simplifies our work. But looking carefully, you will notice that the two clusters have substantially different geometries. The first, in the bottom-left seems to have a circular geometry, while the second, in the upper-right shows an elliptical geometry.

All this is indicative of a multimodal distribution, in which there are regions of large probability mass and regions of smaller probability mass. As previously mentioned, such cases can be handled with the mixture models approach. Now, we fit a two-component GMM using the `fitgmdist()` function, simply specifying that there are two components:

```
>> GMModel = fitgmdist(Data,2)
GMModel =
Gaussian mixture distribution with 2 components in 2 dimensions
Component 1:
Mixing proportion: 0.568761
Mean:    27.2418    21.9020
Component 2:
Mixing proportion: 0.431239
Mean:     9.8755     9.5890
```

In this model, the bivariate Gaussian component is defined by its mean and covariance, and the mixture is defined by a vector of mixing proportions. The `fitgmdist()` function has several options for choosing initial conditions, including random component assignments for the observations and the k-means ++ algorithm. To obtain a complete list of these options, consult MATLAB help by simply typing:

```
>> help fitgmdist
```

To get a confirmation of the two different distributions of the clusters obtained, we can plot the estimated probability density contours for the two-component mixture distribution. Firstly, we get a scatter plot of the source data; then, we add a contour plot of the model data. A contour plot is drawn using the `ezcontour()` function:

```
>> gscatter(Data(:,1),Data(:,2))
>> hold on
>> ezcontour(@(x1,x2)pdf(GMModel,[x1 x2]),[0 45 0 30])
```

In the following figure, a distribution of the data source and the estimated probability density contours of the model are shown:

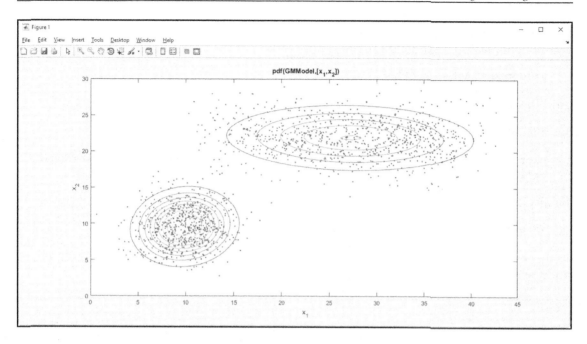

Figure 6.20: Estimated probability density contours of the model

The two bivariate Gaussian components are well distinguished; the geometries of them are clearly different. This confirms that the data can reasonably be divided into two clusters.

Cluster membership by posterior probabilities

To estimate cluster membership posterior probabilities, and to assign each point to the cluster corresponding to the maximum posterior probability, the cluster() function can be used. This method assigns each data point to exactly one cluster, which corresponds to one of the two mixture components in the Gaussian mixture model. The center of each cluster is the corresponding mixture component mean:

```
>> IdCluster = cluster(GMModel,Data);
```

The cluster() function assigns data to clusters based on a cluster membership score. Each cluster membership score is the estimated posterior probability that the data point came from the corresponding component. This function assigns each point to the mixture component corresponding to the highest posterior probability. Let's see the two clusters identified by drawing a scatter plot:

```
>> gscatter(Data(:,1), Data(:,2), IdCluster, 'bg', 'xo')
```

Let's now add the centers of the two clusters, which, as they say, correspond to the mixture component mean. To extract this data, simply type:

```
>> CenterCluster = GMModel.mu;
```

Add the data to the initial scatter plot:

```
>>   hold on
>>
plot(CenterCluster(:,1),CenterCluster(:,2),'x','LineWidth',4,'MarkerEdgeCol
or','k','MarkerSize',25)
```

Finally, add the estimated probability density contours of the model:

```
>> ezcontour(@(x1,x2)pdf(GMModel,[x1 x2]),[0 45 0 30])
```

In the following figure, the scatter plot of clustering, the position of each cluster's center, and the estimated probability density contours of the model are shown:

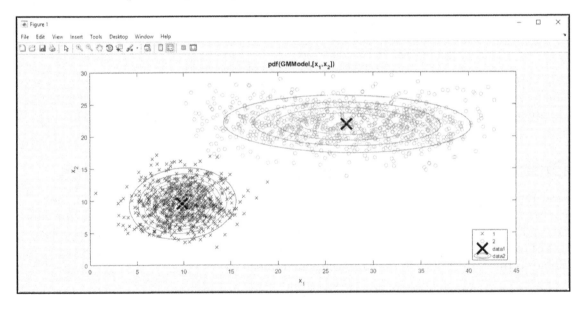

Figure 6.21: The scatter plot of clustering, position of each cluster's center, and estimated probability density contours of the model

All we have to do is represent the two Gaussian distributions at the base of our cluster analysis. For this purpose, we can use the `gmdistribution()` function. This function constructs an object of the `gmdistribution` class, defining a Gaussian mixture distribution. We must first recover the characteristics of the two distributions; I mean, `mu` and `sigma`. This data is contained in the model we created; we just extract it using point notation:

```
>> mu = GMModel.mu;
>> sigma = GMModel.Sigma;
>> DistObj = gmdistribution(mu,sigma);
```

Finally, we draw a three-dimensional plot of the two distributions:

```
>> ezsurf(@(x,y)pdf(DistObj,[x y]),[0 45],[0 30])
```

In the following figure two Gaussian distributions at the base of our cluster analysis are shown:

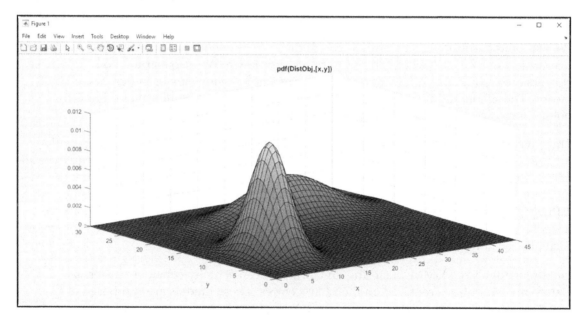

Figure 6.22: Two Gaussian distributions of the model

In Figure 6.22, the geometries of the two distributions are clearly represented.

Summary

In this chapter, we learned how to perform an accurate cluster analysis in the MATLAB environment. First, we explored how to measure similarity. We learned concepts such as proximity between elements, similarity and dissimilarity measures, and Euclidean, Minkowski, Manhattan, and cosine distance metrics. We looked at a couple of methods for grouping objects: hierarchical clustering and partitioning clustering. In the first method, clusters are constructed by recursively partitioning the instances in either a top-down or bottom-up fashion. The second one decomposes a dataset into a set of disjoint clusters.

We discovered hierarchical clustering in MATLAB using the `pdist`, `linkage`, and `cluster` functions. These functions perform agglomerative clustering. We learned how to calculate the distance between the objects through the `pdist` function. To determine the proximity of objects to each other, we used the linkage function. With the cluster function, we cut the ramifications from the bottom of the hierarchy tree and we assigned all the objects below each cut to a single cluster. Finally we learned how to read a dendrogram and how to verify hierarchical clustering to improve performance.

We explored partitioning clustering through the `kmeans` method. We learned how to locate *k* centroids, one for each cluster, by an iterative procedure. We also learned how well these clusters are separated and how to make a silhouette plot using cluster indices issued by K-means. The silhouette value for each point is a measure of how similar that point is to points in its own cluster when compared to points in other clusters.

Thus, we discovered K-medoids clustering and how to locate the center of clusters with medoids. A medoid can be defined as an object of a cluster whose average disparity over all objects in the cluster is minimal; thus, it will be the most central point of a given dataset. K-medoids is more robust to noise and outliers than K-means, because a mean is easily influenced by extreme values. We learned to use the `kmedoids` function; it partitions the observations of a matrix into *k* clusters and returns a vector containing the cluster indices of each observation.

Finally, we analyzed GMM clustering. In GMM, we can actually consider clusters as Gaussian distributions centered on their barycentres. These models are composed of *k* (positive integer) multivariate normal density components. Each component has an n-dimensional mean, *n-by-n* covariance matrix, and mixing proportion. We used the `fitgmdist` function to return a Gaussian mixture distribution model with *k* components (fixed by the user) fitted to the input dataset. Then, we used the cluster function. Finally, we drew a three-dimensional plot of the distributions identified.

In the next chapter, we will learn the basic concepts of artificial neural networks and how to implement them in the MATLAB environment. We will also see how to prepare data for neural network analysis; how to perform data fitting, pattern recognition, and clustering analysis in MATLAB; and how to perform preprocessing, postprocessing, and network visualization to improve training efficiency and assess network performance.

7

Simulation of Human Thinking - Artificial Neural Networks

Artificial Neural Networks (ANN) are mathematical models for the simulation of typical human brain activities such as image perception, pattern recognition, language understanding, sense-motor coordination, and so on. These models are composed of a system of nodes, equivalent to the neurons of a human brain, which are interconnected by weighted links, equivalent to the synapses between neurons. The output of the network is modified iteratively from link weights to convergence. The original data is provided to the input layer and the result of the network is returned from the output level. The input nodes represent the independent or predictor variables that are used to predict the dependent variables, that is, the output neurons.

The MATLAB Neural Network Toolbox provides algorithms, pretrained models, and apps to create, train, visualize, and simulate artificial neural networks. We can perform classification, regression, clustering, dimensionality reduction, time series forecasting, and dynamic system modeling and control. ANNs include data structures and algorithms for learning and classification of data. Through neural network techniques, a program can learn by examples and create an internal structure of rules to classify different inputs.

This chapter shows us how to use neural networks to fit data, to classify patterns, and for clustering. You'll learn preprocessing, postprocessing, and network visualization for improving training efficiency and assessing network performance. We'll also analyze how to properly divide the data before submitting it to the network.

We will cover the following topics:

- Creating, training, and simulating neural networks
- Fitting data
- Using neural network GUI
- Neural network command-line functions

At the end of the chapter, we will understand the basic concepts of artificial neural networks and how to implement them in the MATLAB environment. We will learn how to prepare data for neural network analysis. We will know how to perform data fitting analysis in MATLAB and perform a command-line neural network analysis to understand how specific functions work.

Getting started with neural networks

Serial computers and their programs are very powerful tools used to perform tasks requiring the repetition of a number of well-defined operations where accuracy, reliability, and speed are important features. These information processing systems are very useful but not intelligent; the only element of intelligence in the whole process is the programmer who has analyzed the task and created the program. For an artificial system to be intelligent, it should at least be able to solve problems that humans find simple, trivial, and natural.

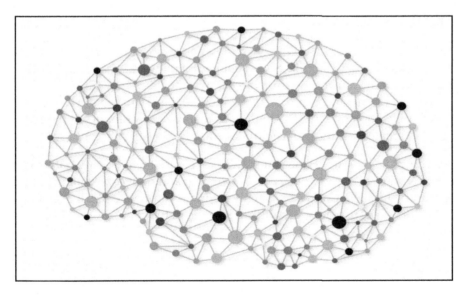

Figure 7.1: A biological neural network scheme

ANNs are information processing systems that try to simulate within a computer system the functioning of biological nervous systems that are made up of a large number of nerve cells, or neurons, connected to each other in a complex network. Each neuron is connected, on an average with tens of thousands of other neurons, with hundreds of billions of connections. Intelligent behavior emerges from the many interactions between these interconnected units.

Some of these units receive information from the environment, others emit responses to the environment, and others--if they are there--communicate only with the units within the network. These three are defined as **input** units, **output** units, and **hidden** units, respectively.

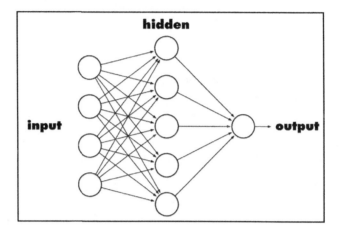

Figure 7.2: Neural network architecture

Each unit performs a very simple operation that involves activating if the total amount of signal received exceeds an activation threshold. If a unit becomes active, it emits a signal that is transmitted along the communication channels to other units to which it is connected. Each connection point acts as a filter that transforms the received message into an excited or inhibitory signal, increasing or decreasing at the same time the intensity according to its individual characteristics. The input-output link (in other words, the network transfer function) is not programmed but is simply obtained from a learning process based on empirical data that may be of these kinds: supervised, unsupervised, and reinforcement learning.

Neural networks work in parallel and are therefore able to deal with lots of data at the same time, as opposed to serial computers, in which each one is processed individually and in succession. Although each individual neuron is relatively slow, parallelism partly explains the higher brain velocity in performing tasks that require the simultaneous processing of a large amount of data, such as visual object recognition. This is essentially a complicated statistical system with good noise immunity. If some of the system's units malfunction, the network as a whole has performance reductions but is unlikely to encounter a system shutdown. In the following figure is a comparison between **serial processing** and **parallel processing**:

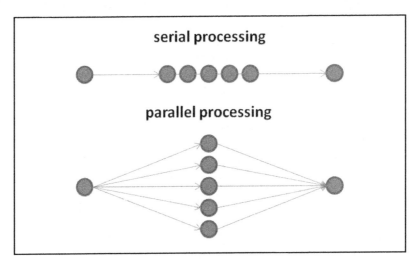

Figure 7.3: Comparison between serial and parallel processing

However, the latest-generation software for neural networks requires good statistical knowledge. The degree of immediate usability must not mislead, even allowing the user to immediately make predictions or classifications, albeit within the limits of the case. From an industrial standpoint, they are effective when we have historical data that can be handled with neural algorithms. This is of interest to production because it allows extraction of data and models.

Models produced by neural networks, though very efficient, cannot be explained in human symbolic language; the results must be accepted *as they are*, from which the definition of neural networks as black box, as is shown in the following figure:

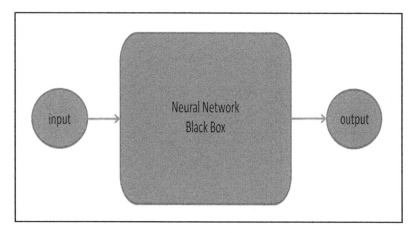

Figure 7.4: Neural network as a black box

As with any modeling algorithm, neural networks are also efficient only if predictive variables are carefully chosen. They require a system training phase that sets the weights of individual neurons, and this phase can take a long time if the number of records and variables analyzed is very large. There are no theorems or models that allow us to define the network, so the success of a network depends greatly on the creator's experience.

Neural networks are usually used in situations where data may be partially incorrect, or where no analytic models are available to deal with the problem. Their typical use is in OCR software, facial recognition systems, and, more generally, in systems dealing with handling data that is subject to error or noise. They are also one of the most used tools in data mining analysis. Neural networks are also used as a means of forecasting financial or meteorological analysis. In recent years, their significance has increased considerably in the field of bioinformatics, where they are used to find functional and/or structural patterns in nucleic acids and proteins. By providing a long set of input data, the network is able to return the most likely output.

Basic elements of a neural network

The atomic computational unit of a neural network is the artificial neuron. It simulates several basic functions of the biological neuron, evaluates the intensity of each input, sums up the different inputs, and compares the result with an appropriate threshold. Finally, it determines what the output value is. The basic anatomy of the neuron is known and the main biochemical reactions that govern its activity have been identified. A neuron can be considered the elemental computational unit of the brain. In the human brain, about *100* different classes of neurons have been identified. The following figure shows the scheme of a single neuron:

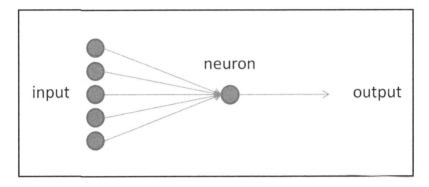

Figure 7.5: Neural network scheme

The main feature of the neuron is to generate an electric potential propagating along the axon (neuron output) when electrical activity at the neuron body level exceeds a certain threshold. Neuron input is a set of fibers called **dendrites**; they are in contact with the axons of other neurons from which they receive electrical potentials. The connection point between an axon of a neuron and the dendrite of another neuron is called **synapse**. In the following figure, a biological neuron structure is shown:

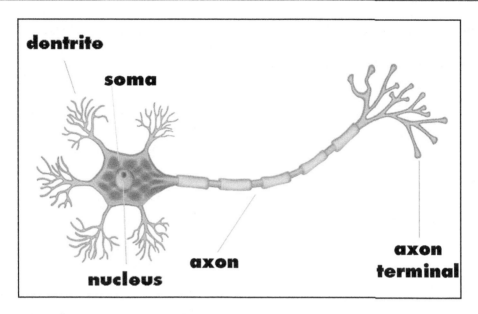

Figure 7.6: Biological neuron structure

The synapse also has the property of modulating the electrical pulse from the axon. The electrical potential generated by a neuron is, in fact, of the kind on/off; if the electrical activity of the neuron exceeds a certain threshold, the impulse is generated; otherwise, not.

The generated pulse does not differ by intensity from one neuron to another. The potential propagates along the axon and reaches the synapse with the dendrite of another neuron. The post-synaptic potential of dendrites depends on the biochemical characteristics of the synapses. In the presence of the same pre-synaptic potential, two different synapses generate different post-synaptic potentials. In other words, the synapse weighs the input potential by modulating it. Post-synaptic potentials propagate through neuron dendrites. At the soma level, they add up, and only if the result of that sum is greater than a certain threshold will the neuron trigger the potential that propagates through its axon.

A biological neuron, as we have said, receives various inputs through dendrites. An artificial neuron also receives different input values. All inputs are added and the result is the value counted by the neuron. If this value exceeds a certain threshold, the neuron produces an output signal, or potential; otherwise, it remains silent.

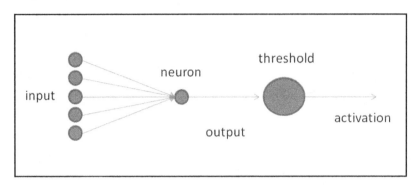

Figure 7.7: Scheme of a single neuron with the threshold of activation

The algebraic sum of its inputs is the first function implemented by the artificial neuron. This sum allows you to build the system response. In the case of an error in the simulation of the phenomenon, an appropriate correction is required. To do this, each input must be assigned a weight, that is, a numeric value that modulates the impact that this input has on the total sum to determine the potential of the neuron. In other words, each input contributes more or less to the determination of the threshold value being exceeded and the potential triggering. This property is also inspired by a characteristic of biological neurons. The feature in question concerns the synapses that the axon of a neuron does with the dendrite of another neuron.

From the point of view of the post-synaptic neuron, inputs, constituted by the potential of other neurons whose axons synapse on its dendrites, are modulated precisely by such synapses. Some of them will have a greater effect on the total sum. Others will even have a character inhibitory; that is, they will have the effect of lowering the value of the total sum of the inputs, consequently decreasing the probability that it exceeds the threshold value and triggers a potential.

This property of biological systems is modeled in connection systems with the mathematical weight concept. The weight of a connection is a numeric value for which to multiply the input value. In this way, the input will have a greater or lesser effect on the total amount depending on the weight entity.

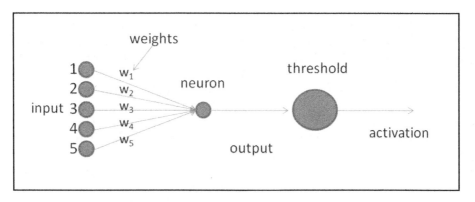

Figure 7.8: Scheme of a single neuron with weights of connections

In this way, the sum of the inputs will become their weighted sum. We can sketch this concept through this simple formula:

```
Output = input1*w1+input2*w2+input3*w3+input4*w4+input5*w5
```

Consider the input and the corresponding weight as two vectors:

```
INPUT = (input1, input2, input3, input4, input5)
W = (w1, w2, w3,w4, w5)
```

The total input signal to the neuron, which we identified as the sum of the inputs, will be the scalar product of these two vectors:

```
Output = INPUT * W
```

Each component of the `INPUT` vector is multiplied with the corresponding component of the `W` vector and all the products obtained are added. The result will be a scalar, the weighted sum of inputs.

Geometrically, the scalar product of two vectors can be considered a measure of their similarity. If the vectors are in the same direction, the scalar product is maximum; if the vectors have opposite directions, the scalar product is null. In the weighted sum, each entry participates in the sum in a proportional manner to the weight.

Previously, we have illustrated the sum function, which then becomes weighted sum by introducing the weight concept. Now, we will introduce another property of the artificial neuron, once again inspired by a biological neuron property. It has been said that the biological neuron at the soma level sums up all the potential post-synaptic dendrites. In fact, this sum is not really the sum of algebraic values of such potentials.

Several factors, including the passive resistance of the neuron membrane, affect it; this means that the sum of these values is not the exact algebraic sum but a function, usually nonlinear, of that sum. In other words, artificial neurons sum up the weighed inputs and then modify the result based on a particular function. This function is called the **transfer function** and, applied to the output of the neuron, it determines its actual potential.

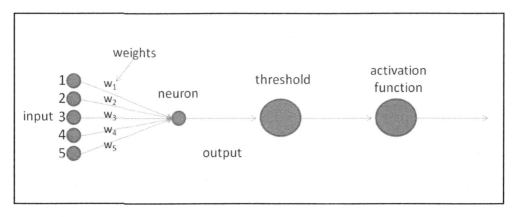

Figure 7.9: Scheme of a single neuron with the activation function

There are several types of transfer functions applied to the neurons of artificial neural networks. Some of these are listed here:

- **A**: Linear function
- **B**: Step function
- **C**: Sigmoid function
- **D**: Hyperbolic tangent function

In the following figure is a graphical representation of the activation functions just listed:

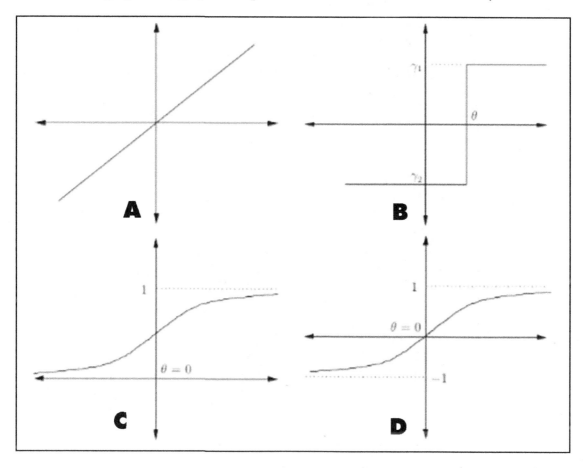

Figure 7.10: A graphical representation of activation functions

After describing the properties of an artificial neuron, we now describe the architecture of a neural network. This means, on one hand, we will physically illustrate the architecture of an ANN; and on the other hand, we will determine the role of each neuron within that structure.

Suppose you have different inputs and different nodes in such a way that each input is connected to all output nodes. Each output node has all the properties described before and performs its activity alongside those of the other nodes. By introducing an input pattern, you will have values for the outputs that depend on either the input values or the weights of the network. Generally, a weight will determine how much the relative input can affect a particular node. The set of nodes in the structure gets the name layer. The following figure shows this structure:

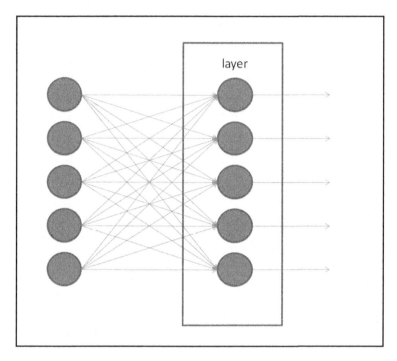

Figure 7.11: One-layer neural network architecture

Neural networks can also have multiple layers. Each layer added to the network increases its computational capacity. Inputs are numeric values that are evaluated by the weights of connections with the first layer of nodes, also called hidden layer. Here, each node performs the computation as described so far and eventually produces a potential that, in turn, propagates to the nodes of the output layer. The potential produced by output nodes is the output calculated by the neural network. In general, when talking about the architecture of a neural network, one refers to the way the different nodes are connected to each other. The architecture by layers, as shown in the previous figure, it is typical of feed-forward neural networks. Such networks are characterized by the fact that the activation of the input nodes propagates forward to those of the hidden layer, and from those to the ones of the output layer.

Changing the way the nodes are connected to each other changes the network architecture. This not only has practical consequences, as it changes the computational capacity of the network, but also has important theoretical consequences that involve the concept of learning. The following figure shows a deep neural network with two hidden layers:

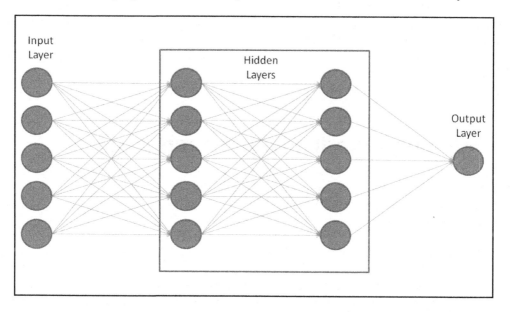

Figure 7.12: Deep neural network with two hidden layers

In *Figure 7.12*, we have a network with five **Input Layers**, two **Hidden Layers** with five nodes for each, and finally one, **Output Layer**. It's easy to understand that there are several things that need to be set in building a network's architecture. Essentially, we will have to set the following features:

- The number of hidden layers
- The number of nodes within each layer
- The network training algorithm

Each listed feature assumes a particular importance with respect to the result. Greater and more complex networks are able to simulate more complex models, at least in general terms. But this is not always true; we can only say that the position of each unit determines the functionality of the network. In this regard, network training is of utmost importance, which must be done by trying to find the most reliable solution.

The number of hidden layers

By analyzing *Figure 7.12*, we notice that two layers (input and output) are imposed by the problem and nothing can be done. So, it all depends on the number of hidden layers that we're staring at. The number of hidden neurons characterizes the size of a neural network. Choosing an optimal size of the network is an actual problem because no analytical solution has been found so far. One way to proceed can be the heuristic one: different networks are formed with increasing complexity by using a subset of learning of the training data and simultaneously observing the error of a validation subset. Once the training is completed, the network with the lowest validation error is preferred.

The number of nodes within each layer

To start, we can say what is said about choosing the number of layers. The number of input nodes is predetermined by the number of features in the input data. As well, the number of output nodes is predetermined by the number of outcomes to be modeled or the number of class levels in the outcome.

Again, everything is played in the hidden layers. There is no analytical approach to determine the number of neurons in the hidden layer. The appropriate number depends on the number of input nodes, the amount of training data, and the complexity of the learning algorithm, among many other factors. A greater number of neurons will result in a model that more closely simulates the training data, but this runs a risk of overfitting; it may generalize poorly to future data. Furthermore, neural networks with many nodes can also be computationally expensive and slow to train. Once again, we can adopt a heuristic approach by trying.

The network training algorithm

As already mentioned, the ANNs are composed of simple elements operating in parallel. Connections between network elements are fundamental as they decide network functions. These connections affect the result through its weight, which is regulated in the neural network training phase.

Then, in the training phase, the network is regulated by changing the connection weights so that a particular input will lead to a specific destination. For example, the network can be adjusted by comparing the output (what we calculate practically) and the target (what we want to get) until the network output matches the target. To get sufficiently reliable results, many input-target pairs are needed to form a network.

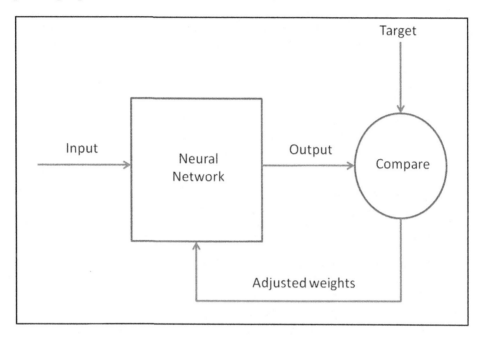

Figure 7.13: Flow chart of the training phase

The way these weights are adjusted is defined by the particular algorithm we will adopt. We will refer to the various algorithms when we use them in practical examples.

Neural Network Toolbox

The Neural Network Toolbox provides algorithms, pre-trained models, and apps to create, train, visualize, and simulate neural networks with one hidden layer (called **shallow neural networks**) and neural networks with several hidden layers (called **deep neural networks**). Through the use of the tools offered, we can perform classification, regression, clustering, dimensionality reduction, time series forecasting, and dynamic system modeling and control.

There are several ways to use the Neural Network Toolbox software; the essential ones are the four ways that are listed here:

- The most comfortable one uses MATLAB graphical user interfaces. We can start the main window through the `nnstart` command. In this way, we can automatically perform the following tasks: function fitting (`nftool`), pattern recognition (`nprtool`), data clustering (`nctool`), time series analysis (`ntstool`).
- We can use basic command-line operations. Command-line operations offer greater flexibility but require more knowledge. This is why you will need to remember all the necessary functions without the help of menus and icons that typically appear in the GUI.
- We can customize the toolbox. In fact, we can create our own neural networks. You can create networks with arbitrary connections and continue training them using existing toolbox training features in GUI.
- Finally, we can modify the functions in the toolbox. Each computational component is written in MATLAB code and is completely accessible.

As you can see, there is something for everyone, from the novice to the expert. Simple tools are available to guide the new user through specific applications, and more complex tools that allow the network to be customized to test new architectures.

Whatever the way we deal with these problems, a proper analysis with the use of neural networks should include the following steps:

1. Collect data.
2. Create the network.
3. Configure the network.
4. Initialize the weights and biases.
5. Train the network.
6. Validate the network.
7. Test the network.

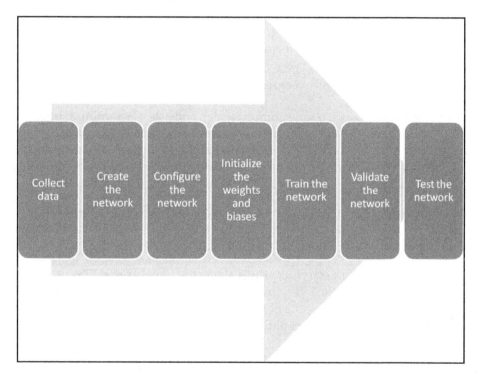

Figure 7.14: Workflow for neural network design

The first step involves collecting the data we want to analyze; this is usually performed outside the MATLAB environment. This phase is obviously of paramount importance for the final result as the quality of the collected data will allow us to extract the knowledge adequately.

Then, we are going to create the network; in this case, we can use a number of functions available in the toolbox that allow us to create a neural network through one of the expected algorithms. This procedure leads to the creation of a neural network object. This object is used to store all of the information that defines a neural network. It has a number of properties which define its features. For example, some of them are listed here with brief descriptions:

- **General**: General properties of neural networks
- **Architecture**: The number of network sub-objects (inputs, layers, outputs, targets, biases, and weights) and how they are connected
- **Subobject structures**: Cell arrays of structures that define each of the network's inputs, layers, outputs, targets, biases, and weights
- **Functions**: These define the algorithms to use when a network is to adapt, is to be initialized, is to have its performance measured, or is to be trained
- **Weight and bias values**: These define the network's adjustable parameters (its weight matrices and bias vectors)

The third step involves network configuration, which consists of examining input and output data, setting the input and output dimensions of the network to fit data, and choosing input and output processing settings that allow for better network performance. The configuration phase is normally performed automatically when the training function is called. However, it can be executed manually, using the configuration function.

The fourth step involves the initialization of weights and bias, which consists of setting the initial values from which to start and then train the network. This step occurs automatically once the training algorithm has been decided, but may be set by the user.

The fifth step involves network training; at this stage, the weights and bias must be tuned to optimize the network performance. It represents the most important phase of the whole process as the better the network is, the better the generalization will be able to operate with new data unknown to it. At this stage, part of the collected data is taken randomly (usually *70* percent of the available cases).

The sixth step involves the network validation, in which a fraction of the randomly collected data (usually *15* percent of the available cases) is passed to the network in order to estimate how well our model has been trained. From the results obtained in this phase, it will be possible to decide whether the model chosen adequately reflects the initial expectations or whether you need to go back on your steps and choose a different model.

The final step involves the use of the network; part of the collected data taken randomly (usually *15* percent of the available cases) is passed to the network to test it. Then the neural network object can be saved and used as many times as you want with any new data.

The following figure shows how the original dataset has been divided:

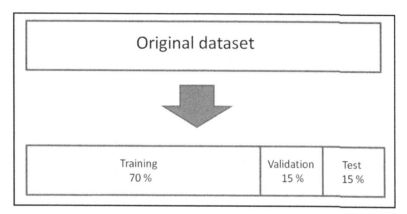

Figure 7.15: Original data subdivision in training, validation, and test stages

In describing the different steps in which the workflow for neural network design is divided, we have referred to a breakdown of the collected data into three sets: training, validation, and test. We now describe them in detail:

- **Training set** (usually *70* percent of the available cases): A set of examples used for learning, to fit the parameters of the neural network. We use the training set to find the optimal values of weights and biases.
- **Validation set** (usually *15* percent of the available cases): A set of examples used to tune the parameters of a network. We use the validation set to find the optimal number of hidden units or to determine a stopping point for the used algorithm.
- **Test set** (usually *15* percent of the available cases): A set of examples used only to assess the performance of a fully trained network. We use the test set to estimate the error rate after we have chosen the final model. After assessing the final model on the test set, we must not tune the model any further.

At this point, the workflow is sufficiently clear, so it is time to get down to work. But before you start, note one last thing about the data to be analyzed. We have previously pointed out that the data collection process is often done outside by the MATLAB environment. This means that you need to have a properly collected data file available to initiate an analysis in MATLAB. But we are here to learn, so we do not have the data available--at least not now. No fear, as always MATLAB comes to the rescue.

Indeed, several sample datasets are available in the Neural Network Toolbox software. We can use this data to experiment with the functionality of the toolbox. To view the datasets that are available, use the following command:

```
>> help nndatasets
Neural Network Datasets
   ------------------------
   simplefit_dataset    - Simple fitting dataset.
   abalone_dataset      - Abalone shell rings dataset.
   bodyfat_dataset      - Body fat percentage dataset.
   building_dataset     - Building energy dataset.
   chemical_dataset     - Chemical sensor dataset.
   cho_dataset          - Cholesterol dataset.
   engine_dataset       - Engine behavior dataset.
   vinyl_dataset        - Vinyl bromide dataset.
```

The code just seen shows a brief summary of what is shown on video. Notice that all the datasets have file names of the form `name_dataset`. Inside these files will be the arrays `nameInputs` and `nameTargets`. For example, we can load a dataset into the workspace with the following command:

```
>> load abalone_dataset
```

This will load `abaloneInputs` and `abaloneTargets` into the workspace. If you want to load the input and target arrays with different names, you can use the following command:

```
>> [Input,Target] = abalone_dataset;
```

This will load the inputs and targets into the arrays `Input` and `Target`. You can get a description of a dataset with this command:

```
>> help abalone_dataset
```

In the following figure is the result of this command in the MATLAB environment:

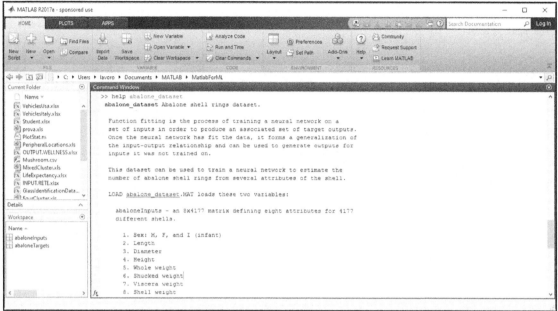

Figure 7.16: Brief summary of the abalone_dataset content

As can be seen in *Figure 7.16*, a description of the contents of the dataset is proposed: number of attributes, number of items, variables' list, and so on. Also, possible uses are suggested.

A neural network getting started GUI

A GUI is an interface that allows users to interact with computers through graphical icons and visual indicators instead of text-based interfaces. GUIs were introduced to make interactive operations more convenient in comparison to the more challenging procedures required by command-line interfaces, which require commands to be typed on a computer keyboard. The actions in a GUI are usually performed through direct manipulation of the graphical elements.

To make the application of neural networks as simple as possible, the toolbox gives us a series of GUIs. Seeing is believing. The main one is the `nnstart()` function, which opens a window with launch buttons for neural network fitting, pattern recognition, clustering, and time series tools:

```
>> nnstart
```

This command opens the **Neural Network Start** GUI, as shown in the following figure:

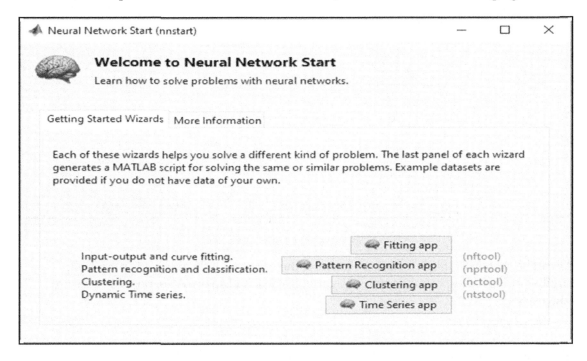

Figure 7.17: The Neural Network Start GUI

This GUI represents the dashboard of the entire toolbox, in the sense that, from here, it is possible to perform any kind of analysis involving the use of neural networks through the use of graphical interfaces. As can be seen in *Figure 7.17*, four types of problems are available:

- Function fitting (`nftool`)
- Pattern recognition (`nprtool`)
- Data clustering (`nctool`)
- Time series analysis (`ntstool`)

For each task, a GUI is available and it guides us step by step throughout the analysis process. The first tool (`nftool`) resolves a fitting problem. In a fitting problem, a neural network to map between a set of numeric inputs and a set of numeric targets is created. The Neural Fitting app helps us to select data, create and train the network, and evaluate its performance using mean square error and regression analysis. In the following, we will address a fitting problem in detail.

The second tool (`nprtool`) resolves pattern recognition problems. In pattern recognition problems, we use a neural network to classify inputs into a set of target categories. This app will help us select data, create and train a network, and evaluate its performance using cross-entropy and confusion matrices. We will address this type of problem in the last chapter.

The third tool (`nctool`) resolves clustering problems. In clustering problems, we use a neural network to group data by similarity. This app will help us to select data, create and train a network, and evaluate its performance using a variety of visualization tools. We will address this issue in the last chapter.

The last tool (`ntstool`) solves nonlinear time series problems with dynamic neural networks. Dynamic neural networks are used for nonlinear filtering and prediction. Prediction is a kind of dynamic filtering, in which past values of one or more time series are used to predict future values. This tool allows us to solve three kinds of nonlinear time series problems:

- Nonlinear autoregressive with external input
- Nonlinear autoregressive
- Nonlinear input-output

Data fitting with neural networks

Data fitting is the process of building a curve or a mathematical function that has the best match with a set of previously collected points. Curve fitting can relate to both interpolations, where exact data points are required, or smoothing, where a flat function that approximates the data is built. We are talking about curves fitting in a regression analysis, which is most concerned with statistical inference problems, as well as the uncertainty that a curve coincides with observed data that has random errors. The approximate curves obtained from the data fitting can be used to help display data, to predict the values of a function where no data is available, and to summarize the relationship between two or more variables.

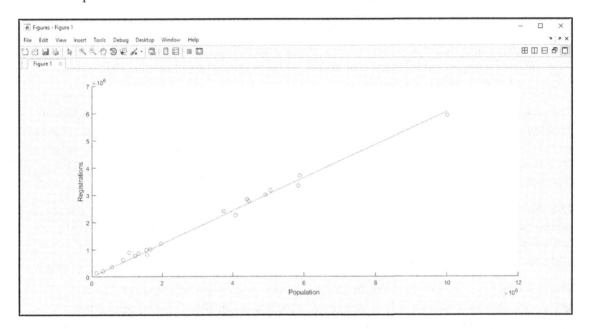

Figure 7.18: Linear interpolation of collected data

We have seen some examples of curve fitting in the regression chapter. On that occasion, we could see that the mathematical formulas that allow us to predict the trend of a particular distribution are very complicated, and often they are not able to represent all data. At least we cannot predict the trend of data over the entire range of its existence. In these cases, it is useful to use machine learning algorithms, which, as we know, are able to build a model without resorting to complicated mathematical formulas. In particular, ANNs are suitable for data fitting operations to predict the trend of data. Indeed, a simple neural network can adapt to any practical function.

Function fitting is the process of training a neural network on a set of inputs in order to produce an associated set of target outputs. Once the neural network has fitted the data, it forms a generalization of the input-output relationship and can be used to generate outputs for inputs it was not trained on.

As we have already said, in the Neural Network Toolbox, you can solve a data fitting problem in several ways. In particular, the most used ones are:

- Use a graphical user interface (nftool)
- Use command-line functions

For beginners, it is best to start with the nftool app (graphical user interface). The usefulness of such an approach, at least in the preliminary stages, is due to the ability to acquire the skills needed to be able to do the same later without the help of the graphical interface.

In fact, the GUI helps us by offering a series of windows in which we will only have to make our choices by using the menus and icons typical of a graphical interface operating system. In other words, we will not be required to remember all the commands to create the network and then train it.

Later, once we have created the network, we can generate the script. From the script's analysis we can access the functions we need to perform all the operations. In this way, we will be able to know all the functions involved in the different phases and how they will be used.

As always, before you start, regardless of the method you choose to use, you must first define the problem by selecting a suitable dataset. To get started, we will be able to use one of the sample datasets that we have previously mentioned. There is one for every use of the toolbox, especially so for the curve fitting. In fact, accessing the help dataset is done as follows:

```
>> help nndatasets
```

A list of all available datasets is grouped by category. Specifically for curve fitting, we will find the following dataset:

- `simplefit_dataset`: Simple fitting dataset
- `abalone_dataset`: Abalone shell rings dataset
- `bodyfat_dataset`: Body fat percentage dataset
- `building_dataset`: Building energy dataset
- `chemical_dataset`: Chemical sensor dataset
- `cho_dataset`: Cholesterol dataset
- `engine_dataset`: Engine behavior dataset
- `vinyl_dataset`: Vinyl bromide dataset

After using the examples in the first learning phase, we will pass on real cases. If we have a specific problem that we want to resolve, we can upload our data into the MATLAB workspace. To do this, we can use all the lessons learned in Chapter 2, *Importing and Organizing Data in MATLAB*.

How to use the Neural Fitting app (nftool)

In a fitting problem, a neural network to map between a set of numeric inputs and a set of numeric targets is created. The Neural Fitting app helps us to select data, create and train the network, and evaluate its performance using mean square error and regression analysis. To start, we launch the app by simply typing the following command at the MATLAB prompt:

```
>> nftool
```

This is the welcome page of the **Neural Fitting** app:

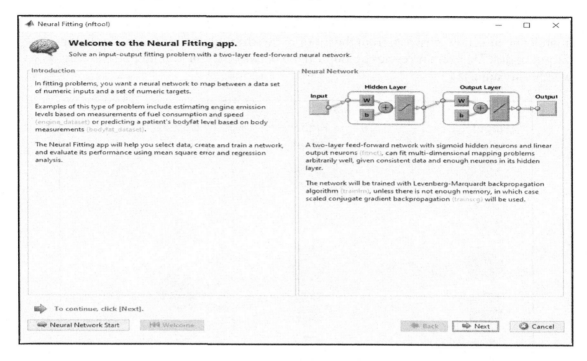

Figure 7.19: The welcome page of the Neural Fitting app

The welcome page of the **Neural Fitting** app (*Figure 7.19*) introduces the topic by explaining what the application will be able to help us with and reminds us of the ready-to-use examples we can adopt to understand the analysis mechanisms; but most importantly, it describes the architecture of the network that will be created.

The **Neural Fitting** app solves an input-output fitting problem with a two-layer feed-forward neural network. But what is it about? In a feed-forward neural network, the connections between the units do not form a cycle. In this network, the information moves in only one direction, forward, from the input nodes through the hidden nodes to the output nodes. There are no cycles or loops in the network. In the training phase, only weights are adjusted.

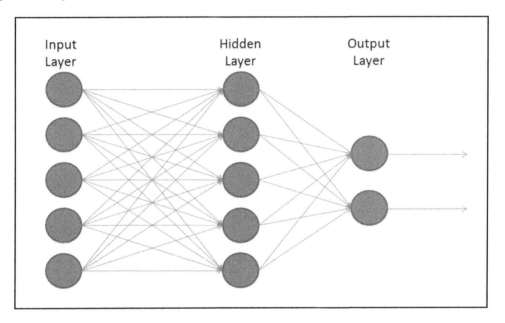

Figure 7.20: A feed-forward neural network architecture

At the bottom of the welcome page of the **Neural Fitting** app (*Figure 7.19*) are the buttons needed to go ahead in the analysis. In particular, at the bottom right are the buttons that let us go to the next page or go back on our steps. As suggested by the same app, we click on the next button to continue.

A new window is opened (*Figure 7.21*), where we can select the data to process: inputs and targets that define our fitting problem. Two options are available:

- **Get Data from Workspace**
- **Load Example Data Set**

The first option allows us to use data already available in the MATLAB workspace. This data must be loaded into two different arrays: one for input, one for output. To understand how our data must be formatted, we can take a look at the example datasets already mentioned before.

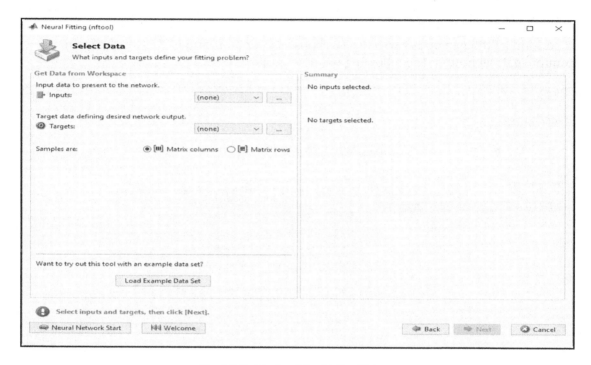

Figure 7.21: The Select Data window of the Neural Fitting app

As can be seen in *Figure 7.21*, in the **Get Data from Workspace** area, two clearly distinct fields are available:

- **Input data to present to the network.**
- **Target data defining desired network output.**

In both cases we can use the drop-down menu to select the data already available in the workspace, or click on the three-point button to import new data into MATLAB. Let me make a final clarification on the **Get Data from Workspace** area. Two radio buttons are there:

- **Matrix columns**
- **Matrix rows**

Select **Matrix columns** (default option) if the data is collected by columns, that is, if each column represents an observation. Select **Matrix rows** if the data is collected by rows, I mean, if each row represents an observation. The second option allows us to load an example dataset to understand how to proceed. This is the option to use in the first stage of learning, in which we do not have to worry about the quality of the source data, not even its format. We can draw on the resources that the toolbox provides us with to understand how to perform a fitting analysis correctly. To choose this option, simply click on the **Load example dataset** button. The following window is opened:

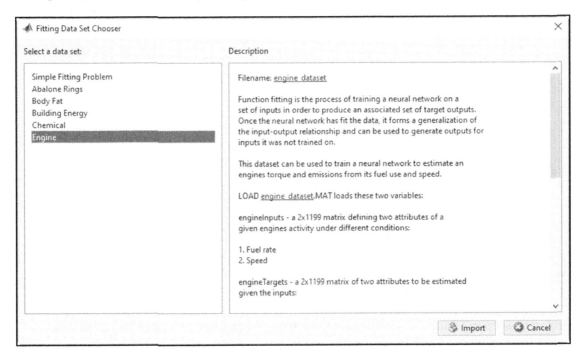

Figure 7.22: Fitting Data Set Chooser window

In this window, a list of available datasets is presented. For each item selected, a complete description of the dataset is proposed. To begin, we will use this second approach by loading `engine_dataset`. This dataset can be used to train a neural network to estimate an engine's torque and emissions from its fuel use and speed. This dataset contains two variables:

- `engineInputs`: A *2x1199* matrix defining two attributes of a given engines activity under different conditions: fuel rate and speed
- `engineTargets`: A *2x1199* matrix of two attributes to be estimated given the inputs: torque, and nitrous oxide emissions

Recapitulating, to upload the engine_dataset, we simply have to select that item in the **Fitting Data Set Chooser** window (*Figure 7.22*) and click the **Import** button. This returns you to the **Select Data** window. Two matrices are imported into the MATLAB workspace: engineInputs and engineTargets. At the same time, these matrices are loaded into their respective fields on the **Get Data from Workspace** area in the **Select Data** window of the **Neural Fitting** app (*Figure 7.21*). Click on **Next** to display the **Validation and Test Data** window, shown in the following figure:

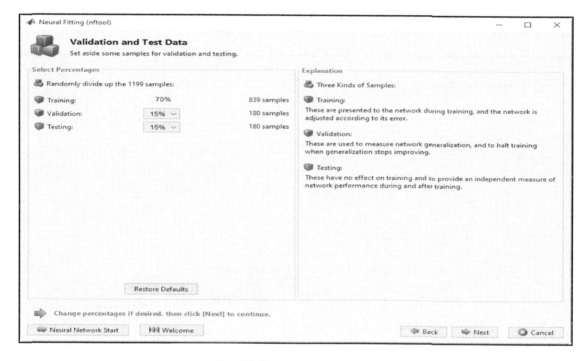

Figure 7.23: The Validation and Test Data window

In the **Validation and Test Data** window (*Figure 7.23*) is the random subdivision of the *4,177* samples in **Training**, **Validation**, and **Testing**. The percentage of the Training set is locked, while the other two can be set by the user.

Remember: the training set is presented to the network during training, and the network is adjusted according to its error. The validation set is used to measure network generalization and to halt training when generalization stops improving. Finally, the testing set has no effect and so provides an independent measure of network performance during and after training.

Change the percentages if desired, and then click on the **Next** button to display the **Network Architecture** window, shown in the following figure:

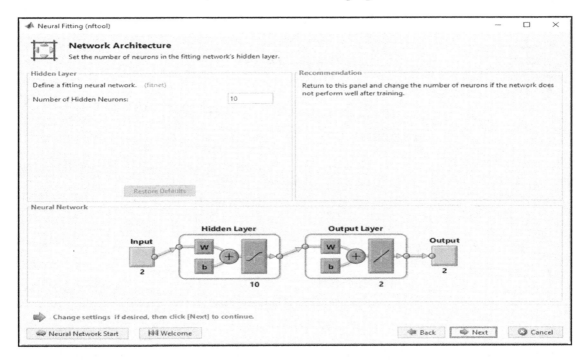

Figure 7.24: The Network Architecture window

The default network that is used for function fitting is a two-layer feed-forward network, with a sigmoid transfer function in the hidden layer and a linear transfer function in the output layer. The default number of hidden neurons is set to **10**. You might want to increase this number later if the network training performance is poor. Once we have chosen the number of neurons in the hidden layer, we can proceed to building the network simply by clicking on the **Next** button. The **Train Network** window is opened, as shown in this figure:

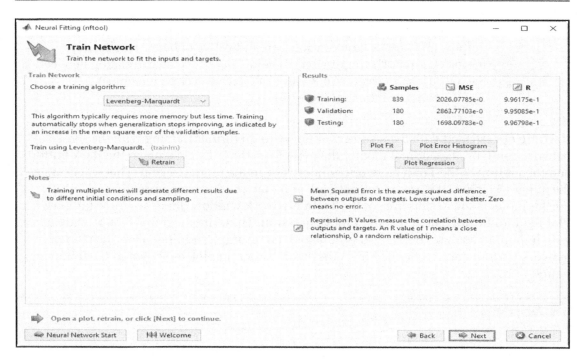

Figure 7.25: The Train Network window

In this window, we can choose the training algorithm. Three options are available:

- **Levenberg-Marquardt** (`trainlm`) is recommended for most problems
- **Bayesian Regularization** (`trainbr`) can take longer but obtains a better solution for some noisy and small problems
- **Scaled Conjugate Gradient** (`trainscg`) is recommended for large problems, as it uses gradient calculations, which are more memory efficient than the Jacobian calculations the other two algorithms use

This time, we use the default **Levenberg-Marquardt**. Once we have chosen the algorithm, we can start the network training simply by clicking on the **Train** button. The training continues until the validation error fails to decrease for six iterations (validation stop). When the training stops, the **MSE** and **R** values are displayed in the **Results** area of the **Train Network** window.

Mean Sqared Error (MSE) is the average squared difference between the outputs and targets. Lower values are indicative of better results. Zero means no error. The regression (R) value measures the correlation between the outputs and targets. An R value of *1* means a close relationship, and *0* means a random relationship.

If we are not satisfied with the results, we can try to do further training with the same network configuration, or first modify the network settings by clicking on the **Back** button and then return to the **Train Network** window to run the training again. This will change the initial weights and biases of the network and may produce an improved network. Furthermore, in the Results area of the **Train Network** window, there are three buttons: **Plot Fit**, **Plot Error Histogram**, and **Plot Regression**. These are diagrams that provide us with important analyses of the results obtained. For example, additional verification of network performance is obtained from the error histogram plot, as shown in the following figure:

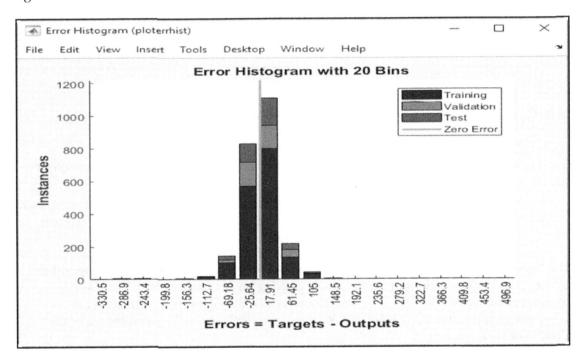

Figure 7.26: The Error Histogram plot

In the **Error Histogram** plot, the blue bars represent training data, the green bars represent validation data, and the red bars represent testing data. This plot can give us an indication of the error distribution; a normal distribution is indicative of good results. Also, the histogram can give us an indication of outliers, which are data points where the fit is significantly worse than the majority of data. Another plot used to validate the network performance is the **Regression** plot:

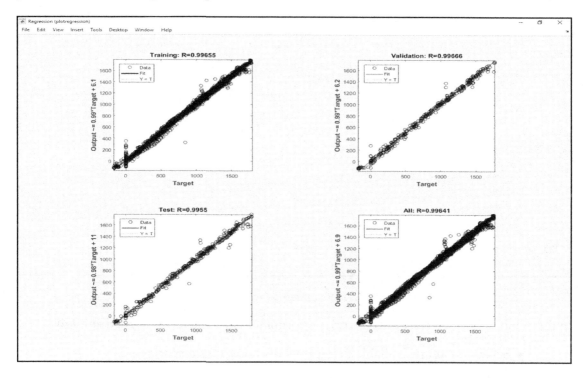

Figure 7.27: A regression plot

The regression plots display the network outputs with respect to targets for training, validation, and test sets. For a perfect fit, the data should fall along a 45-degree line, where the network outputs are equal to the targets. For this problem, the fit is reasonably good for all datasets, with R values of *0.99* or above in each case. From the regression plot analysis, we can see if more accurate results are needed. If necessary, we can do the training again, as indicated before.

Click on **Next** in the **Train Network** window to evaluate the network. The **Evaluate Network** window is opened, as shown in the following figure:

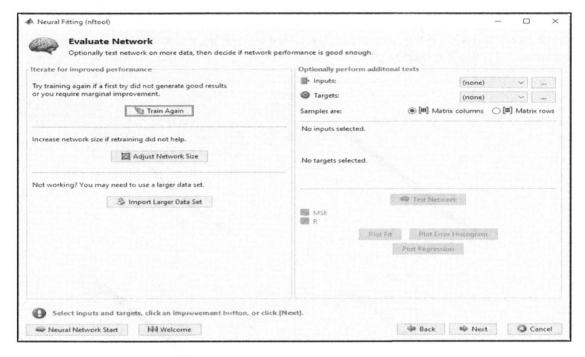

Figure 7.28: The Evaluate Network window

In this window, you can test the network performance to evaluate if it is good enough:

- Several tools are available to improve the network's performance
- Test the network on more data
- Train it again
- Increase the number of neurons
- Get a larger training dataset

Remember: good performance on the training set and worse performance on the test set is indicative of overfitting. Reducing the number of neurons can improve your results. If the training performance is poor, then we can increase the number of neurons.

Click on **Next** in the **Evaluate Network** window to generate the deployable solutions of your trained network. The **Deploy Solution** window is opened, as shown here:

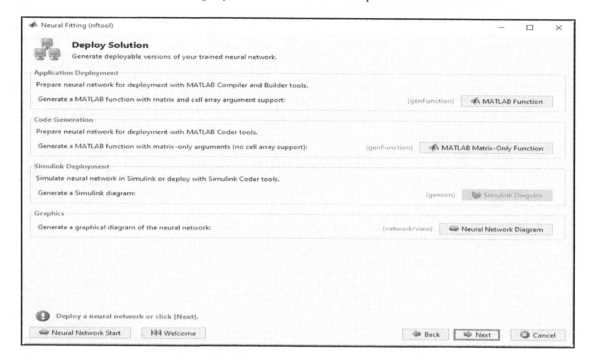

Figure 7.29: The Deploy Solution window

Four options are available:

- **Generate a MATLAB function with matrix and cell array argument support**
- **Generate a MATLAB function with matrix-only argument (no cell array support)**
- **Generate a Simulink diagram**
- **Generate a graphical diagram of the neural network**

We use these options to generate a **MATLAB Function** or **Simulink Diagram** for simulating our neural network. Also, we can use the generated code or diagram to better understand how our neural network computes outputs from inputs, or deploy the network with MATLAB compile tools and other MATLAB code generation tools. To choose one option, simply click on the relative button to the right of the window (MATLAB function, MATLAB Matrix-Only Function, Simulink Diagram, and Neural Network Diagram).

Click on **Next** in the **Deploy Solution** window to generate scripts or to save your results. The **Save Results** window is opened as shown in the following figure:

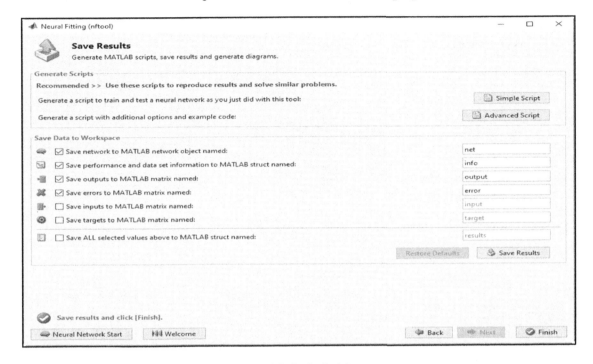

Figure 7.30: The Save Results window

Several options are available:

- **Generate a script to train and test a neural network as you just did with this tool**
- **Generate a script with additional options and example code**
- **Save Data to Workspace**

To generate a script, click on the relative button to the right of the window. To save data obtained in the MATLAB Workspace, select the desired options and then click on the **Save Results** button. The data selected is stored in the MATLAB workspace with the name present in the box to the right. Finally, click on the **Finish** button to end the analysis.

It's amazing! We ended our first analysis with neural networks and we have not even noticed it. Thanks to MATLAB and the nftool app.

Script analysis

As we have said before, by analyzing the script just created, we can access the functions we need to perform all the operations. In this way, we will be able to know all the functions involved in the different phases and how they will be used. We can modify them to customize the network training. As an example, let's take a look at the simple script that was created in the previous section:

```
inputs = engineInputs;
targets = engineTargets;
hiddenLayerSize = 10;
net = fitnet(hiddenLayerSize);
net.divideParam.trainRatio = 70/100;
net.divideParam.valRatio = 15/100;
net.divideParam.testRatio = 15/100;
[net,tr] = train(net,inputs,targets);
outputs = net(inputs);
errors = gsubtract(outputs,targets);
performance = perform(net,targets,outputs)
view(net)
figure, plotperform(tr)
figure, plottrainstate(tr)
figure, plotfit(targets,outputs)
figure, plotregression(targets,outputs)
figure, ploterrhist(errors)
```

After seeing how easy it is to perform neural network analysis using the nftool app, we might think that script analysis was a lot more difficult. The first thing to note is the extreme compactness of the code generated by MATLAB. Only seventeen lines of code! It's amazing! Let's analyze it in detail, line by line. Let's start with the first two rows; they define the input and output data already present in the MATLAB workspace:

```
inputs = engineInputs;
targets = engineTargets;
```

The third and fourth rows create the network. The third row defines the number of neurons of the hidden layer. We have assigned 10 neurons to one hidden layer in the previous section. The fourth row creates the network. As we've said later, the default network for function fitting problems, using the `fitnet()` function, is a feed-forward network with the default tan-sigmoid transfer function in the hidden layer and linear transfer function in the output layer. The network created has two output neurons, because there are two target values associated with each input vector (torque and nitrous oxide emissions):

```
hiddenLayerSize = 10;
net = fitnet(hiddenLayerSize);
```

The next three rows (5,6,7) randomly divide the data available in the following three sets--training, validation, and test:

```
net.divideParam.trainRatio = 70/100;
net.divideParam.valRatio = 15/100;
net.divideParam.testRatio = 15/100;
```

The eight row trains the network. During training, the **Neural Network Training** window is opened. This window displays the training progress and allows you to interrupt training at any time by clicking on **Stop Training**. To train the network, we have used the default **Levenberg-Marquardt** algorithm (`trainlm`). As we've said later, there are two other algorithms available: **Bayesian Regularization** (`trainbr`) and **Scaled Conjugate Gradient** (`trainscg`): To set this algorithm, simply type `net.trainFcn = 'trainbr'`, or `net.trainFcn = 'trainscg'`:

```
[net,tr] = train(net,inputs,targets);
```

The next three rows (9,10,11) test the network. After the network has been trained, you can use it to compute the network outputs. The following code calculates the network `outputs`, `errors`, and overall `performance`:

```
outputs = net(inputs);
errors = gsubtract(outputs,targets);
performance = perform(net,targets,outputs)
```

The twelfth row gives a view of the network diagram:

```
view(net)
```

The last rows display the plots described in the previous section:

```
figure, plotperform(tr)
figure, plottrainstate(tr)
figure, plotfit(targets,outputs)
figure, plotregression(targets,outputs)
figure, ploterrhist(errors)
```

 We've previously said that to improve the network performance, we can repeat the training session several times. This is due to different initial weight and bias values and different divisions of data into training, validation, and test sets used each time.

Summary

In this chapter, we learned how to simulate typical human brain activities through the ANN. We understood the basic concept of ANN. We saw how to build a simple neural network architecture. We explored topics such as input, hidden, and output layers; weights of connections; and the activation function.

We learned how to choose the number of hidden layers, the number of nodes within each layer, and the network training algorithm. Then, we took a tour into of the Neural Network Toolbox (which provides algorithms), pre-trained models, and apps to create, train, visualize, and simulate shallow, as well as deep, neural networks. We checked out the neural network *getting started* GUI, the starting point for our neural network fitting, pattern recognition, clustering, and time series analysis.

Finally, we focused on fitting data with a neural network. We saw how to use the Neural Fitting app (`nftool`). Then, we ran a script analysis to learn how to use neural network functions from the command line.

In the next chapter, we will learn the different types of dimensionality reduction techniques. We will understand the difference between feature selection and feature extraction. We will see how to perform the correct operation of dimensionality reduction. We'll also learn topics such as **Principal Component Analysis (PCA)** and factor analysis.

8
Improving the Performance of the Machine Learning Model - Dimensionality Reduction

When we handle large volumes of data, some issues occur spontaneously. How to build a representative model of a set of hundreds of variables? How to view data across countless dimensions? To address these issues, we must adopt a series of techniques called **dimensionality reduction**. Dimensionality reduction is the process of converting a set of data with many variables into data with lesser dimensions while ensuring similar information. The aim is to reduce the number of dimensions in a dataset through either feature selection or feature extraction without significant loss of details. Feature selection approaches try to find a subset of the original variables. Feature extraction reduces the dimensionality of the data by transforming it into new features.

Dimensionality reduction techniques are used to reduce two undesirable characteristics in data, namely noise (high variance values) and redundancy (highly correlated variables). These techniques help identify sets of unrelated predictive variables that can be used in subsequent analyses. Reducing a high-dimensional dataset, I mean a dataset with many predictive variables, to one with fewer dimensions improves conceptualization. Above three dimensions, visualizing the data becomes difficult or impossible.

This chapter shows us how to select the feature that best represents a set of data. You will learn feature extraction techniques for dimensionality reduction when transformation of variables is possible. We will cover the following topics:

- Stepwise regression
- **Principal Component Analysis (PCA)**

At the end of the chapter, we will have learned the different dimensionality reduction techniques and understood the difference between feature selection and feature extraction. We will discover how to perform correct operation of dimensionality reduction.

Feature selection

In general, when we work with high-dimensional datasets, it is a good idea to reduce the number of features to only the most useful ones and discard the rest. This can lead to simpler models that generalize better. Feature selection is the process of reducing inputs for processing and analyzing or identifying the most significant features over the others. This selection of features is necessary to create a functional model so as to achieve a reduction in cardinality, imposing a limit greater than the number of features that must be considered during its creation. In the following figure, a general scheme of a feature selection process is shown:

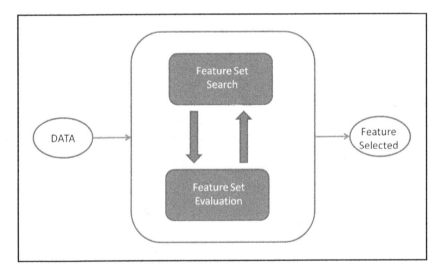

Figure 8.1: General scheme of a feature selection process

Usually, the data contains redundant information, or more than the necessary information; in other cases, it may contain incorrect information. Feature selection makes the process of creating a model more efficient, for example, decreasing the load on the CPU and the memory needed to train the algorithm. Selection of features is used for the following reasons:

- Preparing clean, understandable data
- Simplifying models to make them easier to interpret

- Shorter training times
- General improvement in reducing the problem of overfitting, that is, a reduction in variance

Feature selection is based on finding a subset of the original variables, usually iteratively, thus detecting new combinations of variables and comparing prediction errors. The combination of variables that produces minimum error will be labeled as a selected feature and used as input for the machine learning algorithm.

To do feature selection, we must set the appropriate criteria in advance. Usually, these selection criteria determine the minimization of a specific predictive error measure for models fit for different subsets. Based on these criteria, the selection algorithms seek a subset of predictors that optimally model the measured responses. Such research is subject to constraints such as the necessary or excluded characteristics and the size of the subset.

Function selection is particularly useful in cases where the modeling goal is to identify an influencing subset. It becomes essential when categorical features are present and numerical transformations are inadequate.

Basics of stepwise regression

At the beginning of the chapter on regression techniques, we said that regression analysis can be conducted for dual purposes; one of these is to understand and weigh the effects of the independent variable on the dependent variable. In other words, with this method, we can select predictors that have a greater influence on the response of the model. Stepwise regression is a method of selecting independent variables in order to choose a set of predictors that have the best relationship with the dependent variable. Among variable selection algorithms, we have three methods:

- The **forward method** starts with an empty model in which no predictors are selected; in the first step, the variable with the most significant association at the statistical level is added. At each subsequent step, the remaining variable with the largest statistically significant association is added into the model. This process continues until it is no longer variable with a statistically significant association with the dependent variable.
- The **backward method** begins with a model that includes all the variables. Then, we proceed step by step to delete the variables starting from the one with the least significant association.
- The **stepwise method** moves back and forth between the two processes by adding and removing variables that gain or lose significance in the various model adjustments (with the addition or reinsertion of a variable).

In the following figure, the criteria adopted from these three methods to select the variables are shown:

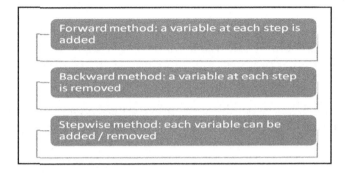

Figure 8.2: Forward, backward, and stepwise methods

To learn how to use a feature selection algorithm, we perform a stepwise regression analysis step by step.

Stepwise regression in MATLAB

Stepwise regression is an automated tool used in the exploratory stages of model building to identify a useful subset of predictors. In MATLAB, to create a stepwise regression model, use the `stepwiselm()` function. This function returns a linear model for the variables in the table or dataset array passed using stepwise regression to add or remove predictors. The `stepwiselm()` function uses forward and backward stepwise regression to determine a final model. The method begins with an initial model, specified using the `modelspec` attribute, and then compares the explanatory power of incrementally larger and smaller models. The most significant variable is added, or the least significant variable is removed during each step.

Indeed, at each step, the function searches for terms to add to or remove from the model based on the value of the `Criterion` argument, and the p-value of an F-statistic is computed to test models with and without a potential term. If a term is not currently in the model, the null hypothesis is that the term would have a zero coefficient if added to the model. If there is sufficient evidence to reject the null hypothesis, the term is added to the model. Conversely, if a term is currently in the model, the null hypothesis is that the term has a zero coefficient. If there is insufficient evidence to reject the null hypothesis, the term is removed from the model.

The following steps are performed:

1. Fit the initial model.
2. If any terms not in the model have p-values less than the entrance tolerance, add the one with the smallest p-value and repeat this step; otherwise, go to step 3.
3. If any terms in the model have p-values greater than the exit tolerance, remove the one with the largest p-value and go to step 2; otherwise, end the process.

Different models from the same set of potential terms can be built depending on the terms included in the initial model and the order in which terms are moved in and out. The method terminates when no single step improves the model.

We begin, as always, by getting the data to be analyzed.

 To get the data, we draw on the large collection of data available at the UCI Machine Learning Repository, at the following link: http://archive.ics.uci.edu/ml

We use a Yacht Hydrodynamics dataset, used to predict the hydrodynamic performance of sailing yachts from dimensions and velocity. Predicting the residuary resistance of sailing yachts at the initial design stage is of great value for evaluating the performance of the ship and for estimating the required propulsive power. Essential inputs include the basic hull dimensions and the boat velocity. The inputs are concerned with hull geometry coefficients and the Froude number, while the output is the residuary resistance per unit weight of displacement. This dataset contains the following fields:

- Longitudinal position of the center of buoyancy, adimensional
- Prismatic coefficient, adimensional
- Length-displacement ratio, adimensional
- Beam-draught ratio, adimensional
- Length-beam ratio, adimensional
- Froude number, adimensional
- Residuary resistance per unit weight of displacement, adimensional

To start, we download the data from the UCI Machine Learning Repository and save it in our current folder. To do this, we will use the `websave()` function; it saves content from the web service specified by the URL address and writes it to file. We insert the URL address to the specific dataset into a variable named `url`:

```
>> url =
'https://archive.ics.uci.edu/ml/machine-learning-databases/00243/yacht_hydr
odynamics.data';
```

Now, we save the content into a file named `yacht_hydrodynamics.csv`:

```
>> websave('yacht_hydrodynamics.csv',url);
```

We set the names of the variables in accordance with the previous example:

```
>> varnames = {'LongPos'; 'PrismaticCoef'; 'LengDispRatio';
'BeamDraughtRatio'; ' LengthBeamRatio ';'FroudeNumber';'ResResistance'};
```

Read the data into a table and specify the variable names:

```
>> YachtHydrodynamics = readtable('yacht_hydrodynamics.csv');
>> YachtHydrodynamics.Properties.VariableNames = varnames;
```

So, the data is now available in the MATLAB workspace, in table form; now we can perform a stepwise regression. In the following figure, the first rows of the `YachtHydrodynamics` table are shown:

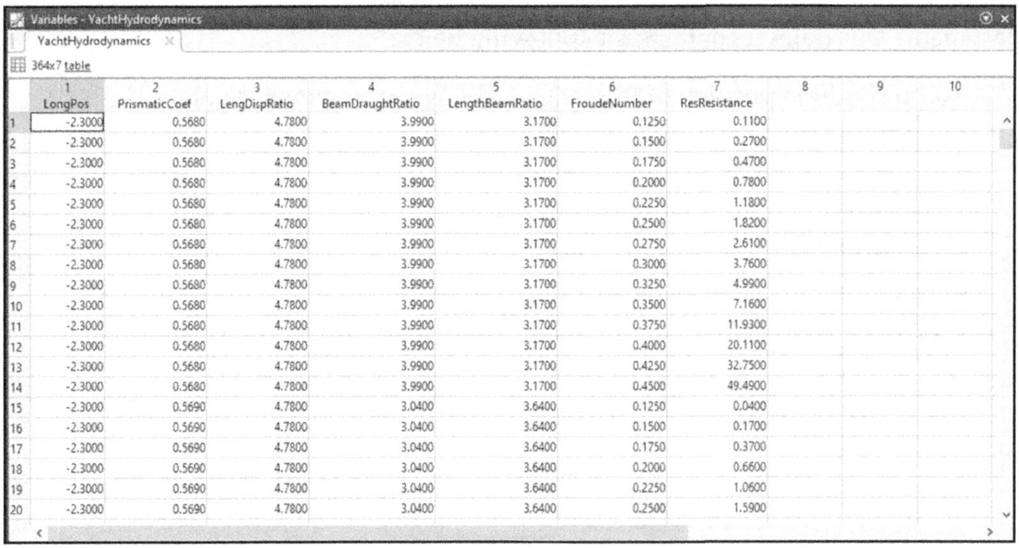

	1 LongPos	2 PrismaticCoef	3 LengDispRatio	4 BeamDraughtRatio	5 LengthBeamRatio	6 FroudeNumber	7 ResResistance	8	9	10
1	-2.3000	0.5680	4.7800	3.9900	3.1700	0.1250	0.1100			
2	-2.3000	0.5680	4.7800	3.9900	3.1700	0.1500	0.2700			
3	-2.3000	0.5680	4.7800	3.9900	3.1700	0.1750	0.4700			
4	-2.3000	0.5680	4.7800	3.9900	3.1700	0.2000	0.7800			
5	-2.3000	0.5680	4.7800	3.9900	3.1700	0.2250	1.1800			
6	-2.3000	0.5680	4.7800	3.9900	3.1700	0.2500	1.8200			
7	-2.3000	0.5680	4.7800	3.9900	3.1700	0.2750	2.6100			
8	-2.3000	0.5680	4.7800	3.9900	3.1700	0.3000	3.7600			
9	-2.3000	0.5680	4.7800	3.9900	3.1700	0.3250	4.9900			
10	-2.3000	0.5680	4.7800	3.9900	3.1700	0.3500	7.1600			
11	-2.3000	0.5680	4.7800	3.9900	3.1700	0.3750	11.9300			
12	-2.3000	0.5680	4.7800	3.9900	3.1700	0.4000	20.1100			
13	-2.3000	0.5680	4.7800	3.9900	3.1700	0.4250	32.7500			
14	-2.3000	0.5680	4.7800	3.9900	3.1700	0.4500	49.4900			
15	-2.3000	0.5690	4.7800	3.0400	3.6400	0.1250	0.0400			
16	-2.3000	0.5690	4.7800	3.0400	3.6400	0.1500	0.1700			
17	-2.3000	0.5690	4.7800	3.0400	3.6400	0.1750	0.3700			
18	-2.3000	0.5690	4.7800	3.0400	3.6400	0.2000	0.6600			
19	-2.3000	0.5690	4.7800	3.0400	3.6400	0.2250	1.0600			
20	-2.3000	0.5690	4.7800	3.0400	3.6400	0.2500	1.5900			

Figure 8.3: YachtHydrodynamics dataset

We print a summary of the main features:

```
>> summary(YachtHydrodynamics)
Variables:
    LongPos: 364x1 double
        Values:
            Min             -5
            Median          -2.3
            Max             60.85
    PrismaticCoef: 364x1 double
        Values:
            Min             0.53
            Median          0.565
            Max             0.6
            NumMissing      112
    LengDispRatio: 364x1 double
        Values:
            Min             0.53
            Median          4.78
            Max             5.14
            NumMissing      56
    BeamDraughtRatio: 364x1 double
        Values:
            Min             2.81
            Median          3.99
            Max             5.35
            NumMissing      56
    LengthBeamRatio: 364x1 double
        Values:
            Min             2.73
            Median          3.17
            Max             4.24
            NumMissing      56
    FroudeNumber: 364x1 double
        Values:
            Min             0.125
            Median          0.325
            Max             3.51
            NumMissing      56
    ResResistance: 364x1 double
        Values:
            Min             0.01
            Median          1.79
            Max             62.42
            NumMissing      56
```

From a preliminary analysis of the statistics, you will notice a fair number of missing values (NaN). This is not a problem, as the `stepwiselm()` function ignores them. However, we recall that it is possible to find, replace, or remove those rows by using the following functions respectively: `ismissing()`, `standardizeMissing()`, and `rmmissing()`. We analyzed these in detail in Chapter 3, *From Data to Knowledge Discovery*.

To avoid problems in subsequent calculations, we should remove the rows with missing values. To this end, we will use the `rmmissing()` function to remove missing entries from an array or table:

```
>> YachtHydrodynamicsClean = rmmissing(YachtHydrodynamics);
```

To confirm the removal, we display the size of the two tables that appear in MATLAB's workspace:

```
>> size(YachtHydrodynamics)
ans =
    364     7
>> size(YachtHydrodynamicsClean)
ans =
    252     7
```

The `YachtHydrodynamicsClean` table contains fewer rows because the rows with missing values have been removed. To get further confirmation, we can print the summary again:

```
>> summary(YachtHydrodynamicsClean);
```

No missing values are listed (I do not propose listing them for space reasons). To better understand how to the MATLAB function works, it is advisable to have the response values in vector form and the predictive terms in matrix form. We have them in the form of a table; they can be transformed into arrays:

```
>> X =table2array(YachtHydrodynamicsClean(:,1:6));
>> Y =table2array(YachtHydrodynamicsClean(:,7));
```

Before passing our data to the `stepwiselm()` function, we need to give a first look to what we've got in the `YachtHydrodynamicsClean` dataset. To do this, we will draw a simple scatter plot for each predictive variable versus the response variable:

```
>> subplot(2,3,1)
>> scatter(X(:,1),Y)
>> subplot(2,3,2)
>> scatter(X(:,2),Y)
>> subplot(2,3,3)
>> scatter(X(:,3),Y)
>> subplot(2,3,4)
```

```
>> scatter(X(:,4),Y)
>> subplot(2,3,5)
>> scatter(X(:,5),Y)
>> subplot(2,3,6)
>> scatter(X(:,6),Y)
```

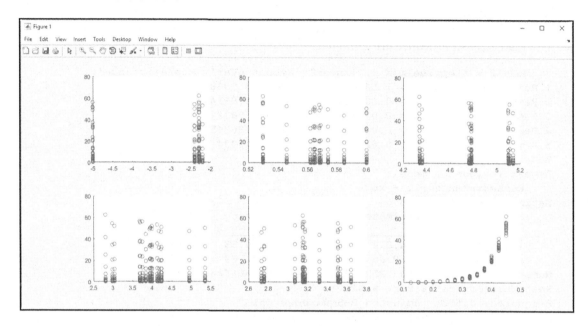

Figure 8.4: A table of scatter plots; each plot represents a scatter plot of predictive variable versus response variable

From a quick analysis of the plots, we can see that the sixth predictive variable (FroudeNumber) seems to be particularly correlated with the response variable (the bottom-right plot of *Figure 8.4*). Let's see if we find confirmation from the feature selection analysis.

To create a residuary resistance stepwise model starting from the constant model, simply type:

```
>> Model1 = stepwiselm(X,Y,'constant','ResponseVar','ResResistance')
1.Adding x6, FStat = 470.0273, pValue = 2.334071e-59
Model1 =
Linear regression model:
    ResResistance ~ 1 + x6
Estimated Coefficients:
                    Estimate       SE       tStat        pValue

    (Intercept)     -24.074     1.6799     -14.33     2.0954e-34
    x6               119.55     5.5142      21.68     2.3341e-59
Number of observations: 252, Error degrees of freedom: 250
```

```
Root Mean Squared Error: 8.82
R-squared: 0.653,   Adjusted R-Squared 0.651
F-statistic vs. constant model: 470, p-value = 2.33e-59
```

As we started from a constant, the function added only the variables that it considered statistically significant (x6 = FroudeNumber). Let's try starting from a linear model that contains an intercept and linear terms for each predictor. Subsequently, step by step, terms with no statistical significance are removed:

```
>> Model2 = stepwiselm(X,Y,'linear','ResponseVar','ResResistance')
1.Removing x5, FStat = 1.568e-05, pValue = 0.99684
2.Removing x4, FStat = 0.0021018, pValue = 0.96347
3.Removing x1, FStat = 0.014617, pValue = 0.90387
4.Removing x3, FStat = 0.029568, pValue = 0.86361
5.Removing x2, FStat = 0.62393, pValue = 0.43034
Model2 =
Linear regression model:
    ResResistance ~ 1 + x6
Estimated Coefficients:
                    Estimate      SE       tStat       pValue

    (Intercept)     -24.074     1.6799    -14.33    2.0954e-34
    x6               119.55     5.5142     21.68    2.3341e-59
Number of observations: 252, Error degrees of freedom: 250
Root Mean Squared Error: 8.82
R-squared: 0.653,   Adjusted R-Squared 0.651
F-statistic vs. constant model: 470, p-value = 2.33e-59
```

Now, let's see what happens if we start from the full interaction model. This model starts with an intercept, linear terms for each predictor, and all products of pairs of distinct predictors (no squared terms). Subsequently, terms with no statistical significance are removed:

```
>> Model3 = stepwiselm(X,Y,'interactions','ResponseVar','ResResistance')
1.Removing x4:x6, FStat = 2.038e-05, pValue = 0.9964
2.Removing x2:x3, FStat = 7.8141e-05, pValue = 0.99295
3.Removing x1:x3, FStat = 0.0030525, pValue = 0.95599
4.Removing x1:x4, FStat = 0.0016424, pValue = 0.96771
5.Removing x4:x5, FStat = 0.006498, pValue = 0.93582
6.Removing x3:x4, FStat = 0.0022245, pValue = 0.96242
7.Removing x2:x4, FStat = 0.031089, pValue = 0.86019
8.Removing x4, FStat = 0.022261, pValue = 0.88152
9.Removing x1:x6, FStat = 0.038943, pValue = 0.84373
10.Removing x2:x5, FStat = 0.051739, pValue = 0.82026
11.Removing x3:x5, FStat = 0.03084, pValue = 0.86074
12.Removing x1:x5, FStat = 0.027003, pValue = 0.86961
13Removing x1:x2, FStat = 0.030884, pValue = 0.86065
```

```
14Removing x1, FStat = 0.014759, pValue = 0.90341
15.Removing x5:x6, FStat = 0.083209, pValue = 0.77324
16.Removing x5, FStat = 0.001841, pValue = 0.96581
17.Removing x3:x6, FStat = 0.18793, pValue = 0.66503
18.Removing x3, FStat = 0.029651, pValue = 0.86342
19.Removing x2:x6, FStat = 1.7045, pValue = 0.1929
20.Removing x2, FStat = 0.62393, pValue = 0.43034
Model3 =
Linear regression model:
    ResResistance ~ 1 + x6
Estimated Coefficients:
                    Estimate      SE        tStat        pValue
                    _____    _____    _____    _____

    (Intercept)     -24.074      1.6799     -14.33    2.0954e-34
    x6               119.55      5.5142      21.68    2.3341e-59
Number of observations: 252, Error degrees of freedom: 250
Root Mean Squared Error: 8.82
R-squared: 0.653,   Adjusted R-Squared 0.651
F-statistic vs. constant model: 470, p-value = 2.33e-59
```

The result is the same, but the procedure followed is different. In this case, we started from a model which contains all variables and their interactions. Subsequently, the function gradually removed the less important variables (high p-value) and their interactions.

Let's finally see what happens by creating a full quadratic model as the upper bound, starting from the full quadratic model. At the beginning, this model contains an intercept, linear terms, interactions, and squared terms for each predictor. Subsequently, terms with no statistical significance are removed. The idea of inserting a quadratic term is suggested by an analysis of *Figure 8.4*, specifically from the bottom-right plot:

```
>> Model4 =
stepwiselm(X,Y,'quadratic','ResponseVar','ResResistance','Upper','quadratic
')
Removing x1:x2, FStat = Inf, pValue = NaN
Removing x1:x3, FStat = Inf, pValue = NaN
Removing x1:x4, FStat = -Inf, pValue = NaN
Removing x4:x6, FStat = 9.5953e-05, pValue = 0.99219
Removing x2^2, FStat = 0.0082475, pValue = 0.92772
Removing x1^2, FStat = 0.040083, pValue = 0.8415
Removing x1:x5, FStat = 0.081041, pValue = 0.77615
Removing x4^2, FStat = 0.11143, pValue = 0.73882
Removing x2:x5, FStat = 0.010871, pValue = 0.91705
Removing x5^2, FStat = 0.023037, pValue = 0.87949
Removing x2:x3, FStat = 0.0091051, pValue = 0.92406
Removing x4:x5, FStat = 0.10571, pValue = 0.74537
Removing x3^2, FStat = 0.05183, pValue = 0.82011
Removing x3:x5, FStat = 0.0016867, pValue = 0.96727
```

```
Removing x3:x4, FStat = 0.0023858, pValue = 0.96108
Removing x1:x6, FStat = 0.18625, pValue = 0.66644
Removing x1, FStat = 0.040299, pValue = 0.84107
Removing x5:x6, FStat = 0.39137, pValue = 0.53217
Removing x5, FStat = 0.0053964, pValue = 0.9415
Removing x2:x4, FStat = 0.56395, pValue = 0.4534
Removing x4, FStat = 0.012446, pValue = 0.91126
Removing x3:x6, FStat = 0.888, pValue = 0.34695
Removing x3, FStat = 0.13971, pValue = 0.70889
Model4 =
Linear regression model:
    ResResistance ~ 1 + x2*x6 + x6^2
Estimated Coefficients:
                 Estimate       SE        tStat         pValue

    (Intercept)   -1.7269     19.175    -0.09006       0.92831
    x2             71.135     33.777     2.106         0.036212
    x6            -198.69     64.67     -3.0723        0.0023618
    x2:x6         -314.14    110.87     -2.8334        0.0049859
    x6^2           861.56     28.389    30.349         2.6482e-85
Number of observations: 252, Error degrees of freedom: 247
Root Mean Squared Error: 4.06
R-squared: 0.927,  Adjusted R-Squared 0.926
F-statistic vs. constant model: 787, p-value = 3.1e-139
```

This time, the return model is more complex. The variable $x6$ is present as the square and it also includes the interaction between this variable and $x2$. Although more complex, it certainly is more representative of the phenomenon given the results obtained (R-squared= 0.927, Adjusted R-Squared =0.926, p-value = 3.1e-139).

We have seen that, starting from different models, the stepwiselm() function returns different results. Let's then compare these results. The first thing we can do is compare the adjusted R-squared values:

```
>> RSquared = [Model1.Rsquared.Adjusted,Model2.Rsquared.Adjusted,
               Model3.Rsquared.Adjusted,Model4.Rsquared.Adjusted]
RSquared =
    0.6514    0.6514    0.6514    0.9261
```

The first three models provide substantially the same results, while the fourth has a significant improvement. To extract more useful information to compare different models, we can draw residual plots of the four models. For this purpose, we will use the `plotResiduals()` function; it plots the raw conditional residuals of the linear mixed-effects model in a plot of type specified by the user. In this case, we will plot residuals versus fitted values:

```
>> subplot(2,2,1)
>> plotResiduals(Model1,'fitted')
>> subplot(2,2,2)
>> plotResiduals(Model2,'fitted')
>> subplot(2,2,3)
>> plotResiduals(Model3,'fitted')
>> subplot(2,2,4)
>> plotResiduals(Model4,'fitted')
```

 Remember, the residual is the difference between the observed value and the predicted value. A residual is an observable estimate of an unobservable statistical error.

In the following figure, the plot of residuals versus fitted values for the four models built earlier is shown:

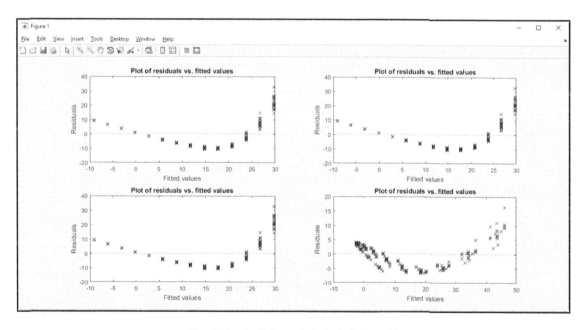

Figure 8.5: Plot of residuals versus fitted values for the four models

The first three models are practically identical. We can get the same result by analyzing the formulas of the models with their intercept. All four plots suggest non-linearity of the distribution. But in the fourth model, the residuals seem more concentrated. To confirm this, we will calculate the deviations of the residuals:

```
>> Rrange1 = [min(Model1.Residuals.Raw),max(Model1.Residuals.Raw)];
>> Rrange2 = [min(Model2.Residuals.Raw),max(Model2.Residuals.Raw)];
>> Rrange3 = [min(Model3.Residuals.Raw),max(Model3.Residuals.Raw)];
>> Rrange4 = [min(Model4.Residuals.Raw),max(Model4.Residuals.Raw)];
>> Rranges = [Rrange1;Rrange2;Rrange3;Rrange4]
Rranges =
   -10.9093    32.6973
   -10.9093    32.6973
   -10.9093    32.6973
    -6.8535    16.3131
```

Indeed, the more complex models have a minimum number of deviations of residuals with respect to the others.

Feature extraction

When the data is too large to be processed, it is transformed into a reduced representation set of features. The process of transforming the input data into a set of features is called **feature extraction**. Indeed, feature extraction starts from an initial set of measured data and builds derivative values that can retain the information contained in the original dataset, but emptied of redundant data, as shown in the following figure:

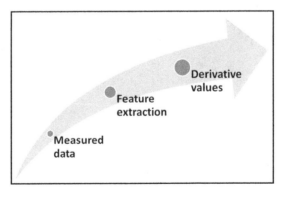

Figure 8.6: Feature extraction workflow

In this way, the subsequent learning and generalization phases will be facilitated and, in some cases, will lead to better interpretations. It is a process of deriving new features from the original features in order to reduce the cost of feature measurement, increase classifier efficiency, and allow higher classification accuracy. If the features extracted are carefully chosen, it is expected that the features set will perform the desired task using the reduced representation instead of the full size input.

Principal Component Analysis

One of the greatest difficulties encountered in multivariate statistical analysis is the problem of displaying a dataset with many variables. Fortunately, in datasets with many variables, some parts of data are often closely related to each other. This is because they actually contain the same information, as they measure the same quantity that governs the behavior of the system. These are therefore redundant variables that add nothing to the model we want to build. We can then simplify the problem by replacing a group of variables with a new variable that encloses the information content. The following figure shows redundant data in a table:

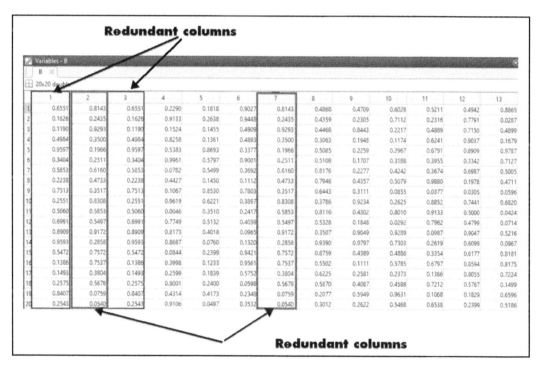

Figure 8.7: Redundant data in a table

PCA generates a new set of variables, among them uncorrelated, called **principal components**; each main component is a linear combination of the original variables. All principal components are orthogonal to each other, so there is no redundant information. The principal components as a whole constitute an orthogonal basis for the data space. The goal of PCA is to explain the maximum amount of variance with the least number of principal components. PCA is a form of multidimensional scaling. It is a linear transformation of the variables into a lower dimensional space which retains maximum amount of information about the variables. A principal component is therefore a combination of the original variables after a linear transformation.

In MATLAB, PCA is performed by using the `pca()` function; it returns the principal component coefficients, also known as **loadings**, for the *n-by-p* data matrix given by the users. Rows of this matrix correspond to observations and columns correspond to variables. The coefficient matrix is *p-by-p*. Each column of `coeff` contains coefficients for one principal component, and the columns are in descending order of component variance. By default, PCA centers the data and uses the **Singular Value Decomposition (SVD)** algorithm.

As always, we begin by getting the data to be analyzed.

 To get the data, we draw on the large collection of data available from the UCI Machine Learning Repository at the following link: `http://archive.ics.uci.edu/ml`

In this study, we use a seeds dataset, which contains measurements of the geometrical properties of kernels belonging to three different varieties of wheat. As reported on the site, the examined group comprises kernels belonging to three different varieties of wheat (Kama, Rosa, and Canadian), with *70* elements each, randomly selected for the experiment. High-quality visualization of the internal kernel structure was detected using a soft X-ray technique. The images were recorded on *13 x 18* cm X-ray KODAK plates. Studies were conducted using combine-harvested wheat grain originating from experimental fields, explored at the Institute of Agrophysics of the Polish Academy of Sciences in Lublin.

The seeds dataset is multivariate, consisting of *210* instances. Seven geometric parameters of the wheat kernel are used as real-valued attributes organizing an instance. These seven attributes are:

- Area *A*
- Perimeter *P*
- Compactness *C = 4*pi*A/P^2*
- Length of kernel
- Width of kernel
- Asymmetry coefficient
- Length of kernel groove

The seeds dataset contains *210* records of *3* kinds of wheat seed specification; there are *70* points of each kind.

To start, we download the data from the UCI Machine Learning Repository and save it in our current folder. To do this, we will use the `websave()` function; it saves content from the web service specified by the URL address and writes it to a file. We insert the URL address to the specific dataset into a variable named `url`:

```
>> url =
'http://archive.ics.uci.edu/ml/machine-learning-databases/00236/seeds_datas
et.txt';
```

Now, we save the content into a file named `seeds_dataset.csv`:

```
>> websave('seeds_dataset.csv',url);
```

We set the names of the variables in accordance with the previous example:

```
>> varnames = {'Area'; 'Perimeter'; 'Compactness'; 'LengthK';
'WidthK';'AsymCoef';'LengthKG';'Seeds'};
```

Read the data into a table and specify the variable names:

```
>> Seeds_dataset = readtable('seeds_dataset.csv');
>> Seeds_dataset.Properties.VariableNames = varnames;
```

So, the data is now available in the MATLAB workspace in table form. Now we can perform a PCA. Before we start, just a moment! Do you remember the missing values in the dataset used in stepwise regression? Let's see if they are also in this dataset:

```
>> MissingValue = ismissing(Seeds_dataset);
```

This command returns a logical array that indicates which elements of an array or table contain missing values. To extract only the rows that contain missing values, simply type:

```
>> RowsMissValue = find(any(MissingValue==1,2));
```

This command returns a *22x1* column vector representing the number of the rows that contain missing values. To avoid problems in subsequent calculations, we should remove these 22 rows from `Seeds_dataset`. To this end, we will use the `rmmissing()` function to remove missing entries from an array or table:

```
>> Seeds_dataset =  rmmissing(Seeds_dataset);
```

From a *221x8* table, the `Seeds_dataset` now contains *199x8* double data. The first 15 rows of the `Seeds_dataset` table have been cleaned, as shown here:

	1	2	3	4	5	6	7	8	9
	Area	Perimeter	Compactness	LengthK	WidthK	AsymCoef	LengthKG	Seeds	
1	15.2600	14.8400	0.8710	5.7630	3.3120	2.2210	5.2200	1	
2	14.8800	14.5700	0.8811	5.5540	3.3330	1.0180	4.9560	1	
3	14.2900	14.0900	0.9050	5.2910	3.3370	2.6990	4.8250	1	
4	13.8400	13.9400	0.8955	5.3240	3.3790	2.2590	4.8050	1	
5	16.1400	14.9900	0.9034	5.6580	3.5620	1.3550	5.1750	1	
6	14.3800	14.2100	0.8951	5.3860	3.3120	2.4620	4.9560	1	
7	14.6900	14.4900	0.8799	5.5630	3.2590	3.5860	5.2190	1	
8	16.6300	15.4600	0.8747	6.0530	3.4650	2.0400	5.8770	1	
9	16.4400	15.2500	0.8880	5.8840	3.5050	1.9690	5.5330	1	
10	15.2600	14.8500	0.8696	5.7140	3.2420	4.5430	5.3140	1	
11	14.0300	14.1600	0.8796	5.4380	3.2010	1.7170	5.0010	1	
12	13.8900	14.0200	0.8880	5.4390	3.1990	3.9860	4.7380	1	
13	13.7800	14.0600	0.8759	5.4790	3.1560	3.1360	4.8720	1	
14	13.7400	14.0500	0.8744	5.4820	3.1140	2.9320	4.8250	1	
15	14.5900	14.2800	0.8993	5.3510	3.3330	4.1850	4.7810	1	

Figure 8.8: First 15 rows of the Seeds_dataset table cleaned (no NaN values are included)

Before passing our data to the `pca()` function, we need to give a first look to what we've got in the `Seeds_dataset` table. The first seven columns contain the measured variables, while the eighth variable is the type of seed. Let's first try to find out whether the variables are related to each other. We can do this using the `plotmatrix()` function to create a matrix of sub-axes containing scatter plots of the columns of a matrix. But we have a table, so they need to extract only the measured variables into a single matrix:

```
>> VarMeas = table2array((Seeds_dataset(:,1:7)));
>> SeedClass = table2array((Seeds_dataset(:,8)));
```

Now we can use the `plotmatrix()` function:

```
>> plotmatrix(VarMeas)
```

The sub-axes along the diagonal are histogram plots of the data in the corresponding column of the matrix, while the rest of the plots are scatter plots of the columns of a matrix (the subplot in the ith row and j^{th} column of the matrix is a scatter plot of the ith column against the jth column), as shown in the following figure:

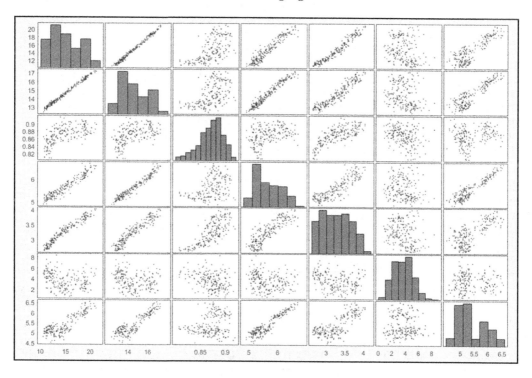

Figure 8.9: Scatter plot matrix of the measured variables

As we can see in *Figure 8.9*, scatter plot matrices are a great way to roughly determine whether you have a linear correlation between multiple variables. This is particularly helpful in locating specific variables that might have mutual correlations, indicating a possible redundancy of data. As already mentioned, in the diagonal are histogram plots of the measured variables, which provide us with a measure of the distribution of its values. The rest of the plots are scatter plots of the matrix columns. Specifically, each plot is present twice; the plots on the ith row are the same as those in the ith column (mirror image).

From a first analysis of *Figure 8.8*, you can see several plots showing a linear relationship between the variables. This is the case of the plot showing the relationship between Area and Perimeter, as well as between Perimeter and LengthK, just to name a couple; while no correlation can be found for other pairs of variables. For example, the variable LengthKG has no correlation with any variable; in fact, the data is distributed throughout the plot area.

This first visual analysis can be confirmed by calculating the linear correlation between the measured variables. We will use the corr() function to return a matrix containing the pairwise linear correlation coefficient (r) between each pair of columns in the matrix given by the user:

```
>> r = corr(VarMeas)
r =
 1.0000    0.9944    0.6099    0.9511    0.9710   -0.2228    0.8627
 0.9944    1.0000    0.5318    0.9729    0.9455   -0.2110    0.8895
 0.6099    0.5318    1.0000    0.3740    0.7622   -0.3294    0.2270
 0.9511    0.9729    0.3740    1.0000    0.8627   -0.1697    0.9321
 0.9710    0.9455    0.7622    0.8627    1.0000   -0.2531    0.7482
-0.2228   -0.2110   -0.3294   -0.1697   -0.2531    1.0000   -0.0033
 0.8627    0.8895    0.2270    0.9321    0.7482   -0.0033    1.0000
```

The correlation coefficient has to be between -1.0 and 1.0 (*0= no correlation; -1/1=high negative/positive correlation*). What is suggested in *Figure 8.8* is confirmed by the preceding table. To better understand the concept of correlation, we analyze in detail the first row of plots shown in *Figure 8.9*; for each of them, we provide the value of the newly calculated correlation coefficient, as shown in the following figure:

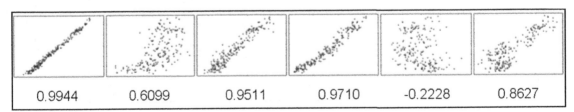

| 0.9944 | 0.6099 | 0.9511 | 0.9710 | -0.2228 | 0.8627 |

Figure 8.10: Scatter plot of the first variable versus the others with relative correlation coefficient

From *Figure 8.10*, we can understand a lot:

- In the first plot to the left, the data points are placed on a straight line, showing a correlation of nearly +1, as confirmed by the correlation coefficient (**0.9944**).
- In the second plot, the data shows an increasing trend but is less grouped on the straight line, indicating a moderate linear relationship (**0.6099**).
- In the third plot, the data is again placed on a straight line showing a correlation of nearly +1, but to a lesser extent than the first plot, as confirmed by the correlation coefficient (**0.9511**).
- A similar thing happens for the fourth plot (**0.9710**).
- The fifth plot, however, shows a different trend than the ones seen so far. In it, the trend is decreasing (r is negative) and the data is extremely scattered. Indeed, the correlation coefficient is close to zero (**-0.2228**).
- Finally, the sixth plot shows a strong uphill (positive) linear relationship (**0.8627**).

One may ask why we must analyze both the graphs and the coefficients. In some cases, the plots tell us what r does not. Indeed, if the scatter plot doesn't indicate there's at least somewhat of a linear relationship, the correlation calculation doesn't mean much. Then, two things can happen:

- If no relationship at all exists, calculating the correlation doesn't make sense, because correlation only applies to linear relationships
- If a strong relationship exists but it's not linear, the correlation may be misleading, because in some cases a strong curved relationship exists

That's why it's critical to examine the scatter plot. As we can notice in the r matrix, the correlation among some variables is as high as *0.85*. This means that there is a good linear correlation between some variables, so there is some data redundancy in the data matrix measured. PCA constructs new independent variables that are linear combinations of the original variables. It's time to run PCA:

```
>> [coeff,score,latent,tsquared,explained,mu] = pca(VarMeas);
```

This code returns the following information:

- coeff: The principal component coefficients
- score: The principal component scores
- latent: The principal component variances

- `tsquared`: Hotelling's T-squared statistic for each observation
- `explained`: The percentage of the total variance explained by each principal component
- `mu`: The estimated mean of each variable

When the variables are in different units or the difference in the variance of different columns is substantial, scaling of the data or use of weights is often preferable. By default, the `pca()` function centers the matrix given by the user by subtracting column means before computing singular value decomposition or eigenvalue decomposition.

Furthermore, to perform our PCA, three different algorithms are available:

- Singular value decomposition (`'svd'`)
- Eigenvalue decomposition of the covariance matrix (`'eig'`)
- Alternating least squares algorithm (`'als'`)

By default, the `pca()` function uses the singular value decomposition algorithm.

Now, we analyze the results obtained by applying the `pca()` function in detail. Let's start with the `coeff` variable, which contains the principal component coefficients:

```
>> coeff
coeff =
0.8852     0.0936    -0.2625     0.2034     0.1394    -0.2780    -0.0254
0.3958     0.0532     0.2779    -0.5884    -0.5721     0.2922     0.0659
0.0043    -0.0030    -0.0578     0.0581     0.0524     0.0452     0.9942
0.1286     0.0285     0.3967    -0.4293     0.7905     0.1267     0.0003
0.1110     0.0008    -0.3168     0.2392     0.1268     0.8986    -0.0804
-0.1195     0.9903    -0.0659    -0.0262     0.0030    -0.0027     0.0011
0.1290     0.0832     0.7671     0.6057    -0.0973     0.1078     0.0092
```

The rows of `coeff` contain the coefficients for the seven variables contained in the `VarMeas` matrix, and its columns correspond to seven principal components. Each column of `coeff` contains coefficients for one principal component, and the columns are in descending order of component variance. Each column contains coefficients that determine the linear combination of the starting variables that represent the information in the new dimensional space.

A generic principal component is defined as a linear combination of the original variables p weighed for a vector u. The first principal component is the linear combination of p variables with higher variance; the second is the linear combination of p variables with an immediately lower variance, subject to the constraint of being orthogonal to the previous component; and so on. For example, the first principal component is represented by the following equation:

```
PC1 = 0.8852* Area + 0.3958   * Perimeter + 0.0043 * Compactness + 0.1286 *
LengthK + 0.1110 * WidthK - 0.1195 * AsymCoef + 0.1290 * LengthKG
```

There are as many principal components as there are observed variables, and each one is obtained as a linear combination at maximum variance under the non-correlation constraint with all the previous ones.

The second output, score, contains the coordinates of the original data in the new dimensional space defined by the principal components. The score matrix is of the same `size` as the input data matrix:

```
>> size(VarMeas)
ans =
    199     7
>> size(score)
ans =
    199     7
```

Our purpose was to represent the dataset in the new space characterized by a smaller number of dimensions. Then, we create a plot of the first two columns of score (the first two principal components).

Remember, the score contains the coordinates of the original data in the new coordinate system defined by the principal components.

To make the graph more understandable, we group the data per class:

```
>> gscatter(score(:,1),score(:,2),SeedClass,'brg','xo^')
```

In the following figure, the scatter plot for the new feature obtained (the first two principal components) is shown:

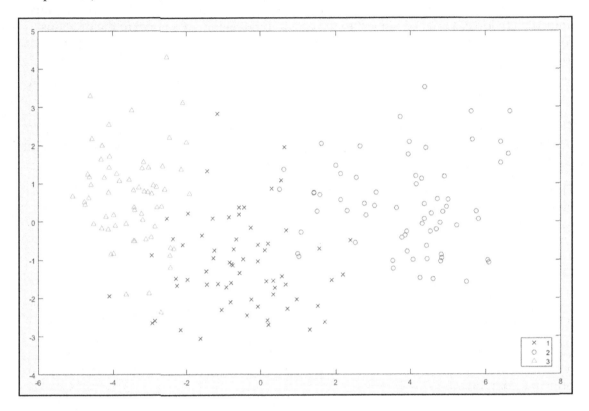

Figure 8.11: The scatter plot for the first two principal components

Figure 8.11 clearly classifies the seeds into three relative classes. The different points are distributed in different areas of the plot, leaving only minimal uncertainty in border areas. To locate such points, we can use the gname() function. This function displays a figure window and waits for you to press a mouse button. Moving the mouse over the plot displays a pair of cross hairs. If you position the cross hairs near a point with the mouse and click once, the plot displays the label corresponding to that point (right-click on a point to remove its label). When you are done labeling points, press *Enter* or *Esc* to stop labeling.

The window with the scatter plot is already open, so we can type the command:

```
>> gname
```

By clicking on the points near the borders that seem uncertain, we can locate the record number for that observation (row number of the dataset), as shown in the following figure:

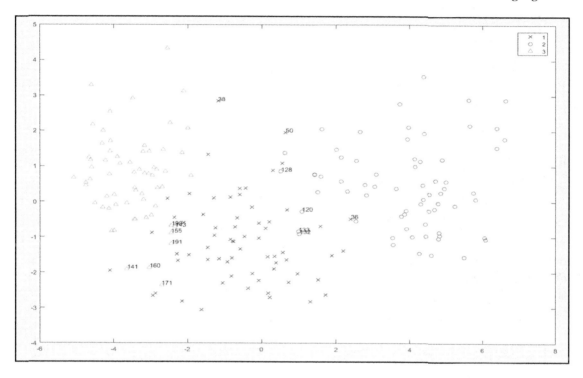

Figure 8.12: Points with classification uncertainty

From an analysis of *Figure 8.12*, we can derive the number of the row corresponding to the observation that, according to the plot, is suitable for uncertain classification. The purpose is to analyze the variable's values for such occurrences so as to understand the reason for its ambiguous positioning.

We now return to the results provided by using the `pca()` function. The third output obtained, named latent, is a vector containing the variance explained by the corresponding principal component. Each column of score has a sample variance equal to the corresponding row of latent. As already mentioned before, the column is in descending order of component variance:

```
>> latent
latent =
    10.8516
     2.0483
     0.0738
     0.0127
     0.0028
     0.0016
     0.0000
```

It is convenient to chart these values to understand the meaning:

```
>> plot(latent)
>> xlabel('Principal Component')
>> ylabel('Variance Explained ')
```

A scree plot displays the explained variance associated with a principal component in descending order versus the number of the principal component. We can use scree plots in PCA to visually assess which components explain most of the variability in the data, as shown in the following figure:

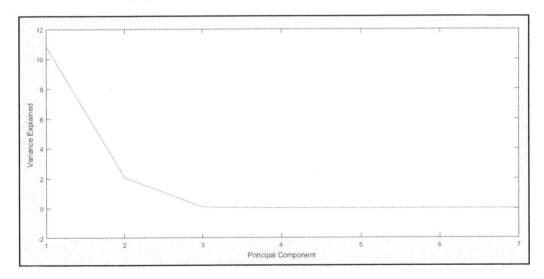

Figure 8.13: Variance explained for each principal component

Generally, we extract the components on the steep slope. The components on the shallow slope contribute little to the solution. The last big drop occurs between the second and third components, so we choose the first two components.

To better understand this choice, we can make a scree plot of the percent variability explained by the first two principal component. The percent variability explained is returned in the explained variables from the `pca()` function.

```
>> figure()
>> pareto(explained(1:2))
>> xlabel('Principal Component')
>> ylabel('Variance Explained (%)')
```

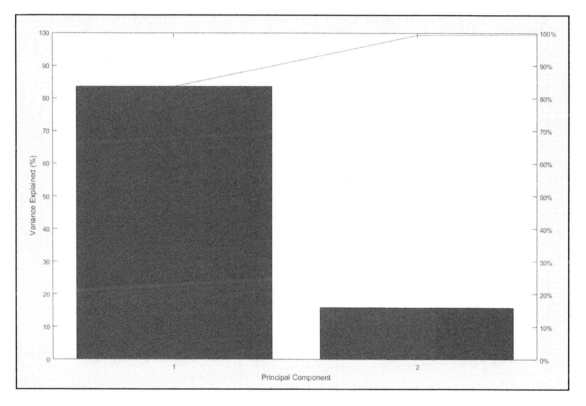

Figure 8.14: Scree plot of the percent variability explained by each principal component

In *Figure 8.14*, there are two pieces of information; the bar plot shows the proportion of variance for each principal component, while the upper line shows the cumulative variance explained by the first two components. An analysis of *Figure 8.14* confirms the choice made earlier, since the first two main components offer more than *99* percent of the explained variance.

Finally, we just have to visualize both the principal component coefficients for each variable and the principal component scores for each observation in a single plot. This type of plot is named `biplot`:

 Biplots are a type of exploration plot used to simultaneously display graphic information on the samples and variables of a data matrix. Samples are displayed as points, while variables are displayed as vectors.

```
>>biplot(coeff(:,1:2),'scores',score(:,1:2),'varlabels',varnames(1:7));
```

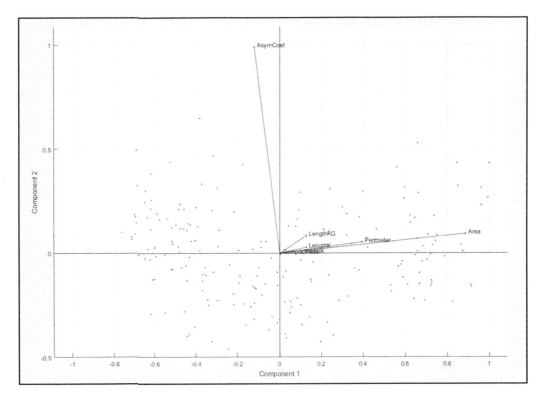

Figure 8.15: Biplot of the principal component coefficients for each variable and principal component scores for each observation

All seven variables are represented in this biplot by a vector, and the direction and length of the vector indicate how each variable contributes to the two principal components in the plot. For example, the first principal component, on the horizontal axis, has positive coefficients for six variables; only the `AsymCoef` variable has a negative coefficient. That is why six vectors are directed into the right half of the plot and only one is directed into the left half. The largest coefficient in the first principal component is the first element, corresponding to the variable `Area`.

The second principal component, on the vertical axis, has positive coefficients for six variables and only one negative coefficient for the `Compactness` variables (close to zero). Moreover, the length of the vectors makes us understand clearly what the weight of each variable is in the corresponding principal component. It is clear then, that the `Area` variable assumes a preponderant weight over the others in the first principal component. The same applies to the `AsymCoef` variable for the second principal component.

Summary

In this chapter, we learned how to select a feature that best represents a set of data. We gained an understanding the basic concept of dimensionality reduction. We saw how to perform a feature extraction procedure for dimensionality reduction when transformation of variables is possible. We also explored stepwise regression and PCA.

We learned how to use the `stepwiselm()` function to create a linear model and automatically add/remove variables from the model. We also saw how to create a small model starting from a constant model, and how to create a large model starting from a model containing many terms. We reviewed the methods to remove missing values from a dataset.

Subsequently, we covered the techniques for extracting features. In particular, we analyzed PCA. PCA is a quantitatively rigorous method for achieving this simplification. The method generates a new set of variables, called principal components. Each principal component is a linear combination of the original variables. All the principal components are orthogonal to each other, so there is no redundant information. The principal components as a whole form an orthogonal basis for the space of the data.

We learned how to use the `pca()` function to perform PCA. We learned how to calculate the coefficients, the scores, and the variances of each principal component. Furthermore, we discovered how to extract the Hotelling's T-squared statistic for each observation, the percentage of the total variance explained by each principal component, and the estimated mean of each variable.

Finally, we learned how to read a scree plot and a biplot to explain the feature obtained from PCA.

In the next chapter, after analyzing the different machine learning algorithms in detail, we will apply them by performing practical examples. This last chapter is meant to be a short reference, covering some of the major machine learning algorithms. In it, you will just apply what you've learned to real-world cases. You can explore regression, classification, and clustering algorithms applied to datasets resulting from such cases.

Machine Learning in Practice

In Chapter 1, *Getting Started with MATLAB Machine Learning*, we said that machine learning is based on the concept of learning by example--knowledge gained by starting from a set of positive examples or instances of the concept to be learned, and negative examples or non-instances of the concept. In this regard, let's not forget that this concept is borrowed from the human experience, which has always been based on learning on analysis through the series of examples.

After analyzing in detail the different machine learning algorithms, it is time to put them to practice. This last chapter is meant to be a short reference, covering some of the major machine learning algorithms. In this chapter, you will just apply what has been learned. You can explore regression, classification, and clustering algorithms applied to datasets resulting from real cases. The basic concepts we have learned from the previous chapters, we will now put them into practice. If we need to reinforce these concepts, we can safely go back on our footsteps and review the topics already discussed. We will look at practical examples from raw data to extract as much knowledge as possible.

This chapter starts with solving a real-world fitting problem. Then you'll learn how to use neural networks to classify patterns. Finally, we'll perform a clustering analysis. In this way, we'll analyze supervised and unsupervised learning algorithms.

We will cover the following topics:

- Example of fitting data
- Pattern recognition
- Clustering

At the end of the chapter, we will understand the techniques required to perform fitting analysis, pattern recognition, and clustering through a series of real cases. We will learn how to prepare data for machine learning analysis. We will also know how to perform fitting, pattern recognition, and clustering analysis in MATLAB, and how to perform preprocessing, postprocessing, and visualization to improve training efficiency and assess model performance.

Data fitting for predicting the quality of concrete

Concrete is the most important material in civil engineering. Its compressive strength is a highly nonlinear function of age and ingredients. These ingredients include cement, blast furnace slag, fly ash, water, superplasticizer, coarse aggregate, and fine aggregate. The test to calculate compressive strength is carried out either on a concrete cube or cylinder through the use of a compression testing machine (2000 kN). The test is destructive and takes a long time, so the possibility of predicting the compressive strength takes on a significant importance. The following figure shows a compressive strength test:

Figure 9.1: The concrete compressive strength test

In this study we want to create a model that allows us to calculate the compressive strength according to the ingredients used in the mixture. We begin, as always, by getting the data to be analyzed.

 To get the data, we draw on the large collection of data available at the UCI Machine Learning Repository at the following link:

`https://archive.ics.uci.edu/ml/machine-learning-databases/`
`concrete/compressive/`

To predict the compressive strength of concrete from the ingredients of the mixture, we can use the concrete compressive strength dataset containing eight quantitative input variables, and one quantitative output variable.

This dataset contains the following fields:

- Cement (component 1) -- quantitative -- kg in a m^3 mixture -- input variable
- Blast Furnace Slag (component 2) -- quantitative -- kg in a m^3 mixture -- input variable
- Fly Ash (component 3) -- quantitative -- kg in a m^3 mixture -- input variable
- Water (component 4) -- quantitative -- kg in a m^3 mixture -- input variable
- Superplasticizer (component 5) -- quantitative -- kg in a m^3 mixture -- input variable
- Coarse Aggregate (component 6) -- quantitative -- kg in a m^3 mixture -- input variable
- Fine Aggregate (component 7) -- quantitative -- kg in a m^3 mixture -- input variable
- Age -- quantitative -- Day (1~365) -- input variable
- Concrete compressive strength -- quantitative -- MPa, megapascals -- output variable

After downloading the `Concrete_Data.xls` file from the previously mentioned URL, be sure to have it saved in the MATLAB current folder. Now we can import data into MATLAB. We will do this by using the **Import Wizard**. The **Import Wizard** is very useful for beginners, since it helps us in the data import process and, depending on the nature of the data, various import ways are offered. This tool will guide you step by step in the data import process. So, we can specify the type of data that we are going to import from many different file types recognizable. The wizard allows us to view the contents of a file in order to select the variables to be imported, and possibly to discard those deemed unnecessary.

To import the data contained in the `Concrete_Data.xls` file, follow these steps:

1. By selecting the **Import Data** button, open the import data dialog box.
2. After selecting the file (in our case, `Concrete_Data.xls`), the **Import Tool** window opens. In the following figure, the **Import Data** button and the **Import Tool** window are shown:

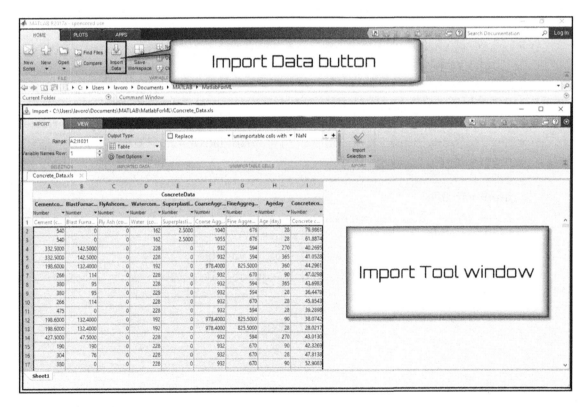

Figure 9.2: Import Data and Import Tool

3. The **Import Tool** window (*Figure 9.2*), shows a preview of the data in the selected file; we can only select the ones that interest us or do nothing to import the entire file content.

4. In the **Import Data** section (*Figure 9.2*), in the drop-down menu below the **Output Type** label, it's possible to select how we want the data to be imported. The following options are available: **Table**, **Column vectors**, **Numeric Matrix**, **String Array**, and **Cell**.

5. Select **Column vectors**, for example.

6. Now just click on the **Import Selection** button (*Figure 9.2*); in this way, the **Import Tool** creates variables in our workspace.

In step 4, we will select the table entry to import the data into a table that we will find at the end of the procedure in the MATLAB workspace. Let's take a look at its simple contents by clicking on it. As we anticipated, the table contains *1,030* observations and *9* variables. Of these, the first *8* are the ingredients of the concrete mix and the last is the concrete compressive strength, as is shown in the following figure:

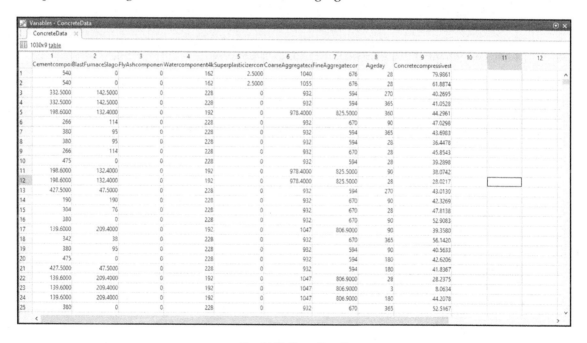

Figure 9.3: The ConcreteData table

The table also includes the names of the variables as they are in the original dataset. As anticipated earlier, the concrete compressive strength is a highly nonlinear function of age and ingredients. Let's look at the data contained in the table through a brief description, accompanied by some statistical indexes that give us the summary() function:

```
>> summary(ConcreteData)
Variables:
    Cementcomponent1kginam3mixture: 1030x1 double
        Values:
            Min             102
            Median          272.9
            Max             540
    BlastFurnaceSlagcomponent2kginam3mixture: 1030x1 double
        Values:
            Min             0
            Median          22
            Max             359.4
    FlyAshcomponent3kginam3mixture: 1030x1 double
        Values:
            Min             0
            Median          0
            Max             200.1
    Watercomponent4kginam3mixture: 1030x1 double
        Values:
            Min             121.75
            Median          185
            Max             247
    Superplasticizercomponent5kginam3mixture: 1030x1 double
        Values:
            Min             0
            Median          6.35
            Max             32.2
    CoarseAggregatecomponent6kginam3mixture: 1030x1 double
        Values:
            Min             801
            Median          968
            Max             1145
    FineAggregatecomponent7kginam3mixture: 1030x1 double
        Values:
            Min             594
            Median          779.51
            Max             992.6
    Ageday: 1030x1 double
        Values:
            Min             1
            Median          28
            Max             365
```

```
Concretecompressivestrength MPamegapascals: 1030x1 double
    Values:
        Min        2.3318
        Median     34.443
        Max        82.599
```

The first thing we can notice is that there are no missing values, so we can skip its removal procedure. As a second step, we can perform a preliminary exploratory visualization. In this respect, we remember that by tracing appropriate charts we can identify from our data specific trends even before applying machine learning algorithms. What we will be able to draw from this analysis can serve to focus our study on specific areas rather than performing generic simulations. We will create a matrix of sub-axes containing scatter plots of the mixture ingredients against the concrete compressive strength. To use this function, we have to extract the data from the table as matrices:

```
>> X = table2array(ConcreteData(:,1:8));
>> Y = table2array(ConcreteData(:,9));
>> plotmatrix(X,Y)
```

In the following figure, we can see the scatter plots of the mixture ingredients against the concrete compressive strength:

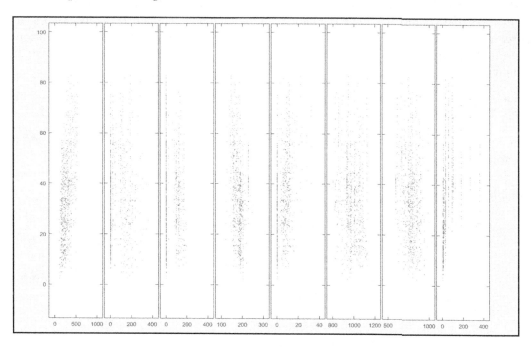

Figure 9.4: Scatter plots of mixture ingredients against concrete compressive strength

As we can see from an analysis of *Figure 9.4*, it is still too early to identify trends. So, let's take help from machine learning. But one thing we can say for sure--this is a distribution that is particularly suited to data fitting with neural networks.

As described in detail in Chapter 7, *Simulation of Human Thinking - Artificial Neural Networks*, data fitting is the process of building a curve or a mathematical function that has the best match with a set of previously collected points. Data fitting can relate to both interpolations, where exact data points are required, or smoothing, where a flat function that approximates the data is built. We are talking about curves fitting in the regression analysis, which is most concerned with statistical inference problems, as well as the uncertainty that a curve coincides with observed data that has random errors. The approximate curves obtained from data fitting can be used to help display data, predict the values of a function where no data is available, and summarize the relationship between two or more variables.

Unlike what we did in Chapter 7, *Simulation of Human Thinking - Artificial Neural Networks*, this time, we'll go by entering commands from the command line; by now, we've become experts in the procedure. Let's start by defining the data. We have already imported them into MATLAB and we have also separated the mix ingredients from the concrete compressive strength, saving them into two arrays (X and Y respectively). Only a clarification that we already gave in Chapter 7, *Simulation of Human Thinking - Artificial Neural Networks*... Remember that MATLAB assumes variables as rows and observations as columns by default. Nothing serious will simply transpose the two arrays we already have in the workspace:

```
>> X = X';
>> Y = Y';
```

Then, X will be our input data while Y will represent the target. We must now proceed to the choice of training function. To fix a neural network's training algorithm, set the `net.trainFcn` property to the name of the corresponding function. Several algorithms are available:

- Levenberg-Marquardt backpropagation (`'trainlm'`) is usually fastest.
- Bayesian regulation backpropagation (`'trainbr'`) takes longer but may be better for challenging problems.
- Scaled conjugate gradient backpropagation (`'trainscg'`) uses less memory. It is suitable for low-memory situations.

For a list of all training functions, type:

```
>> help nntrain;
```

In our case, we will choose Levenberg-Marquardt backpropagation:

```
>> trainFcn = 'trainlm';
```

Once we have chosen the training algorithm, we can create the network. To do this, we will have to fix the number of nodes in the hidden layer. We decide to construct a function-fitting neural network with one hidden layer of size 10:

```
>> hiddenLayerSize = 10;
```

To construct a function-fitting neural network, we can use the `fitnet()` function, which returns a function-fitting neural network with a hidden layer size of `hiddenLayerSize`:

```
>> net = fitnet(hiddenLayerSize,trainFcn);
```

In this way, we have only defined the network architecture; we have not brought the network into the input data in the target. It is true that if we display the network, by using the `view()` function:

```
>> view(net)
```

We will notice that the input and output sizes are zero, as shown in the following figure:

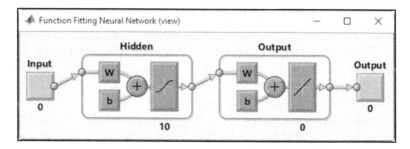

Figure 9.5: Architecture of fitting a neural network

Before proceeding with training of the network with the data in our possession, we do preprocessing of the data to avoid any problems later on. A list of functions available to preprocess the data is shown here:

- `fixunknowns`: Processes matrix rows with unknown values
- `mapminmax`: Maps the matrix row minimum and maximum values to [*-1 1*]

- `mapstd`: Maps the matrix row means and deviations to standard values
- `processpca`: Processes rows of a matrix with principal component analysis
- `emoveconstantrows`: Removes matrix rows with constant values
- `removerows`: Removes matrix rows with specified indices

For example, we can process input and target data by removing rows with constant values, if present. Constant values do not provide a network with any information and can cause numerical problems for some algorithms:

```
>> net.input.processFcns = {'removeconstantrows','mapminmax'};
>> net.output.processFcns = {'removeconstantrows','mapminmax'};
```

After creating the network and preprocessing the data, it is time to divide the data. But why divide the data into subsets? The fitting data algorithms, but more generally machine learning algorithms, train a model based on a finite set of training data. In the training phase, the model is evaluated based on how well it predicts the observations contained in the training set. But the goal of the algorithm is to produce a model that predicts previously unseen observations, in other words, one that is able to generalize the problem by starting from known data and unknown data. Overfitting occurs when a model fits the data in the training set well (already known data) but incurs larger errors when working with new data (unknown data).

To avoid overfitting when training a model with an iterative method, we can use the validation-based early stopping procedure. These early stopping rules work by splitting the original dataset into three subsets. The first subset is the training set, which is used for computing the gradient and updating the network weights and biases. The second subset is the validation set. The error on the validation set is monitored during the training process. The validation error normally decreases during the initial phase of training, as does the training set error. However, when the network begins to overfit the data, the error on the validation set typically begins to rise. The network weights and biases are saved at the minimum of the validation set error. The third subset is the test set, which is used for the application phase; now, we will apply our model to the real-world data and will get the results. Since we normally don't have any reference value in this type of data, we can only speculate about the quality of our model output using the results of your validation phase. If the error on the test set reaches a minimum at a significantly different iteration number than the validation set error, this might indicate a poor division of the dataset.

MATLAB provides four functions for dividing data into training, validation, and test sets:

- `dividerand`: Divide the data randomly (default)
- `divideblock`: Divide the data into contiguous blocks
- `divideint`: Divide the data using an interleaved selection
- `divideind`: Divide the data by index

Each function provides specific properties. For example, to access or change the division function for our network, we can use the following property:

```
net.divideFcn
```

Instead, to customize the behavior of each of the division functions, use this property:

```
net.divideParam
```

Finally to define the target data dimensions to divide up when the data division function is called, use the following property:

```
net.divideMode
```

Its default value is `sample` for static networks and `time` for dynamic networks. It may also be set to `sampletime` to divide targets by both sample and timestep, `all` to divide up targets by every scalar value, or `none` to not divide up data at all (in which case, all of the data is used for training and none for validation or testing).

Let's start by dividing the data randomly using the `dividerand()` function:

```
>> net.divideFcn = 'dividerand';
```

Then, let's divide up every sample:

```
>> net.divideMode = 'sample';
```

Finally, let's create the three subsets:

```
>> net.divideParam.trainRatio = 70/100;
>> net.divideParam.valRatio = 15/100;
>> net.divideParam.testRatio = 15/100;
```

Let's now worry about evaluating the performance of the model that we are going to train. MATLAB provides several performance function types:

- `mae`: Mean absolute error performance function
- `mse`: Mean squared error performance function

- `sae`: Sum absolute error performance function
- `sse`: Sum squared error performance function
- `crossentropy`: Cross-entropy performance
- `msesparse`: Mean squared error performance function with L2 weight and sparsity regularizers

We will choose the mean squared normalized error performance function, which measures the network's performance according to the mean of squared errors:

```
>> net.performFcn = 'mse';
```

We then set the charts to be displayed to evaluate the simulation results. There are a number of charts available; for a list of all plot functions, type:

```
>> help nnplot
```

For the fitting neural network, the available plots are:

```
>> net.plotFcns = {'plotperform','plottrainstate','ploterrhist',
'plotregression', 'plotfit'};
```

The time has finally come to train the network using the `train()` function, which trains a network according to `net.trainFcn` and `net.trainParam`:

```
>> [net,tr] = train(net,X,Y);
```

The `train()` function takes:

- `net`: Network
- `X`: Network inputs
- `Y`: Network targets

It returns:

- `net`: Newly trained network
- `tr`: Training record (epoch and perf)

During the training, the neural network training window is shown. In this window, four areas are available: neural network, algorithms, progress, and plots. Each one provides useful information during the training phase.

The neural network area shows us a network plot that we are training. Comparing this plot to the one shown in *Figure 9.5*, it can be seen that now the input and output show the correct number of variables (`input = 8` and `output = 1`).

The algorithms area shows us the essential features of the training phase. For example, there are: the function chosen for the division (`dividerand`), the chosen training algorithm (`trainlm`), and the function chosen to measure performance (`mse`). In the progress area, we see the progress in the training phase in real time. Finally, in the **Plots** area, all available plots are listed through a set of buttons. By clicking on them, the relative plot is opened in a new window. The following figure shows the **Neural Network Training** window:

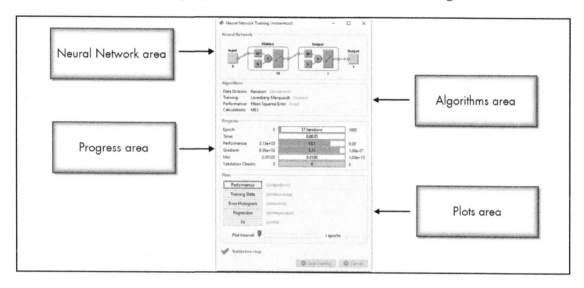

Figure 9.6: The Neural Network Training window

As we have seen before, the `train()` function returns two results: `net` and `tr`. The first (`net`) is the neural network object; the second (`tr`) contains the training record. We can see the contents of the variable using the plot returned by the `plotperform()` function. This is the first plot that is proposed in the Plots area of the **Neural Network Training** window:

```
>> figure, plotperform(tr)
```

The `plotperform()` function shows the network performance by using the training record returned by the specific training function. The second plot listed in the **Neural Network Training** window is the **Training State** plot (`plottrainstate`); it plots the training states returned by the `train()` function:

```
>> figure, plottrainstate(tr)
```

Both the plots we've displayed provide us with useful information about the network performance we've just trained, as shown in the following figure:

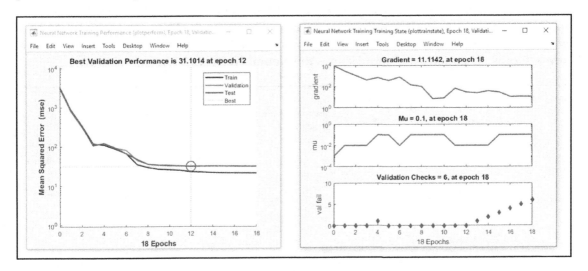

Figure 9.7: The Neural Network Training Performance plot (to the left), and the Neural Network Training plot (to the right)

The network is made; now we just have to use it. We recall that the purpose of this study is to build a model for predicting the concrete compressive strength according to the ingredients used in the mixture. The first simulation can be done precisely with the data already used for its construction. In this way, we can make a comparison between the real and the simulated values of the network to calculate its performance:

```
>> Ytest = net(X);
>> e = gsubtract(Y,Ytest);
>> performance = perform(net, Y,Ytest);
```

The first row of code uses the constructed net (the net object) to compute the output from the data in matrix X. Recall that the construction of a network leads to the formation of a neural network object.The second row of code uses the gsubtract() function, which takes two arrays, and subtracts them in an element-wise manner. In this way, we get a first estimate of the error, that is, the error that is obtained for each observation.The last row of code calculates the performance of the network using the perform() function. This function returns the network performance calculated according to the net.performFcn property values ('mse'), which we have already set before.

To evaluate the network, we still have so many tools; we previously talked about the error made in data simulation. A good way to evaluate this error is to represent it using a histogram. To do this, we will use the `ploterrhist()` function, which plots the error histogram:

```
>> figure, ploterrhist(e)
```

Finally, to evaluate the network's ability to estimate the model target, we can use the `plotregression()` function. This function plots the linear regression of targets relative to outputs. The following commands extract the outputs and targets that belong to the training, validation, and test subsets. The final command creates four regression plots for training, testing, validation, and the whole data:

```
>> trOut = Ytest(tr.trainInd);
>> vOut = Ytest(tr.valInd);
>> tsOut = Ytest(tr.testInd);
>> trTarg = Y(tr.trainInd);
>> vTarg = Y(tr.valInd);
>> tsTarg = Y(tr.testInd);
>> plotregression(trTarg, trOut, 'Train', vTarg, vOut, 'Validation',
tsTarg, tsOut, 'Testing',Y,Ytest,'All')
```

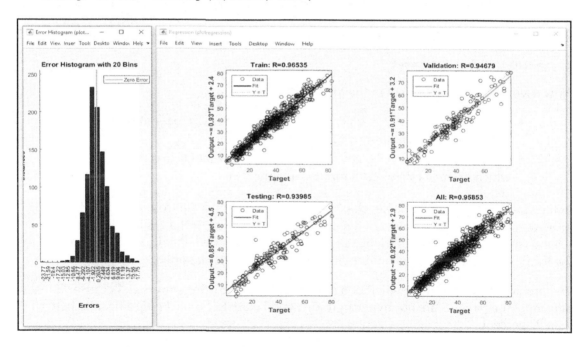

Figure 9.8: The neural network training Error Histogram plot and the neural network training Regression plot

Classifying thyroid disease with a neural network

Thyroid activity has many effects in our body. For example, the thyroid gland regulates metabolism and controls very important functions such as heart rate, nervous system development, body growth, muscular strength, sexual function, and more. Because of the central role of the thyroid in regulating bodily metabolism, when this gland does not work properly, the whole body suffers.

The causes of thyroid dysfunction can be many. First of all, your thyroid may increase or slow down your activity, producing excess or defective hormones over the actual body needs. These conditions are called hyperthyroidism (that is, an excessive production of thyroid hormones) and hypothyroidism (which is the opposite condition in which there is a deficiency of thyroid hormones).

In this study, we want to create a model that allows us to classify thyroid disease according to patient data. We begin, as always, by getting the data to be analyzed. This time we will use a dataset already available in the MATLAB distribution. As we said in previous chapters on the MATLAB environment, some ready-to-use databases are available. To import them into the MATLAB workspace, just use the load command followed by the name of the database. In this case, we will use the database named `thyroid_dataset`:

```
>> load thyroid_dataset;
```

Now, two variables are present in the MATLAB workspace:

- `thyroidInputs`: A *21x7200* matrix consisting of *7,200* patients characterized by *15* binary and *6* continuous patient attributes
- `thyroidTargets`: A *3x7200* matrix of *7,200* associated class vectors defining which of three classes each input is assigned to

In the `thyroidTargets` variable, classes are represented by a 1 in row 1, 2, or 3. If the 1 is located in the first row, normal not hyperthyroid is classified. If the 1 is located in the second row, `hyperfunction` (`hyperthyroidism`) is classified. Finally, if the 1 is located in the third row, subnormal functioning (`hypothyroidism`) is classified.

The problem is to determine whether a patient in the clinic is hypothyroid. Because *92* percent of the patients are not hyperthyroid, a good classifier must be significantly better than *92* percent.

Let's start by defining the input and target:

```
>> InputData = thyroidInputs;
>> TargetData= thyroidTargets;
```

We must now proceed to the choice of training function. To fix the neural network's training algorithm, set the net.trainFcn property to the name of the corresponding function. Several algorithms are available; for a complete list, type:

```
>> help nntrain
```

In our case, we will choose scaled conjugate gradient backpropagation:

```
>> trainFcn = 'trainscg';
```

Once we have chosen the training algorithm, we can create the network. To do this, we will have to fix the number of nodes in the hidden layer. We decide to construct a function-fitting neural network with one hidden layer of size 10:

```
>> hiddenLayerSize = 10;
```

To build a pattern recognition network, we can use the patternnet() function. Pattern recognition networks are feed-forward networks that can be trained to classify inputs according to target classes. The target data for pattern recognition networks should consist of vectors of all zero values except for a 1 in element k, where k is the class they have to represent. This function takes the following arguments:

- hiddenSizes: Row vector of one or more hidden layer sizes (default = 10)
- trainFcn: Training function (default = 'trainscg')
- performFcn: Performance function (default = 'crossentropy')

A pattern recognition neural network is returned:

```
>> net = patternnet(hiddenLayerSize, trainFcn);
```

After creating the network and preprocessing the data, it is time to set up division of data for training, validation, and testing:

```
>> net.divideFcn = 'dividerand';
>> net.divideMode = 'sample';
>> net.divideParam.trainRatio = 70/100;
>> net.divideParam.valRatio = 15/100;
>> net.divideParam.testRatio = 15/100;
```

As you may have noticed in the last steps, we have not focused on the significance of operations and the types of functions used. This is because these steps were thoroughly detailed in the previous section, which we recommend revising if doubts arise.

To measure the network performance, we will choose the cross-entropy performance function. This performance function is recommended for classification and pattern recognition problems. It calculates the network performance with a measure of the `crossentropy` value of estimated and actual class memberships:

```
>> net.performFcn = 'crossentropy';
```

We now choose plot functions to visualize the results of the simulation:

```
>> net.plotFcns = {'plotperform','plottrainstate','ploterrhist',
'plotconfusion', 'plotroc'};
```

It's time to train the network using the `train()` function:

```
>> [net,tr] = train(net,InputData,TargetData);
```

During the training, the **Neural Network Training** window is shown. In this window, four areas are available: **Neural Network**, **Algorithms**, **Progress**, and **Plots**. Each one provides useful information during the training phase, as shown in the following figure:

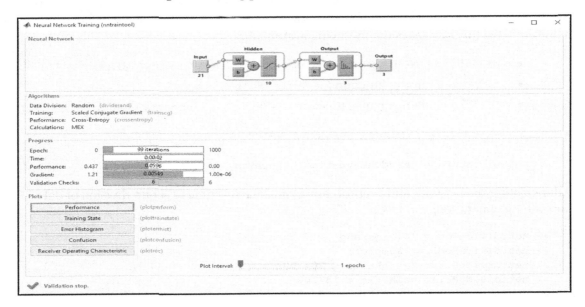

Figure 9.9: The Neural Network Training window for pattern recognition

To assess the quality of the training phase we have just done, we can test the trained network with the same input data already used for the training. The results can be used for evaluation in the following way:

```
>> OutputData = net(InputData);
>> e = gsubtract(TargetData, OutputData);
>> performance = perform(net, TargetData, OutputData);
>> TargetInd = vec2ind(TargetData);
>> OutputInd = vec2ind(OutputData);
>> percentErrors = sum(TargetInd ~= OutputInd)/numel(TargetInd);
```

The functions that appear in the first three rows of code just seen are explained in the previous paragraph. Instead, the `vec2ind()` function is new. This function converts vectors to indices, allowing indices to be represented either by themselves or as vectors containing a 1 in the row of the index they represent. In this way, `TargetInd` and `OutputInd` are vectors with 1, 2, or 3 depending on the relative classes. The last row contains the percentage of errors.

So let's go through the evaluation of the network. The following commands extract the outputs and targets that belong to the training, validation, and test subsets. This data will help us in the next step to build the confusion matrix:

```
>> trOut = OutputData(:,tr.trainInd);
>> vOut = OutputData (:,tr.valInd);
>> tsOut = OutputData (:,tr.testInd);
>> trTarg = TargetData(:,tr.trainInd);
>> vTarg = TargetData (:,tr.valInd);
>> tsTarg = TargetData (:,tr.testInd);
```

The following command plots the confusion matrix for each phase and for the whole process:

```
>> figure, plotconfusion(trTarg, trOut, 'Train', vTarg, vOut, 'Validation',
tsTarg, tsOut, 'Testing', TargetData,OutputData,'All')
```

In a confusion matrix, our classification results are compared to real data. The advantage of a confusion matrix is that it identifies the nature of the classification errors as well as their quantities. In this matrix, the diagonal cells show the number of cases that were correctly classified; all other cells show the misclassified cases.

In an ideal situation, it is expected that a machine learning algorithm can perfectly discriminate between two populations (healthy and diseased) that are not overlapping (mutually exclusive). However, what usually happens is that the two populations overlap in part, and the test will necessarily identify some unhealthy subjects (false positives) as positive and some diseased subjects (false negatives) as negative.

In the following figure, the confusion matrices for training, testing, and validation, and the three kinds of data combined are shown:

Figure 9.10: Confusion matrix for training, testing, and validation, and the three kinds of data combined

In *Figure 9.10*, the blue cell in the bottom right shows the total percentage of correctly classified cases, which are those positioned diagonally and colored in green, and the total percent of misclassified cases, which are those placed in the other cells and colored in red. In the confusion matrix, the rows represent the current values while the columns have the predicted values. For example, in the top-left plot in *Figure 9.10*, the first row tells us that *91* cases are correctly classified as *1* (normal), *6* cases were incorrectly classified as *2* (hyperfunction), and *12* cases were classified incorrectly as *3* (subnormal). If we look at the cell at the bottom right of each plot in the confusion matrix (colored in blue), we can notice that the accuracy of the classification is in any case high (greater than *93* percent). The results show very good recognition. If we need even more accurate results, we can retrain the data.

Another way of evaluating the network performance is provided by the receiver operating characteristic. The following command plots the **Receiver Operating Characteristic (ROC)** for each phase and for the whole process:

```
>> figure, plotroc(trTarg, trOut, 'Train', vTarg, vOut, 'Validation',
tsTarg, tsOut, 'Testing', TargetData,OutputData,'All')
```

The ROC is a metric used to check the quality of classifiers. For each class of a classifier, ROC applies threshold values across the interval *[0,1]* to outputs. In the following figure, the plot ROCs for training, testing, and validation, and the three kinds of data combined are shown:

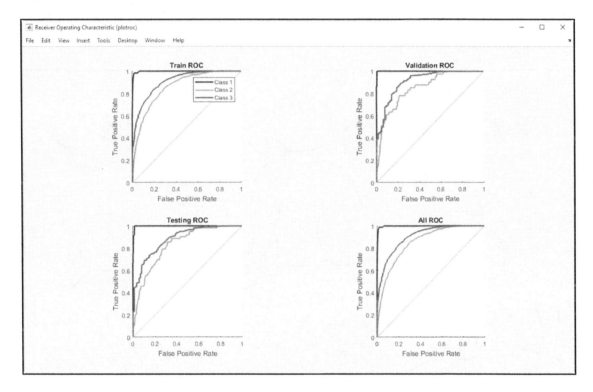

Figure 9.11: Plot ROC for training, testing, and validation, and the three kinds of data combined

The colored lines in each axis represent the ROC curves. The ROC curve is a plot of the true positive rate versus the false positive rate, as the threshold is varied. A perfect test would show points in the upper-left corner, with *100* percent sensitivity and *100* percent specificity. Better the lines approach the upper-left corner, better is the network performance.

Identifying student groups using fuzzy clustering

An effective didactic activity presupposes in-depth and methodical programming. Didactic programming aims to develop a series of coordinated actions that contribute to achieving, through efficiency and cost-effectiveness, a goal. It allows the teacher to overcome improvisation, operational causalities, and to organize rationally and consistently the educational interventions, to organize the content and the various school activities, including verifications. Programming, therefore, adjusts programs to students, identifies interdisciplinary links, and chooses methodologies that effectively facilitate the process of learning and growth, as well as cultural, emotional, relational, and civil. In the following figure, different degrees of motivation in a classroom are depicted:

Figure 9.12: Different degrees of motivation in a classroom

To make effective teaching programs, you need to individualize your study programs by building a specific suit for each student. To do this, you need to collect information about each student who can describe his/her features. To this end, information on students in a course was collected, characterizing their cognitive and motivational skills. These data were then normalized. The purpose of this study is to identify groups of students to whom a specific study path will be directed.

This time, we will use a dataset named `ClusterData.dat`. To import it into the MATLAB workspace, just use the load command, followed by the name of the database. Make sure the file is available in the MATLAB current folder, otherwise we can add the folder that contains it to the MATLAB path:

```
>> load ClusterData.dat
```

Let's first look at the data by drawing a chart:

```
>> scatter(ClusterData(:,1),ClusterData(:,2))
```

In the following figure is shown a distribution of dataset under analysis:

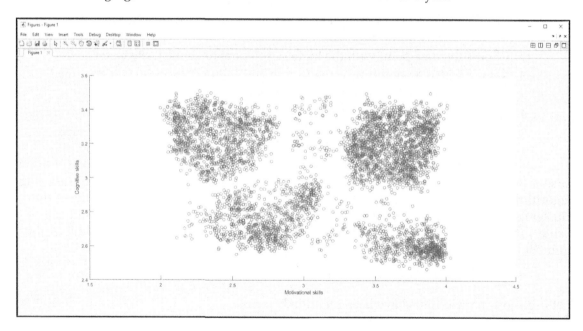

Figure 9.13: Scatter plot of the data distribution

In the *Figure 9.13*, the motivational skills versus the cognitive skills of an entire institute's students are shown.

The goal is to identify student groups in order to plan specific actions to improve their skills. We can use the Fuzzy Logic Toolbox software to identify clusters within this data using either **fuzzy c-means (FCM)** or subtractive clustering.

Analyzing *Figure 9.13*, the points seem to focus on four regions characterized by different values of the two variables. This suggests performing the cluster analysis by fixing $k = 4$. If we do not have a clear idea of how many clusters can be present for a particular set of data, we can use subtractive clustering. It represents a fast transition algorithm for estimating the number of clusters and cluster centers for a dataset. The cluster estimates, obtained from the subclust() function, will be used later to initialize an optimization-based clustering method (fcm).The subclust() function locates the clusters using the subtractive sliding method.

Subtractive clustering is based on the idea that each data point is a potential cluster center. To identify groups, the algorithm performs the following steps:

1. Calculates the probability that each data point defines a cluster center based on the density of the surrounding data points.
2. Choose the data point with the highest potential to be the first cluster center.
3. Removes all data points near the first cluster center. Proximity is determined using clusterInfluenceRange argument.
4. Choose the remaining point with the highest potential as the next cluster center.
5. Repeat steps 3 and 4 until all the data is within the range of a cluster center.

The subclust() function clusters input data using subtractive clustering with the specified cluster influence range, and returns the computed cluster centers. The subtractive clustering algorithm estimates the number of clusters in the input data. The range of influence of the cluster center is a scalar value in the range *[0, 1]*. Specifying a smaller range of influence usually creates more and smaller data clusters, producing more fuzzy rules. We will fix this number to *0.6*.

```
>> C = subclust(ClusterData,0.6);
```

Let's see how many centers have been identified:

```
>> size(C)
ans =
     4     2
```

A vector with 4 rows and 2 columns is returned to indicate that 4 centers have been identified. Add these centers to the scatter plot that we had previously traced:

```
>> hold on
>>
plot(C(:,1),C(:,2),'x','LineWidth',4,'MarkerEdgeColor','k','MarkerSize',25)
```

In the following figure are shown a scatter plot of the data distribution and the centers of the identified groups:

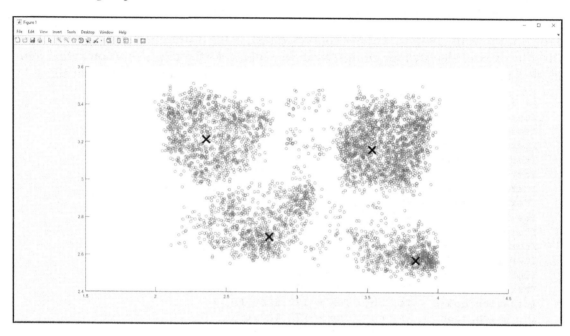

Figure 9.14: The centers of the identified groups on the scatter plot of the data distribution

Now that we have obtained an estimate of the number of clusters through the prior use of the subtractive clustering analysis, as anticipated, we can perform the FCM clustering. This is a data clustering where each data point belongs to a cluster at a certain level specified by a degree of membership. This technique was originally introduced by Jim Bezdek in 1981 (Bezdec, J.C., *Pattern Recognition with Fuzzy Objective Functional Algorithms*, Plenum Press, New York, 1981). Bezdek proposed this technique as an improvement over the latest cluster methods. FCM provides a method that shows how to group data points that populate a multidimensional space in a specific number of different clusters.

In MATLAB, FCM is obtained using the `fcm()` function that begins with an initial idea for cluster centers, which are meant to mark the average position of each cluster. The initial hypothesis for these cluster centers may be incorrect. Additionally, `fcm` assigns each data point a degree of membership for each cluster. By upgrading cluster centers and membership degrees for each data point, `fcm()` will transfer iteratively the cluster centers to the right position within a dataset. This iteration is based on minimizing an objective function that represents the distance from a given data point to a cluster centered by the degree of membership of that data. Finally, the `fcm()` function returns a list of cluster centers and different degrees of membership for each data point.

From the previous analysis, we have confirmed that, in the distribution of data at our disposal, we can identify four groups. Next, we will invoke the `fcm()` function to find four clusters in this dataset until the objective function is no longer decreasing much at all:

```
>> [center,U,objFcn] = fcm(ClusterData,4);
Iteration count = 1, obj. fcn = 639.087543
Iteration count = 2, obj. fcn = 486.601783
Iteration count = 3, obj. fcn = 480.554758
Iteration count = 4, obj. fcn = 439.805998
Iteration count = 5, obj. fcn = 330.894442
Iteration count = 6, obj. fcn = 255.239315
Iteration count = 7, obj. fcn = 226.771134
Iteration count = 8, obj. fcn = 215.201692
Iteration count = 9, obj. fcn = 209.017026
Iteration count = 10, obj. fcn = 203.135041
Iteration count = 11, obj. fcn = 194.039521
Iteration count = 12, obj. fcn = 182.176261
Iteration count = 13, obj. fcn = 174.674374
Iteration count = 14, obj. fcn = 172.526911
Iteration count = 15, obj. fcn = 172.100916
Iteration count = 16, obj. fcn = 172.021407
Iteration count = 17, obj. fcn = 172.006325
Iteration count = 18, obj. fcn = 172.003342
Iteration count = 19, obj. fcn = 172.002717
Iteration count = 20, obj. fcn = 172.002576
Iteration count = 21, obj. fcn = 172.002542
Iteration count = 22, obj. fcn = 172.002533
```

Three output arguments are returned: `centers, U, objFunc`.

- `centers`: Final cluster centers, returned as a matrix with a number of rows equal to the number of clusters we have provided as inputs (N), containing the coordinates of each cluster center. The number of columns in centers (M) is equal to the dimensionality of the data being clustered.
- `U`: Fuzzy partition matrix, returned as a matrix with N rows and M columns. Element `U(i,j)` indicates the degree of membership of the jth data point in the ith cluster. For a given data point, the sum of the membership values for all clusters is one.
- `objFunc`: Objective function values for each iteration, returned as a vector.

We have said that the `fcm()` function proceeds iteratively; to analyze how the clustering algorithm proceeds, we now draw the objective function:

```
>> figure
>> plot(objFcn)
>> title('Objective Function Values')
>> xlabel('Iteration Count')
>> ylabel('Objective Function Value')
```

In the following figure, the objective function values are shown:

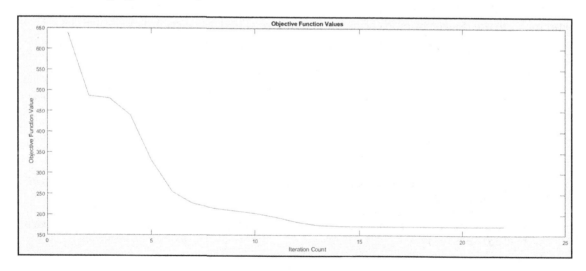

Figure 9.15: The objective function values

The plot has a very steep part to indicate that the algorithm is evolving toward the solution and a partially horizontal part indicating that the algorithm has gone to convergence. Now, we plot the starting data divided into the four groups identified with the four centers found by the `fcm()` function. The large characters in the plot indicate cluster centers.

The first thing to do is attribute to each observation their cluster membership. We have said that variable U, returned by the `fcm` function, contains the degree of membership. For each observation there are four numbers between zero and one. The line that contains the maximum number indicates the membership. We first get this value for each observation and store it in a vector:

```
>> maxU = max(U);
```

Once this is done, we must derive the membership index, that is, the row number that contains that maximum value. To do this we will use the `find()` function that find indices and values of nonzero elements:

```
>> index1 = find(U(1,:) == maxU);
>> index2 = find(U(2,:) == maxU);
>> index3 = find(U(3,:) == maxU);
>> index4 = find(U(4,:) == maxU);
```

At this point we have everything we need: we can then start building the plot. First of all, we will plot the points of representation of the distribution (scores awarded to students who indicate the degree of motivation and cognitive skills). These points will be marked with a different color and marker to indicate belonging to a specific cluster:

```
>> figure
>>
line(ClusterData(index1,1),ClusterData(index1,2),'linestyle','none','marker
','o','color','g')
>>
line(ClusterData(index2,1),ClusterData(index2,2),'linestyle','none','marker
','x','color','b')
>>
line(ClusterData(index3,1),ClusterData(index3,2),'linestyle','none','marker
','^','color','m')
>>
line(ClusterData(index4,1),ClusterData(index4,2),'linestyle','none','marker
','*','color','r')
```

Then, we will add the cluster centers that the `fcm()` function has calculated and stored in the center variable. These points will also be indicated with a different color and marker to indicate belonging to a specific cluster:

```
>> hold on
>> plot(center(1,1),center(1,2),'ko','markersize',15,'LineWidth',2)
>> plot(center(2,1),center(2,2),'kx','markersize',15,'LineWidth',2)
>> plot(center(3,1),center(3,2),'k^','markersize',15,'LineWidth',2)
>> plot(center(4,1),center(4,2),'k*','markersize',15,'LineWidth',2)
```

Finally, a title to the plot and the labels for the axes will be added:

```
>> title('Student groupings')
>> xlabel('Motivational skils')
>> ylabel('Cognitive skills')
```

In the following figure are the four clusters identified and their centers:

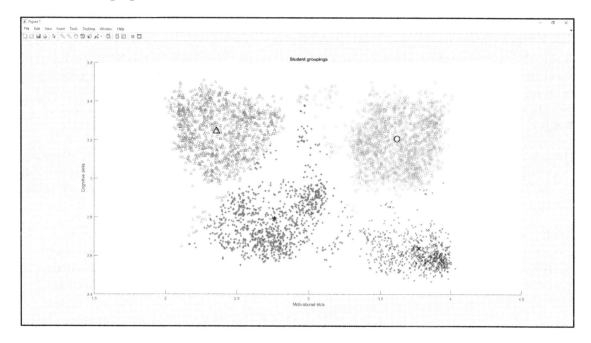

Figure 9.16: Student groupings through the motivational and cognitive skills

From analysis of *Figure 9.16*, the four groups in which the algorithm has divided the distribution is evident. Such clusters are also those that were suggested at the beginning from the simple scatter plot display in *Figure 9.13*. But now we have labeled every student with his group and we can then adopt a specific study plan built on the basis of his needs. It is clear that a motivational deficit requires precise actions different from those necessary to fill a cognitive deficit.

As always, a certain insecurity can be seen in the boundaries between a cluster and the adjacent one. For such cases, further analysis can be undertaken, perhaps by adopting an individualized study plan.

Summary

This final chapter has served us to revise the concepts learned in previous chapters; this time, without any introductions, but starting with a real-life case and analyzing the workflow that allows us to extract knowledge from a database.

In this chapter, we started with solving a fitting problem. We created a model that allows us to calculate the concrete compressive strength according to the ingredients used in the mixture. We learned how to import data in the MATLAB workspace and how to prepare it for subsequent analysis. Then, we resolved a fitting problem using Neural Network Toolbox.

Then, we learned how to use neural network to classify pattern. In this study, we created a model that allows us to classify thyroid diseases according to a lot of patient data. This time, we used a dataset that was already available in the MATLAB distribution. We also learned to build and understand the confusion matrices and the ROC.

Finally, we performed a clustering analysis. The purpose of this study was to identify groups of students to whom a specific study path will be directed, starting from scores of motivational and cognitive skills. Two fuzzy clustering techniques were used: subtractive clustering and FCM clustering. Both functions are contained in the Fuzzy Logic Toolbox.

Index

Made in the USA
Middletown, DE
30 October 2022

13780262R00212